# On the Margins

# On the Margins

*The Art of Exile in
V. S. Naipaul*

**Timothy F. Weiss**

*The University of Massachusetts Press / Amherst*

Copyright © 1992 by
The University of Massachusetts Press
All rights reserved
Printed in the United States of America
LC 92–5719
ISBN 0–87023–820–5
Designed by Edith Kearney
Set in Bodoni Book by Keystone Typesetting, Inc.
Printed and bound by Thomson-Shore

Library of Congress Cataloging-in-Publication Data
Weiss, Timothy. 1949–
On the margins: the art of exile in V. S. Naipaul / Timothy F. Weiss.
p. cm.
Includes bibliographical references (p.   ) and index.
ISBN 0–87023–820–5 (alk. paper)
1. Naipaul, V. S. (Vidiadhar Surajprased), 1932–   —Criticism and interpretation. 2. Marginality, Social, in literature. 3. Exiles in literature. I. Title.
PR9272.9.N32Z96   1992
823'.914—dc20      92–5719      CIP

British Library Cataloguing in Publication data are available.

Excerpts from "The City" in *The Complete Poems of Cavafy*, copyright © 1961 and renewed 1989 by Rae Dalven, is reprinted by permission of Harcourt Brace Jovanovich, Inc.

*For Charlotte*

# Contents

*Acknowledgments*    *ix*

*Introduction*    *3*

1   Carnival    *21*

2   A House for Mr Biswas    *46*

3   Metahistory and Marginality    *65*

4   The Greater Shipwreck    *87*

5   An Exile in the Motherland    *113*

6   The Recursive Voyage    *133*

7   The Fourth World    *165*

8   Exile and Enigma of Arrival    *194*

9   Toward a New Pluralism    *215*

*Notes*    *227*

*Bibliography*    *259*

*Index*    *273*

# Acknowledgments

I am grateful to and wish to thank those who were part of the writing of this book, especially Zohreh Sullivan, Jim Hurt, Herbert Marder, Bruce Michelson, and other colleagues at the University of Illinois who read and commented on drafts and helped me think about the material from new perspectives. Although a basic draft of the book was written in 1987–88, new chapters were added and old chapters were revised in 1988–90 while I was a Fulbrighter in Tunisia. I thank the Council for the International Exchange of Scholars for providing me with the opportunity to lecture and write in North Africa and Robert Krill and others at the American Cultural Center in Tunis for making my stay in Tunisia so pleasant and productive. I thank Selwyn R. Cudjoe, who offered significant suggestions that enabled me to bring a more localized historical context to bear on Chapters 1 and 2 of the book, and Robert K. Morris, who offered significant suggestions concerning development, organization, and style. I thank Clark Dougan, Senior Editor, for his counsel and encouragement; Brenda R. Hanning, the copyeditor; and the proofreaders and others at the University of Massachusetts Press who were part of the production process. Finally, I thank Charlotte Weiss for her caring and support.

# On the Margins

# Introduction

> . . . a British intellectual long before I was ten, already an alien in my own environment among my own people, even my own family.
> —C. L. R. James, *Beyond a Boundary*

> The West Indian person is subjected to successive waves of cultural alienation from birth—a process that has its origins embedded in a mosaic of cultural fragments. . . . The European fragment is brought into sharper focus than the others.
> —Jan Carew, "The Caribbean Writer and Exile"

> The old lady cut a sprig for me. I stuck it in the top buttonhole of my open shirt. I smelled it as I walked back to the hotel. Jasmine, jasmine. But the word and the flower had been separate in my mind for too long. They did not come together.
> —V. S. Naipaul, "Jasmine"

That whiff of jasmine and the separation between word and flower focus imagistically the dislocations within the experience and identity of Vidiadhar Surajprasad Naipaul, a colonial Trinidadian of Asian origin writing about the Caribbean and West Indies for metropolitan English readers. Like his native Trinidad, the former British colony, he is part of, yet not part of the English world, both included in and excluded from it by a combination of inheritance and history: he is a writer on the margins.

In "Jasmine" Naipaul recalls that as a youth in Trinidad he was familiar with the scent of the flower without knowing its name, which belonged to other contexts: *jasmine* was "a word in a book, a word to play with, something removed from the dull vegetation." While the plant belonged to the West Indian landscape, its name was part of his British education and the romance of his literary ambitions. For Naipaul the gap between flower and word signified a disjunction between the world of the colony and the "distilling," "distorting" power of English to transform a dull vegetation into a beautiful construct; it signified the immense distance between islands separated by the Atlantic and between his colonial identity and his aspirations to become a metropolitan writer.[1]

Within the English language, Naipaul the colonial was already "in exile," for its "map" of what is and what is of value did not chart the "territory" of his world.[2] As the authors of *The Empire Writes Back* explain, "The gap which opens between the experience of place and the language available to describe it forms a classic and all-pervasive feature of [colonial and] post-colonial texts."[3] Especially in the Englishness of English literature Naipaul encountered an "alien mythology" by way of which Trinidad and the West Indies were rendered invisible, if not nonexistent (23). Although the English of the short stories and novels that he and his Trinidad schoolmates read was their language too, the literature could not be: "Everything in books was foreign; everything had to be subjected to adaptation; and everything in . . . an English novel which worked and was of value . . . at once ceased to be specifically English" (24).[4] That literature from beyond the colony had to be filtered through a differently focused sociocultural lens, and the gap widened between Naipaul's experience of his world and words in books, between his culture and society and his perception of Englishness.

To write about Trinidad and West Indian societies the colonial had to define a new relationship between self and metropolitan other; he had not only to make present what had been set on the margins, but also to show values in the colony in terms other than the values of another, very different world: "it seemed impossible that the life I knew in Trinidad could ever be turned into a book," Naipaul confesses (25). The division between the meaning-giving authority of the imperial center and Naipaul's colonial experience and understanding is symbolized by the gap between *jasmine*, the beautiful word, and *jasmine* the "dull" vegetation. Like other colonials, Naipaul was marginalized through the ideology and myths of Englishness, and through this and other experiences he began to learn to see as an exile.

But that was almost three decades ago—"Jasmine" was first published

# Introduction 5

in *The Times Literary Supplement*, 4 June 1964. Then, exile could be viewed as a response to the dichotomy of metropolis and colony; today it can be seen as a larger response to a rapidly changing postcolonial world with its collision of cultures and powers and its splintering and remaking of societies. The experience of exile has innumerable variations; in this study of V. S. Naipaul's exile, only some of them will be considered, but it is important to understand from the beginning that exile is not one but many things. In general, exile is a division between self and others; it is the loss, or the renunciation, of close ties with the others—family, community, society—among whom one lives or has lived. Exile can result in the self's fragmentation, yet it can also lead to a syncretism of old and new aspects of self-identity. The exile feels the pain of leaving home, yet goes forward into a world of new possibilities. Exile is more than living life away from one's home; it is a break with the center and a manner of perception from the margins of other worlds. It is a phenomenological reduction in which all that is familiar recedes into the background, replaced in the foreground by the strange or the new.[5] The exile leaves home, yet in that "reduction" goes outward and experiences an opening up of self and world. In *Nous et les autres* (Ourselves and others), Tzvetan Todorov defines the exile as one who interprets his or her life in a foreign country as an experience of not-belonging and cherishes it for that very reason. Like Naipaul, the exile may remain keenly interested in his former community and society, but he has discovered that to cultivate this interest and to probe its depths he needs to live in a foreign land. Todorov, expanding upon this definition, explains that one can be an exile even in one's own country, for it is the same sentiment of exile, though of a lesser intensity, that motivates certain people to move from a town to a big city in order to be anonymous, to be a stranger among others of one's own nation, and thus, to resist integration within a community and to have one's private world.[6] Exile is a process of becoming, in between origins and destinations, and because the exile is in-between, his journey can be a two-directional movement.[7]

Although exile begins with a split, it carries the possibility for new exchanges and connectedness: the understanding of one's self, culture, and society through the lens of other persons, cultures, and societies. As a manner of perception, exile is the understanding of one entity through the lens of another entity; one's self, culture, and society through the lens of other persons, cultures, and societies. It is the potential plurality of the exile's perception that intrigues Naipaul, who in an interview with Ian Hamilton remarks on its opposite, a closure to foreignness: "Since I went to India [in the early 1960s] I've become interested in the way different cultures have different ways of seeing. Columbus, a medieval man, voyaging in a miraculous world, which causes him no surprise. Gandhi coming to England and leaving not a word of description, remembering only that when he arrived at Southampton, he was dressed in white."[8] Exile can afford an experience of diversity. "Each time I go to a place I have not seen before, I hope it will be as different as possible from the places I already know," writes Paul Bowles in *Their Heads Are Green and Their Hands Are Blue*.[9] Exile can lead to an awakening to heterogeneity and the basic connection between self and others. To paraphrase Urbain Chauveton, each of us regards the self through others; we know the self, dialogically, through others.[10] The exile has a heightened awareness of this, which can lead, variously, to wonder or estrangement, to a bond or a Disneyland search for exotic others, to an embrace of the "stranger within" or a frightened depiction of monsters and a fear of the self's annihilation by alien others.

In actuality, choosing exile and being forcibly exiled are not the same, but in Naipaul's works this distinction is less clear-cut. In *The Mimic Men*, for example, Ralph Singh is exiled from Isabella, his West Indian island home, because of his political views and his party's failures, but Singh has an exile's mentality long before he is put on a plane for London. His departure fulfills a wish and continues a flight from the colony motivated by a long history of empire. To what extent does any person choose exile? This seems to be the idea behind Julia Kristeva's remark that a wound (*"une blessure"*) pushes the exile to wander.[11] For many exiles today that wound begins as a force from without, a violation of human rights or a threat of extinction. For some, Edward Said notes, exile would seem "without cause or rationale": "Think . . . of the uncountable masses for whom UN agencies have been created, or refugees without urbanity, with only ration cards and agency numbers.[12] For Singh, exile begins in his colonial inheritance and the many flights of exiles before him from colony to metropolis.

## Introduction

For various reasons—war, tyranny, the breakup of empires, the democratization of the world—the twentieth century has been an age of writers in exile:[13] in English literature, Joyce, Beckett, and Conrad, for example, none of whom was an Englishman; in American literature, Hemingway, Pound, and Eliot; in German literature, Rilke and Grass; in Latin American literature, García Márquez and Vargas Llosa, to mention but a few. Caribbean writers, too, have a tradition of exile; by "the early 1950s," Kenneth Ramchand notes, "the pattern was established of emigration to the Mother Country for West Indian writers seeking the stamp of approval and wishing to live by their pens; nearly every West Indian novel since then has been first published by London publishing houses for sale to members of the British public."[14] A short list of Caribbean writers who have lived in exile would include Eric Walrond, Claude McKay, Jean Rhys, Edward Mittelholzer, Leon Damas, Aimé Césaire, Samuel Selvon, George Lamming, Roger Mais, Edward Brathwaite, Wilson Harris, Derek Walcott, Shiva Naipaul, and, of course, V. S. Naipaul. For these writers it is not merely that the prospects for a successful career lie beyond the Caribbean; there are other considerations. Wilson Harris speculates that exile may be "native" to the Caribbean writer, who lives in "'exile' in his or her own country," an exile that takes place against the social background of what Harris calls a "philistinism," a *persona* adopted by people in a dangerous world where they must "play it safe" and "take no risks."[15] Caribbean writers must constantly confront this philistinism, separating them from their community.

No matter what their nationality or place from which they originate, writers or intellectuals in exile are not a recent phenomenon, nor do all think of exile in the same terms. Todorov cites Descartes as perhaps the first Frenchman to embrace exile and notes that, contrary to what is often believed, Descartes did not leave France because he was persecuted or prevented from publishing, but because, like other intellectuals of a later age, he equated exile, being a stranger among others, with personal liberty. "One foot in one country, the other foot in another," Descartes writes, "I find my situation very agreeable in that I am free." The Prince of Ligne expresses a similar sentiment: "I like my state of being a foreigner everywhere: French in Austria, Austrian in France, either one or the other in Russia, this is the way to enjoy all places and not be dependent anywhere."[16] This experience of liberty and the sense of specialness that it can engender is a prime appeal of exile.

Because the exile is culturally different from the others among whom he lives, he can define himself more sharply against that strangeness. This may lead to a deepening understanding of self and others, as well as to an egocentric or ethnocentric disregard of others: Descartes, for instance, comments that as an exile he took no more notice of people than he did of the trees or animals. Obviously he was not interested in discovering others through exile, but in being free (or rid) of them.[17] At its extreme, this disregard that views others as objects can turn into the exploitation, even destruction, inherent in the many forms of racism. In *La Conquête de l'Amérique: La Question de l'autre* (The conquest of America: The question of the Other), Todorov states that the early Spaniards in America often thought of and treated the Indians as a lower form of life than donkeys. They were a raw material like wood or water; one source recommended irrigating drought-parched fields with Indian blood. The exile's experience of strangeness can result in non-seeing, or seeing only through the blinders of one's preconceptions; in this mode there is no dialogic interaction between self and others because the other is only an object in the self's path of plan and action. In the Americas, the European encounter with others led to extermination: get to know, take from, and destroy—*"comprendre, prendre, et détruire"*—became the equation, Todorov writes.[18] Less extreme, the self's encounter with others may lead to a reinforced ethnocentrism: "the analysis of a foreign culture principally reveals what was sought in it or what the seeker was already prepared to discover," remarks Mircea Eliade. "When one approaches an exotic spirituality, one understands principally what one is predestined to understand by one's vocation, by one's own cultural orientation and that of the historical moment to which one belongs."[19] In a negative sense, then, the traveler or exile may see the other, or another culture or land, only as a variation (often flawed or degenerate) of his or her own. Thus, for example, Columbus renamed each landfall of his voyages so that, rather than an Indian appellation, each place had its appropriate (Spanish) name.[20]

In *Etrangers à nous-mêmes* (Strangers to ourselves) Kristeva considers the exile—the "foreigner" or "stranger"—from a psychological perspective, analyzing the process of estrangement and the response of the stranger "within" to the stranger "without." A disturbance, or a wound, pushes the exile into his wanderings; those who meet him respond with a mixture of fascination and fear, for he plays a double role in their community, on the one hand revealing the hidden meaning of the tribe, and on the other hand, undermining the consensus. The stranger cuts through others' feelings of security and shows them their dark places: "To worry or to smile, such is the choice when the stranger assails us; it depends on our familiarity with our own phantoms." The stranger, Kristeva explains, is within as well as without, for culture implants in us certain values and their opposites, sameness and otherness, identity and strangeness. Whether we flee or confront the stranger, we struggle with our own shadows, our unconscious. In a world that is arguably growing more heteroclite, more cosmopolitan, we are all becoming strangers, she states. Only by recognizing "the stranger in ourselves" can we learn to live with others and achieve a multicultural, multiracial society; although this may sound like a utopian wish, it is also becoming a new world necessity.[21] Should we measure the account of self-other encounters in Naipaul's travel books and social studies against this high, unrealized standard? No matter how we answer this question, we can learn much about these books if we focus on the encounters between strangers—Naipaul and others—and read those encounters as significative of attitudes toward the stranger within.

Exile can provoke extreme responses: just as the stranger can fascinate or frighten, so too strangeness can channel the exile's energies creatively or destructively. Exile can fragment the self, reconstruct it syncretistically, or fragment and reconstruct in cycles. Because the exile breaks ties with others, he lives within a solitude, and although Descartes and other intellectuals have found a freedom through *non-appartenance*, or not-belonging to a community, the experience of exile can produce an intense *déchirement* or a splitting of self and world. In *L'Enfant noir* (The black child) Camara Laye describes a boy's experience of this splitting caused by his departure from his natal village for the city: "I was in Conakry and I was not at all in Conakry: I was still in Kouroussa; and I was no longer in Kouroussa! I was here and I was there; I was torn in two. And I felt very alone."[22] Similarly, the protagonist of Cheikh Hamidou Kane's *L'Aventure ambiguë* laments: "the world is silent, and I no longer resonate with its presence. I am like an open cut, like a broken musical instrument. I feel that nothing can touch me anymore."[23]

As an outcast from the tribe, the exile may feel self-loathing and self-defilement, or he may despise others who rest secure within the tribe for their provincialism. The exile may withdraw into the self, as does Santosh in Naipaul's short story "One Out of Many" when, tired of the strange, bewildering world of America, he retreats into his cabinet/bed.[24] The exile may escape into fantasy as does Singh in his reveries of "Old England" and of a graceful, aesthetic life on an idealized West Indian cocoa plantation. A journey into exile may turn into an endless wandering, as it does for the "world-citizen" of "The Tramp at Piraeus."[25] Like the traveler in C. P. Cavafy's poem "The City"—or the voyager in the Mediterranean fantasy "the enigma of arrival" in Naipaul's novel of that title—the exile may wander the world yet always end up in the same place, because he carries with him, in his mind, his past and the city from which he has escaped physically but can never escape psychologically:

> You said, "I will go to another land, I will go to another sea.
> Another city will be found, a better one than this.
> Every effort of mine is a condemnation of fate;
> and my heart is—like a corpse—buried.
> How long will my mind remain in this wasteland."
> . . . . . . . . . . . . . . . . . .
> You will find no new lands, you will find no other seas.
> The city will follow you. You will roam the same
> streets. And you will age in the same neighborhoods;
> and you will grow gray in these same houses.
> Always you will arrive in this city. Do not hope for any other—
> There is no ship for you, there is no road.
> As you have destroyed your life here
> in this little corner, you have ruined it in the entire world.[26]

Cavafy's traveler-exile tries to escape the past, but the inverse may also occur. Like the Tulsi elders in *A House for Mr Biswas*, the exile may forever seek to return to the past, and, of course, always fail. Here the past is an idealized moment before the fissure of self and world and the expulsion from the "garden" of one's native land; the exile, like Pundit Tulsi, may try to re-create the motherland from which he has been torn and end up living in a world of fantasy instead.

Several of Naipaul's works treat, and are shaped by, the experience of exile as *déchirement* or the splitting of self and world. In the essay "East

Indian," the author alludes to the culturally induced inner turmoil felt by the Indian (and Trinidad Indian) who had left his community for abroad: "To leave India's sacred soil, to cross the 'black water,' was considered an act of self-defilement. So completely did these migrants re-create India in Trinidad that they imposed a similar restriction to those who wished to leave Trinidad."[27] In his initial years in England, Naipaul feels pangs of guilt, believing that he should be back home to help his ailing father and give moral support to his family.[28] In the story "One Out of Many" the author treats variations on these feelings through his exiled, Indian protagonist Santosh, who is struck by pains of an imagined self-defilement after such taboo acts as intercourse with a *"hubshi"* (black woman) and the purchase of a Western hat and suit. After the sexual encounter, the tormented, caste-minded Santosh showers to purify himself; after hastily buying the new clothes, he leaves them in the box, unable to wear them because he believes that to do so would be to overstep his caste boundaries and invite humiliation. The sex and the suit symbolize aspects of his new identity that he has yet to assimilate; he succeeds in remaining in the United States, but he fails to achieve a syncretism in which aspects of India and America are embraced in terms of their values without denying their differences, where self and other exist in difference yet harmony. A sense of difference *and* harmony: this is perhaps the positive outcome of exile as an intercultural process.

The split between exiled self and others is treated in its darkest aspects in the novels of the 1960s, *Mr Stone and the Knights Companion* and *The Mimic Men*, but this split is inherent to the point of view, situations, and sensibility of many of Naipaul's essays and novels. The threat of breakdown, a deepening fissure within the self and between self and others, looms as a possibility in *An Area of Darkness, The Mimic Men, In a Free State, Guerrillas, A Bend in the River, Finding the Center,* and *The Enigma of Arrival*. In "One Out of Many," that possibility is signified by Santosh's fascination with mirrors and their implicit questioning of his identity. (In the Foreword to Seepersad Naipaul's *The Adventures of Gurudeva*, V. S. Naipaul, recalling his father's breakdown, suggests the source of the mirror in Santosh's story: "My father looked in the mirror and thought he couldn't see himself. It was the beginning of a long mental illness that caused him for a time to be unemployed, and as dependent as he had been in his childhood.")[29] In *Finding the Center* and *The Enigma of Arrival* the possibility of breakdown is symbolized by dreams of a crumbling bridge and an exploding head. But like the experience of exile, mirrors and dreams are ambiguous; the mirror of "One Out of Many," for example, may also stand for a vehicle of reconstruction or syncretism of Santosh's Indian-American self. We can view the different, extreme responses to exile—breakdown, or burst of creativity and sense of focused identity—as different aspects of a recursive process or cycle within the self.

Exile offers significant creative possibilities. It offers what Todorov terms the "epistemological privilege" of being a stranger: one is surprised by the new; one examines things more closely because one looks at them in a new way.[30] The exile exercises, potentially, what Bakhtin calls an "exotopy," a vision from the outside through which he or she can see what those "inside" (at anchor, at home) cannot:

There exists a very strong, but one-sided . . . idea that in order better to understand a foreign culture, one must enter it, forgetting one's own, and view the world through the eyes of this foreign culture. . . . Of course, a certain entry as a living being into a foreign culture, the possibility of seeing the world through its eyes, is a necessary part of the process of understanding it; but if this were the only aspect of this understanding, it would merely be a duplication and would not entail anything or be enriching. *Creative understanding* does not renounce itself, its own place in time, its own culture; and it forgets nothing. In order to understand, it is immensely important for the person who understands to be *located outside* the object of his or her creative understanding—in time, in space, in culture. . . . In the realm of culture, outsideness is a most powerful factor in understanding. It is only in the eyes of *another* culture that foreign culture reveals itself more fully and profoundly (but not maximally fully, because there will be cultures that see and understand even more).[31]

Todorov's epistemological privilege and Bakhtin's exotopy convey the basic idea that one can better know the center from the margins, that—to use a metaphor of La Rochefoucauld's—the eye cannot see itself, that a society can only know itself through other societies and through history. To paraphrase Montesquieu, who takes this idea to its logical conclusion: in order to know one's self and one's own community and society, one must in a sense know all the world.[32] An impossible task, of course, but such is the limited, relative nature of all knowing or understanding, which is provisional and contextual.

The "margins" can be "an unprecedented source of creative energy," argue Ashcroft, Griffiths, and Tiffin in *The Empire Writes Back: Theory and Practice in Post-Colonial Literatures*.[33] Although the marginality to which they refer defines the relationship between empire (the center) and its colonies (the margins), we can extend this metaphor to signify a mentality or map that the colonial exile carries with him to the metropolis and to other parts of the world. In *V. S. Naipaul's Later Fiction: The Creative Constraints of Exile*, Ling-Mei Lim argues that while Naipaul "cultivates an 'outsider's' perspective, the authenticity of his work comes from those experiences of living inside the Third World. By maintaining a hold on both the 'inner' and 'outer' perspectives, he transforms the 'fragmented consciousness' into an artistic advantage, rather than a crippling factor."[34] The key idea here is that of dialogue between perspectives and syncretistic transformation. To be on the margins is to be part of yet not part of; in the self's encounter with others, the exile can live a "double exteriority" for he or she belongs to two cultures without identifying wholly with either. The exile can engage in a cross-cultural dialogue and through that dialogue can affirm both his uniqueness and the interrelationship between himself and others.

The exile's attitude toward the stranger "without" and the stranger "within" determines the results of the encounter with the other. One might argue that the traveler or exile prefers difference to sameness, that he wants (in the words of Hugues de Saint-Victor) the "entire world" to be "a foreign country."[35] That is to say that the exile does not want one place to be "like" another; he does not want the landscapes of North Africa to look like a "rather more barren California." As Tangier-based Paul Bowles puts it: "If people and their manner of living were alike everywhere, there would not be much point in moving from one place to another." To perceive strangeness or difference in peoples and places is more fruitful than to project one's self and culture onto them: in the former, the world becomes larger and more interesting, while in the latter, small and boringly the same. Travelers and exiles do not always embrace the stranger, however, even though they may seek the experience of strangeness. For the Westerner, an interest in difference or exotica can turn into a veiled racism or a variation of ethnocentrism in which one's own culture is considered superior to those of the backward "jumblies" of the world.[36] This has often been the case during the history of European empire in Africa, Asia, and the Americas: Westerners perceived the differences between themselves and the peoples they conquered and colonized, but they did not think of these others as their equals. For Naipaul-the-traveler in India and other developing countries, another kind of ethnocentrism is sometimes played out: the stranger "without" is not embraced because the stranger "within" is insufficiently confident to acknowledge a kinship; the kinship is perhaps felt, but an acknowledgment of it is suppressed so that the boundary, the differences, between the impoverished world without and the special world within can be maintained. In the self's encounter with the stranger without, a sense of difference must be coupled with an egalitarianism; there must be some bridge of commonality established across the differences between cultures or there can be no communication. These two attitudes together—recognition of difference, yet a sense of egalitarianism and commonality—can perhaps make for the "perfectly" tolerant, observant, inquiring person envisioned by Hugues de Saint-Victor and for the traveler who applies both an exotopy and an empathy to understand creatively the strangeness of others.

Exile inevitably entails attitudes and modes of cross-cultural perception, encounter, and communication, and as suggested, there are many possibilities for response. In an article entitled "The Double-Swing Model of Intercultural Communication between the East and the West," Muneo Jay Yoshikawa discusses "four modes of intercultural encounter and communication": the ethnocentric, the control, the dialectical, and the dialogical modes.[37] In the ethnocentric mode, Yoshikawa explains, "A [the individual of one culture] perceives B [the individual of another culture] only in A's frame of reference. . . . The cultural integrity of B's culture, its uniqueness, and differences are simply ignored. Communication is one-sided, and feedback is rendered ineffective by well-known psychological processes of selective attention, selective perception, and selective retention." In the control mode, the exchange deteriorates into manipulation: "B is perceived and manipulated as a thing or an object for A's purpose. B's cultural uniqueness and differences are recognized, but they are manipulated in order to achieve A's objectives." In the dialectical mode, three outcomes are possible: A and B create a synthesis, C, of their different viewpoints; a dialectical unity is achieved. The two other outcomes are "pseudo-dialectical," Yoshikawa states, in that either "A fuses into B and loses its identity" or "A coerces B to become part of A." Finally, in the dialogical mode, an "interdependence" is recognized: "A does not appear in its wholeness in isolation but rather in relationship to B. While A and B are separate and independent, they are simultaneously *interdependent*." Yoshikawa cites Buber's concept of dialogism and the Buddhist logic of *Soku* as sources for the "double-swing" model of communication. Similarly, in *Chocs de cultures* (Cultural shocks), Carmel Camilleri states that the basic problem of intercultural communication is how to establish commonality across the differences between interlocutors without emptying those differences of their identity-giving significance.[38] Camilleri explains that a correct approach to the intercultural depends on a long apprenticeship entailing a complex analysis of "others" and a construction of a system of appropriate attitudes toward otherness.

At different times the exile may respond in each of these modes of encounter—ethnocentric, control, dialectic, dialogic. But exile is more than an encounter; it is a manner of perception, more basic than these modes, that involves seeing one entity through the lens of another entity, one culture through another culture, the self through others who are strangers. The perception operates in two directions: the exile understands the self through the lens of strangers, and understands strangers through the lens of the exiled self. Naipaul understands colonial Trinidadian society partly through the lens of metropolitan English society, and colonial and postcolonial societies partly through the lens of Trinidadian society. For Naipaul exile turns into a journey to and testing of the limits of understanding and creativity. "Part of the problem . . . is that you use up your experience," he explains about the challenge of writing. "The great triumph is to go on." Throughout his career he has linked travel, writing, and the knowing of self through others: "I have to travel. Unless my imagination can be released from all these familiar deadening scenes, I will go stale. My travel is so different from that of Graham Greene and others. They're travelers in a world that's been made safe for them by empire. . . . The primary difference between my travel and theirs is that while they travel for the picturesque, I'm *desperately* concerned about the countries I'm in."[39] Several ideas are important here. First, travel can liberate, but it also by definition displaces. "We notice only when we look *for* something," E. H. Gombrich states, "and we look when our attention is aroused by some disequilibrium, a difference between our expectations and the incoming message."[40] Naipaul embraces travel not only because it frees him, but also because it entangles him in the need to understand and respond—chiefly through his writings about himself and others. He also contrasts his travels to those of a writer like Graham Greene, whose identity as an Englishman differentiates him from the colonial or former colonial peoples he meets and whose interest, Naipaul claims, is in the picturesque exotica. Unlike Greene, Naipaul the Trinidad, Asian-Indian must enter into a relationship with the colonial or formerly colonial peoples he observes in India, Pakistan, and other countries; he cannot look only from the safe distance of his difference because he and they do share something in a tangled way. Finally, Naipaul writes that he is "*desperately* concerned about the countries" he travels in; he is, of course, but that does not mean that the relationship he enters into with their people is one that acknowledges their dignity and their meaningfulness in being different from him. Is Naipaul, in his acerbic comments about other peoples and places, ethnocentrist and racist? This question will be considered in subsequent chapters, but here it is worth pointing out that a tag in itself says next to nothing. What is important is to look at the kind of encounter and the entanglement of the relationships between Naipaul and others, the relationship between the stranger without and the stranger within.

The experience of exile holds new possibilities for seeing and understanding, but these can also be painful and paradoxical. The exile believes that in order to find the center, one must look from the margins; and that in order to know one's self and community, one must know all the world, though what one sees and knows is always culturally based and contextual, as seeing itself is always a selection and construction. For Naipaul, exile is often a recurring, reinforcing division between self and others that separates him from his Hindu Indian community in Trinidad, from other Trinidadians, from the English in London, from Indians in India, and from the peoples in the developing countries to which he travels and lives as an observer. He is a person "on the margins" by inheritance and choice: as a child shuffled from house to house,[41] as the son of an iconoclastic journalist, as an East Indian in a primarily black

West Indian society, as a colonial in the English metropolis (where he has lived, in his own words, as a "refugee," as someone "peripheral" and in "limbo"),[42] as an East Indian-West Indian out of place in the "motherland" of India, as a writer from a developing country who writes acerbically about peoples in developing countries, as a nonbeliever among believers during his journeys in India and Islamic countries, as the writer from a distant, former British colony, who by the "exercise of his talent . . . has set himself adrift."[43] Exile, then, as an experience of notbelonging, as an epistemology, and as a manner of perception and encounter informs Naipaul's works, variously shaping their characters, themes, narration, and views of the world.[44] These works emerge from the "double exteriority" of Naipaul's belonging yet not-belonging completely to either colony or metropolis, Third World or First World. They emerge through the tension between recursive voyages of exile and a sense of the past and home, and through the author's construction of a new syncretistic identity for himself and others.

Chapter 1 of this study, "Carnival," reads Naipaul's 1950s novels—*Miguel Street, The Mystic Masseur, The Suffrage of Elvira*—as works that look back on colonial Trinidad through the constructs of an exile's vision of his former home. These novels show the author's new understanding of the West Indian society he has left behind as well as his old insecurities as a colonial and as a member of an ethnic minority in the colony. On the one hand, the novels celebrate the voices, *joie de vivre*, tolerance, and plurality of Trinidad society, whose symbol is carnival as that society has reshaped it into an affirmation of its own heterogeneous identity. On the other hand, they portray a division within the colonial self and society, between fantasy and powerlessness, a symbol of which are the masks and fantastic display of carnival not as theater but as futility and unreality.

Chapter 2, "A House for Mr Biswas," reads Naipaul's masterwork as the writer-son's story of exile and home told through his father's story, and a father's dream of becoming a professional writer told through his son's realization of that dream. The novel overwrites the fictionalized life of Seepersad Naipaul with the experience of not-belonging of the son's exile.

Chapter 3, "Metahistory and Marginality," discusses *The Middle Passage*, the author's travel book and social study of the colonial West Indies and the Caribbean, and *The Loss of El Dorado*, his history of fifteenth-through nineteenth-century Trinidad. These works set paradigms of analysis that recur in later essays and fiction about developing societies: *The Middle Passage* diagnoses cultural and social maladies deriving from colonialism and imperialism, while *The Loss of El Dorado* deconstructs Eurocentered myths distorting Trinidad's and the region's history.

Chapter 4, "The Greater Shipwreck," reads Naipaul's 1960s novels, *The Mimic Men* and *Mr Stone and the Knights Companion*, as works that grow out of and are shaped by the author's experience of exile as *déchirement* or fragmentation, one of whose symbols is the breakup or wreck of the voyager's ship. These novels tell complementary stories of exile, about the absence of belonging to a meaningful community of others. Ralph Singh of *The Mimic Men* is a political exile from the Caribbean island Isabella and an intellectual exile from his youthful, colonial vision of the metropolis as center of the world. The protagonist of *Mr Stone and the Knights Companion*, a middle-class London librarian and office worker, is alienated from nature, society, and his ideas of meaningful work and achievement. The novels convey these aspects of exile as alienation and fragmentation partly through an ironic interplay with literary and mythic discourses such as the story of Robinson Crusoe and the legend of King Arthur.

Chapter 5, "An Exile in the Motherland," treats the author's essays and books about India in terms of two polar aspects of exile, a search for knowledge of self through others and exile as not-belonging. Like *The Middle Passage*, these works diagnose cultural and social maladies and the effects of myths and metahistory on Indian society. They firmly establish Naipaul's persona of exile, of the stranger, among people with whom he is linked through ethnic heritage and history of empire but with whom he shares almost nothing of their sensibility and perception of the world. For the author, India is not precisely a place, but an idea, a state of mind, and a way of seeing the world from which he is exiled and can never return to intellectually but in which, paradoxically, he finds remnants of himself.

Chapter 6, "The Recursive Voyage," considers the original journey of exile as a recurring journey in Naipaul's works; the chapter examines the repetition of themes in a chronologically diverse group of nonfiction spanning more than thirty years, from the 1960s through 1990: themes such as the split identity of the exile and the concomitant split in colonial and postcolonial societies; the trauma of developing societies and the myths that are engendered by that trauma; the relationship between observer and writer, and ethnography and autobiography, in Naipaul's works.

Chapter 7, "The Fourth World," reads Naipaul's 1970s novels, "In a Free State," *Guerrillas,* and *A Bend in the River,* as works that, although referring to the instability and social breakdown of postcolonial nations, superimpose on that actuality a myth of backwardness, of the receding African dawn. Thus, in these works the "Third World" becomes a "Fourth World," at once a dark scenario of the future of the Caribbean and sub-Saharan Africa, and an Afro-Gothic fiction growing out of a myth of the "dark continent" and a mélange of aspects drawn from the author's ethnic, colonial background and his experience of exile as *déchirement.*

Chapter 8, "Exile and Enigma of Arrival," reads the semiautobiographical novel *The Enigma of Arrival* as a meeting of opposites: beginnings and endings, home and exile, life and art. It considers the novel's synthesis of three motifs throughout Naipaul's works: change, journeys, and the interrelationship of life and art. Through a meditation on mutability and the commemoration of a deceased brother and sister, the narrator-author ritualistically heals the split between colony and metropolis, self and others, "man" and "writer" that began with his journey of exile decades ago. He constructs a sense of home in his state of being in-between.

The final chapter, "Toward a New Pluralism," looks at Naipaul's two most recent works, *A Turn in the South* and *India: A Million Mutinies Now,* and concludes this study with a reflection on how exile has shaped Naipaul's works, generating or impacting on their narration, characterization, subject matter, themes, cultural-social evaluations, modes of intercultural encounter and perception. It has shaped the relationship between author and reader during the three phases of Naipaul's works, which can be characterized, respectively, by mediation, alienation, and syncretism. By writing about himself as exile, Naipaul has also written about others; through an autobiographical art, he has tapped experiences that have come to define aspects of people's lives in the colonial and postcolonial world. Spanning several decades, his works are about more than the problems of the developing world that are a deep concern running through every book; they are about a rapidly changing world order and a changing definition of home and belonging in that new order.

# 1

# Carnival

> Carnival has . . . encompassed almost every aspect of life and thought of the Trinidad people, and . . . it is a reservoir of material uniquely valuable. . . . [It] has achieved a synthesis between old and new, between folk forms and art forms, between native and alien traditions. It is considered by many the essential cultural product of Trinidad and Tobago.
> —Errol Hill, *The Trinidad Carnival*

Naipaul has called his 1950s novels "social comedies,"[1] and it is chiefly their equivocal tone that makes them different from later works; specifically, it is the two-sided, "domino" quality of their humor, with its "seriocomical" dark and light sides, that differentiates them from later works. The novels' humor expresses both a *joie de vivre* and a malaise, both a "*joyful relativity*"[2] and a threatening indeterminacy; on one hand, they celebrate the voices and richness of a multicultural society, while on the other hand, they show the author's alienation and his fears of a carnivalistic swallowing of his identity by the colony.

In the gap between the actuality of Trinidad carnival and Naipaul's latent sense of carnival as "inverted real world"[3] lie explanations for the particular shape of his 1950s novels. The author as exile finds some of the keys to an understanding of colonial Trinidad by leaving it and distancing himself from it. Yet, his exile exacerbates fears that he has carried with him from the colony, especially a fear of being entrapped, of losing his special identity (as East Indian and as exile in the metropolis) by being lumped with Trinidadians or West Indians generally—by being rendered carnivalistically one of the "folk." In *Considérations ethno-psychanalytiques sur le Carnaval Haïtien,* Ernest Mirville writes that carnival is a "stew of culture in which masses of unconscious psychic energy ferment in interaction. The individual momentarily loses his personality. Swept up by the dizzy swirl, he throws down the mask, loses himself in the crowd, becomes the crowd and lets go; or escapes the crowd."[4] Metaphorically, Naipaul seeks to escape the carnival, for to him it represents a potential entrapment and belonging in a culture and society that as an exile he has positioned himself outside of. A theater of the people, carnival brings the community together, it calls for mingling, mixing, participation; the exile, however, has chosen to break his ties with his society. Because he has chosen to be someone he cannot easily be were he to remain in the West Indian colony, carnival, this deeply meaningful ritual,[5] this folk celebration, this communal belonging, can seem a "lunacy."

The author's equivocal attitude toward the colony manifests itself in the interplay of voices, the "double-voicedness," of the 1950s novels. Inherent in this double-voicedness and thus double perspective is the possibility of indirection and indeterminacy. "All forms involving a narrator or a posited author," Bakhtin writes, "signify . . . the author's freedom from a unitary and singular language, a freedom connected with the relativity of literary and language systems; such forms open up the possibility of never having to define oneself in language . . . of saying 'I am me' in someone else's language, and in my own language, 'I am other.'"[6] The double-voicedness of the 1950s novels makes them easy to misread, or read incompletely. In "London" (1958), Naipaul mentions a few such "misreadings," reviews that concluded that his purpose in writing was "to show how funny Trinidad Indians are," that he "look[s] down a long Oxford nose" at his own ethnic community, and that he does or does not (depending on the particular reviewer's assessment) write about Trinidad with "warm affection."[7] Naipaul cites the cultures portrayed in these novels as the source of the misreadings, explaining that "exotic writers" face obstacles in getting their work accepted on its literary merits and that only a reader who knows the West Indies will read the novels as they are meant to be read. But the reviewers' disagreement about these novels does suggests something important: it points to their equivocal, two-sided humor and hybrid cultural perspectives as sources of the divergent readings. Still today critics read Naipaul's works from one side only, not hearing their double-voicedness or appreciating their hybridity.[8]

*Miguel Street*, the author's first written but third published novel, portrays a multicultural, inner-city neighborhood of Port of Spain through the eyes of a narrator who tells the story *as if* he were again a boy growing up there; in its narrative perspective and interlinked stories of urban frustration and ironic imprisonment, the collection resembles James Joyce's *Dubliners*.[9] *The Suffrage of Elvira* and *The Mystic Masseur* portray villages in transition from colonialism to independence and rural to urban society. The former depicts a theatrical political campaign and election in a tiny, remote Trinidad town. Although it pokes fun at Elvira's provincialism and satirizes its opportunism, it also sympathizes with a people caught up in unsettling political and economic changes. The latter novel is a history of an ethnic group of the colony written as the satiric biography of a masseur (a healer) who rises from his village origins to become an author and intellectual, politician and statesman.

Through two-sided humor and ironic, satiric perspectives, the 1950s Trinidad novels tell a double story: on the one hand, they celebrate the voices and spirit of a people who, though facing harsh realities, manage to live together in a multicultural, multiracial society; on the other hand, the novels expose a malaise that is partly concealed by, partly expressed by, a people's humor and gaiety. They tell not only stories with "local color," but disturbing stories as well about the trauma of a changing West Indian society.

## *Miguel Street* (1959)

The narrative strategy of *Miguel Street* responds to a split between the author's Trinidad and English cultural selves and attempts to resolve that split through double perspectives. First, by viewing Miguel Street from the perspective of a narrator who tells the story as if he were again a boy growing up in Port of Spain, the author can write from the base of his colonial Trinidad experiences, reentering, reconstructing, and revising that world. Second, by standing outside as well as within the narrator's viewpoint, the author can evaluate that world from the distanced perspective that he has acquired through his life in England. In short, he can write from the double perspective of exile, viewing one culture through the lens of another.

The narrator of *Miguel Street* is both a teller of the story and a character in it. I sometimes refer to him as the boy-adult narrator because he looks from a split perspective, that of a boy and that of an adult selecting and arranging his recollections. In the chapter entitled "The Pyrotechnicist," the narrator alludes to his age and experiences, remarking: "I have travelled in many countries since, but I have seen nothing to beat the fireworks show in Morgan's house that night."[10] The narrator as adult is worldly-wise; he can contrast Miguel Street with other places he has traveled to. However, most of the story is not told from this larger, worldly-wise perspective, but from the narrow perspective of a boy discovering his world, awakening to its dangers and patterns. In this respect the narrator resembles those of "Araby" or "An Encounter" in *Dubliners*. He has been formed by his world to see what he sees, and he sees it as if from the inside only, as if he had never left the "slum" and colony. The deterministic sameness of Miguel Street as an imprisoning milieu is before his eyes all along, but he can only dimly perceive it as such. This is presented symbolically in an incident in which the boy, losing his way while on a walk, discovers something of the extended sameness of his neighborhood, where all streets look alike; "I found about six Miguel Streets, but none seemed to have my house," he remarks (73). Here, as throughout his story, he often says more than he knows—or says one thing by saying another or nothing at all. His neighborhood is full of Miguel Streets, and the plight of the people who live on these streets is no different from those of people who live on the boy's street. Only at the end of his account does he give words to what is there in his environment—and in him—and through this awakening, he resolves to leave the colony. The narrow perspective of the boy shifts to the larger perspective of the adult, who is already in exile at the time of the writing of this story.

Through the counterpoint between the split perspective of the boy-adult narrator and the comprehensive, evaluative attitude of the author, *Miguel Street* sets up a double discourse in which what is said may have two opposed meanings, and what is left unsaid may be as important or more important than what is said. Comprising seventeen chapters or sketches of inhabitants of a multicultural neighborhood, the narrative's form would seem to emphasize the variety of life and richness of human difference in this one street of Port of Spain. The boy wants to impress this variety and difference on the reader: "A stranger could drive through Miguel Street and just say 'Slum!' because he could see no more. But we, who lived there, saw our street as a world, where everybody was quite different from everybody else" (63). The boy is right. He can see what the outsider cannot; he sees details of human difference that the outsider might overlook or dismiss and he feels the neighborhood's special pulse or esprit. But what the boy does not see, though his story shows it, is the essential similarity of the lives of Miguel Street. The narrative's form suggests variety and difference, but its content is a collection of variations on the same story of entrapment, failure, and erasure. Thus, its multistory form contrasts with the depressing sameness of each story's unhappy ending; the play of Miguel Street contrasts with its underlying harsh realities. This is the world that the author in exile constructs—one not without affection, but chiefly a world to justify his and the boy's escape.

Although the boy intends to describe his world's uniqueness and to show its value to outsiders who might think of it as just another slum, the adult-narrator's and author's evaluative attitude impart an ironic accent to his descriptions and thus intimate that Miguel Street may be quite different from what the boy initially perceives. The irony suggests the other side of Miguel Street, its deterministic patterns. Trouble with the law, sadness, and failure abound. The boy's friend, Bogart, admired for his imitation of Humphrey Bogart's "cool" style, is jailed for bigamy. Popo the carpenter, always leisurely making "the thing without a name," is jailed for furniture theft. Hat, the boy's best friend, is imprisoned for murder. George, the father of the boy's friend Elias, batters his wife, who dies prematurely—she "had the shabbiest and saddest and the loneliest funeral Miguel Street had ever seen"—and flogs his son and daughter with a rope soaked in the gutter of a cow pen (24). Thus prepared for failure, Elias has his ambitions for a profession slip away until he ends up a driver of "scavenging carts" (37). The title of Elias's story, "His Chosen Calling," counterpoints the adult-narrator's and author's ironic perspectives with the boy's nonjudgmental account of Elias's failures and sad fate

(30). There is little choice involved in Elias's "calling"; he repeatedly fails because his father and his milieu have programmed him to fail.

The boy's interpretation of Miguel Street often relates inversely to the adult-narrator's, author's, and reader's interpretation of it. Thus, for example, what the boy finds humorous, the author and reader often consider pathetic—or humorous and pathetic—and what the narrator says and describes often turns out to be less important than what he does not. Double-voicedness and double perspectives create a dissonance in the boy's and other characters' humor, a dissonance that we hear in funny or unfunny stories about the failure of human relationships in the slum. For example, the stories of Laura, Mrs. Hereira, and Toni show the damaging effects of the slum on sexual-marital relationships, yet the boy recounts these stories with an unsettling humor. He begins Laura's story with a joke that falls badly flat:

> I suppose Laura holds a world record.
> Laura had eight children.
> There is nothing surprising in that.
> These eight children had seven fathers.
> Beat that! (84)

The boy's remark shows a certain playfulness and esprit, but it also shows a contamination by the macho street attitudes of the slum. Laura is victimized by her ignorance and by a cultural reduction of women to objects, and here in the boy's joke she is turned into an object of sorts, reduced to a "world record." She is the perfect ghetto-female victim; her vivaciousness—the narrator says that she was "quite gay about what was happening to her"—is as unsettling as the boy's bad joke (84). Her ignorance is treated as both laughable and disturbing: "She used to point to [her expanding stomach]," the boy recalls, "and say, 'This thing happening again, but you get use to it after the first three four times. Is a damn nuisance, though'" (84). The humor is counterpointed by a barely audible anger and by the evaluations of the adult-narrator and author: as if slowly succumbing to waves, Laura is suffocating under the burden of pregnancies and children fathered by feckless men. To emphasize the determinism of her predicament, the novel extends it to her child; her daughter Lorna, like her mother, becomes pregnant in her teens. But rather than repeat the cycles of the mother's pregnancies, Lorna drowns herself by swimming out into the ocean that encloses the colony; for her, unlike the boy-narrator, there can be no escape, which is also to say that Lorna is a kind of specter in the narrator's imagination, an emblem of his latent fear of being swallowed by the ghetto and by the colony. "According to the newspapers," Lorna's was "just another week-end tragedy," the boy-narrator explains; like Laura's pregnancies, Lorna's suicide is pushed aside, as if, in this harsh milieu, there is only time for each individual's attention to his or her own survival (91). The adult-narrator and author introduce a dissonance into Laura's (and Lorna's) story; entitled "The Maternal Instinct," the story suggests through its ironic accents that her plight has much to do with something other than instinct as well, that is, with imprisonment in one's milieu.

Toni and Mrs. Hereira's story creates a similar dissonance between the boy as "experiencing self" ("knower") and the adult as "narrating self" ("sayer"), between the evaluations of the narrator and those of the author ("authorial narrator").[11] Toni is a hopeless alcoholic; Mrs. Christiani, alias Mrs. Hereira, is a woman who has temporarily left her husband and middle-class life in a well-to-do Port of Spain suburb. Toni and Mrs. Hereira have a relationship seemingly based on battering and degradation; in drunken fits he batters her, and she accepts it, or accepts it to the point that she continues to live with him. No one on Miguel Street can understand this couple and their living arrangement, which the neighbors interpret according to what their culture has taught them. Hat, for example, expressing the male, streetwise attitude, tells the boy that men need to beat their women occasionally to keep them in line: "Is a good thing for a man to beat his woman every now and then." But even Hat is surprised by the vigor with which Toni batters Mrs. Hereira: "this man does do it like exercise" (106). Hat's "wit and wisdom" create uneasiness, a dissonance caused by the counterpoint of the adult-narrator's and author's attitude and perspectives.[12] Reciting the lines of a calypso, the boy's mother offers another explanation of Mrs. Hereira's submission to Toni's batterings: "Is love, love, love alone / That cause King Edward to leave the throne" (105). But like Laura's "maternal instinct" as an explanation of her repeated pregnancies, "love" as an explanation of Toni's and Mrs. Hereira's relationship explains nothing. Latent in the boy's story of Toni and Mrs. Hereira lies a class-related, milieu-oriented explanation for their violent relationship. As a response to the failure and dehumanization of his lower-class, slum existence, Toni strikes out at Mrs. Christiani, the middle-class woman who can change her identity, so to speak, and return to her secure, suburban world. Unlike her, he cannot escape from the slum and his self-degradation, and therefore he punishes her for this. But such an explanation lies in the text like a dimly perceived puzzle to be pieced together. The boy begins to understand the milieu-related source of violence in male-female relationships in Miguel Street only later, after his best friend, Hat, kills his wife, and after he himself has left the colony and his perspective has changed.

The people of Miguel Street are "romancers," the adult-narrator says, by which he means that they live a "double life" of actuality and fantasy (72). Through some "eccentricity" or "violation of the usual and the generally accepted," they seek to draw life "out of its usual rut."[13] Bogart, Popo the carpenter, Man-man the savior,[14] Morgan the pyrotechnicist, Titus Hoyt the Latinist, Big Foot the pugilist, Hat as Mr. Cool, Edward the would-be American—each character has an eccentricity that raises him out of the rut of ghetto life and imparts to him a stylized, special identity. Shaped by their culture and by imperial forces such as Anglo-American films and advertising, they live out a fantasy as a way of defending against or escaping from a milieu that does not satisfy their desires for meaningful work and identity. B. Wordsworth, for example, who imagines himself the soul-brother of William, has ambitions of writing the "greatest poem" in the English language—at the breathless rate of one line per month. Does Wordsworth mimic the English poetic tradition, or rather, does he try to appropriate and transform it? Is he shaped by his milieu or is he also its shaper? On Miguel Street, hierarchy can be challenged and life raised out of its rut only momentarily. Wordsworth's life ends in erasure, not immortality, with poem unwritten, his death, the demolition of his house, and the cutting down of the mango, plum, and coconut trees around it. "It was just as though B. Wordsworth had never existed," the boy observes with sadness (52).[15]

Even more eccentric than Wordsworth, Morgan has fantastic, impossible ambitions: to make fireworks for the "King of America." Whether by plan or accident, ironically he burns down his own house—setting off a spectacular fireworks display—and is charged with arson. What finally becomes of Morgan no one really knows, the adult-narrator writes: "They said Morgan went to Venezuela. They said he went mad. They said he became a jockey" (72). Morgan, like Wordsworth, disappears, is erased—as if the "romancers" of Miguel Street are finally no more substantial than the stuff of their fantasies. Edward the "American," Eddoes the saga-boy, Bhakcu the mechanical genius, Big Foot the pugilist, Man-man the savior: everyone in Miguel Street seems, at least part of the time, to be dressed in masquerade. And the narrator, viewing the world as if from the perspective of a boy, is fascinated by the play and fantasies of its personages. To him, Bogart is like Bogie, Hat is like Rex Harrison, and Popo—the furniture thief who is always making "the thing without a name"—is a kind of magician. But as the boy's perspective shifts to an adult's-exile's, as it does forcefully at the end of the narrative, the personages of Miguel Street lose their fantastic identities. The masks drop. An implied critique of the double reality in which the people of Miguel Street live is thus built into the novel's narrative strategy; it is situated in the narrator's split, boy-adult perspectives and the author's evaluative attitude expressed, for example, in ironic juxtapositions between the fantastic and the mundane, between romance and actuality. The boy-narrator celebrates a people's unique spirit and voices, but he also shows indirectly the futility of their lives. Gaiety and pathos mix together.

Through the events that overwhelm his best friend, Hat, the boy feels the traps of the slum closing around and within him and determines to escape any way he can. Hat seemed to have succeeded in living life in his own way; "I never knew a man who enjoyed life as much as Hat," the boy says. "He did nothing new or spectacular . . . but he always enjoyed what he did. And every now and then he managed to give a fantastic twist to some very ordinary thing" (157). Hat seems to have the world by the tail, leisurely dividing his time between reading the newspapers and watching cricket, football, or horse races, taking life in a style much admired by the people of Miguel Street. He succeeds in transforming life into play and eluding the slum's stultification; he seems free, "self-sufficient," the boy says admiringly (160). But Hat's luck comes to an end. He marries unhappily, lives a brief, unhappy married life, and eventually kills his unhappy wife. In the end he goes to prison, the pattern of his life repeating the pattern of the lives of other inhabitants of Miguel Street who either go to jail or run from the law. Hat's failure confronts the boy with contradictions: everyone in Miguel Street is different and interesting, yet everyone's life there is shaped similarly by stultification and the threat of imprisonment. Miguel Street has play and gaiety, but it also has a basic, ineluctable harshness against which "romancing" is a feeble mask and no lasting protection. Faced with these conflicting aspects of his world, the boy looks at Miguel Street in a new way: "it was three years . . . in which I had grown up and looked critically at the people around me. I no longer wanted to be like Eddoes. He was so weak and thin, and I hadn't realized he was so small. Titus Hoyt was stupid and boring, and not funny at all" (165). The boy sees the "other side" of Miguel Street, and if he now unfairly diminishes its inhabitants, he does so as a stripping away of his earlier, naive perception of them.

As if by magic, the boy obtains a scholarship to study abroad, and at the end of his collection of portraits of Miguel Street describes himself striding across the runway to the plane that will carry him away to a distant land: "I left them all . . . not looking back, looking only at my shadow before me, a dancing dwarf on the tarmac" (172).[16] He leaves them behind, but he does not walk alone; he is accompanied by his shadow, the past extending into his future. He carries Miguel Street within him in that he has been formed by it and must, through the writing of this story, try to understand his reasons for leaving it. He celebrates it—and exorcises himself of it.

When we read *Miguel Street*, we need to read its double story. The first portrays an inner-city neighborhood alive with a unique spirit and a folk symphony of voices; there is something in it of the street theatricality of the Trinidad carnival. The second, conversely, portrays a pattern of frustration and imprisonment through cultural and social forces turning lives toward fantasy and away from accomplishment; this second story emphasizes the futility beneath the gaiety, the uneasiness within the humor, the entrapment at the end of the imagined escape. The first story shows the author's affection for the personages and voices of his childhood in Port of Spain, while the second manifests an exile's fears and his need to justify leaving the West Indian colony.

## *The Suffrage of Elvira* (1958)

Caricaturing a campaign and election in the "smallest, most isolated . . . most neglected of the nine counties in Trinidad," *The Suffrage of Elvira* takes aim at the mixed-up equation of money-mindedness, profit, and enfranchisement in a predominantly East Indian community.[17] It shows a village losing control of its traditions and itself in a period of political and economic transition. The novel's humor is less laughter *at* East Indians in particular and Trinidadians in general than, in Bakhtin's words, a "carnivalistic laughter . . . directed toward something higher—toward a shift of authorities and truths, a shift of world orders," a laughter that "embraces both poles of change" and has to do with "the very process of change, with *crisis* itself."[18]

The novel's satire depends on the juxtaposition of the characters' words and actions with the narrator's and author's evaluative attitudes. Like *Miguel Street*, *The Suffrage of Elvira* employs double-voicedness and indirection, although there are some differences in the narration of the two works. In the former, the distance between the boy's perspective and the adult-narrator's and author's perspectives diminishes at the end of the novel, while in the latter the distance between the characters' and the narrator-author's perspectives remains more or less the same. This relationship between the characters' attitudes and the narrator-author's evaluative attitude has its subtleties, however. Sometimes what the characters say is inversely related to what the narrator-author suggests and means; at other times a character and the narrator-author may share an attitude, even though they speak different, opposed languages, the one a folksy, Trinidad English, the other the queen's English. The novel's satire depends not only on conjunctions and juxtapositions between characters' attitudes and the narrator-author's attitude, but also on the bond between the author and his intended English audience who, with him, share certain assumptions about politics and democracy against which the campaign and election in Elvira are measured.

Naipaul illuminates the historical context of the novel in his travel book and social study, *The Middle Passage*. There he attributes the political "squalor" of Trinidad in the 1950s to the "picaroon" nature of the colony and to the public confusion that was brought about by the sudden granting of universal adult suffrage in 1946:

> In the colonial society every man had to be for himself; every man had to grasp whatever dignity and power he was allowed; he owed no loyalty to the island and scarcely any to his group. To understand this is to understand the squalor of the politics that came to Trinidad . . . when, after no popular agitation, universal adult suffrage was declared. The privilege took the population by surprise. Old attitudes persisted. . . . The new politics were reserved for the enterprising, who had seen their prodigious commercial possibilities. There were no parties, only individuals. Corruption, not unexpected, aroused only amusement and even mild approval.[19]

Historian Bridget Brereton describes the times in a similar vein: "a proliferation of groups and politicians competed for the new electorate. . . . It was the heyday of the individualist in politics, the independent, the 'broker politician' wheeling and dealing between various interest groups, manipulating the votes and the divisions among them in his own interests, seizing every chance in the confused transition from one system of political authority to another."[20] *The Suffrage of Elvira* caricatures this political confusion, its conflict between "old attitudes" and new politics, its "enterprising" individuals who take advantage of the absence of political parties and are consequently involved in bribery and corruption.

Naipaul's target is not only political topsy-turvydom, but the subworld of predominantly East Indian villages with their narrow loyalties, jealousies, money-mindedness, and philistinism (*MP* 82). Though it is multicultural, Elvira is one such subworld of the colony; a mélange of Hindus and Muslims, Catholics, Jehovah's Witnesses, and African animists, it is a village of ethnic diversity and yet defined group loyalties. Of the main groups, Baksh the tailor speaks for the Muslims, Chittaranjan the goldsmith for the Hindus, the Preacher for the Spanish Catholics and animists. Beliefs and traditions serve to differentiate and separate one group from another, although these differences are less obstacles than convenient tags of identity on the basis of which Elvirans vent their grievances with one another and politicians trump up issues on which to run for election. Thus, for example, Chittaranjan the Hindu berates his neighbor Baksh the Muslim for eating meat less out of principle than out of personal offense at Baksh's apparent belittling of Chittaranjan's daughter: "Smell the beef and all the other nastiness they does cook in this house. . . . A animal spend nine months in his mother belly. It born. The mother feed it. People feed it. It feed itself. It grow up. It come big. It come strong. Then they kill it. Why? . . . To feed Baksh" (114–15). But Chittaranjan's complaint finally has nothing to do with meat; he is merely getting in a few pokes at Baksh, who has implied that his daughter is not good enough to marry the politician's son. Although the ethnic groups in Elvira make a show of standing up for their traditions and beliefs, the differences between the groups are breaking down in the tiny, hybridizing world of Elvira. The mixing of beliefs and traditions is one of its prominent characteristics: "Things were crazily mixed up in Elvira," the narrator remarks. "Everybody, Hindus, Muslims and Christians, owned a Bible; the Hindus and Muslims looked on it, if anything, with greater awe. Hindus and Muslims celebrated Christmas and Easter. The Spaniards and some of the Negroes celebrated the Hindu festival of the lights" (66). In this context, partisanship based solely on ethnic differences would not seem to make much sense, and part of the novel's satire of Harbans's and the Preacher's opposing campaigns derives from the fact that ethnic differences are less important in determining blocks of votes than bribery and deals. The beliefs are partly masks—for show and for concealment of underlying intentions.

The campaign manipulates these differences in conjunction with Elvira's awakened sense that any commodity, whether a vote or a daughter, can be turned to profit. Tradition, political dealing, and profit making unite in the parentally arranged marriage of Chittaranjan's daughter and Harbans's son. According to Hindu tradition, parents and not sons and daughters arrange marriages, but Chittaranjan and Harbans view the prospective marriage less as a traditional match than as a payoff for support of Harbans's candidacy. After he wins the election—and he could not have won without Chittaranjan's block of support—Harbans the political opportunist feigning Hindu traditionalism wriggles out of the deal by implying that Chittaranjan's daughter has sullied herself by secretly meeting a Muslim boy, ironically Harbans's own campaign manager, Foam. He threatens to make this known. More the traditionalist than Harbans and fearful of town prejudice, Chittaranjan does not want a blot on his daughter's reputation and thus allows himself to be blackmailed. The (broken) agreement between Chittaranjan and Harbans focuses the two forces of the campaign: the manipulation of the old ways by the new wiles of profit making, and complementarily, the contamination of the new right to vote by the old patterns of petty feuds and ethnic prejudice.

"Democracy had come to Elvira four years before, in 1946," the narrator recounts, "but it had taken nearly everybody by surprise and it wasn't until 1950, a few months before the second general election under universal adult franchise, that people began to see the possibilities" (13). Here "possibilities" do not mean the challenges of a democratic society, but the opportunities for monetary gain. " 'The people' have learned their power," Naipaul writes caustically in *The Middle Passage*, "and the sensation is still so new that every new voter regards himself as a pressure group. In this way the people . . . who wish to beg, bribe and bully because this is the way they got things done in the past . . . are a threat to responsible government and a threat, finally, to their own leaders. It is part of the colonial legacy" (*MP* 120). In Elvira everyone has a say, a voice, and almost everyone tries to profit from the election in one way or another. Because Foam wants a van and salary, and, above all, relishes being in the spotlight, he begs himself into the position as Harbans's campaign manager. Baksh, after vacillating and raising his demands, settles for a lump-sum payoff to insure his support of Harbans. Chittaranjan negotiates the future marriage of his daughter to Harbans's son. Everyone wants and gets something, and consequently, Harbans's campaign expenses mount—they comprise petty allowances, contributions to humanitarian funds like the sick or dying Negro fund (if a sick or dying Negro can indeed be found), payoffs, and the numerous expenses of the election-day parade. In the past, "People did just go and vote for the man they like," Baksh remarks. "Now is different. People learning. You have to spend on them" (46). Viewed from one perspective, a new money-mindedness corrupts the community; viewed from another, the old survivalist principle of the colony (i.e., every man for himself) corrupts the new democracy.

The politicking in Elvira turns into a fete prefiguring today's media-driven campaigns in which the theatrical and the sensational take the place of a thorough debate of the issues. Foam typifies the spirit, his campaign slogans at once cheers and threats: "VOTE HARBANS OR DIE!" (40). The dress and mood are theatrical: Foam wears sunglasses while he drives the campaign van and broadcasts announcements; the taxi drivers paid to join Harbans's election-day parade sport double-sided "cardboard eyeshades," with "DO YOUR PART" printed on one side and "VOTE THE HEART" on the other (178). This theatricality is expressive of a folk spirit, though there is a point of satire here that should not be missed. Both *Miguel Street* and *The Suffrage of Elvira* critique a culture and society in which, as in the former novel, individuals create fantastic identities in response to their limiting milieu, and in the latter, where a tiny community becomes swept up in a fantasy of power. In *The Suffrage of Elvira* that fantasy is so calculated that it becomes a kind of theater. The townspeople in the election-day parade know what their parts are supposed to be, and they see through the masks that they have been given to wear. The effect of this is that although they can be naive, they are never quite as naive as they seem. All of Naipaul's 1950s novels show a sophisticated sense of mask, play, and theatricality in which the characters' motives and intentions are never quite as determinable as they may appear on a first reading.

Although *The Suffrage of Elvira* satirizes the townspeople's (con)fusion of politics and profit, it does give its characters an ethical reflex. Mrs. Baksh, for example, observes critically the Elvirans' opportunism: "Everybody just washing their feet and jumping in this democracy business" (40). Though she speaks with the voice of the folk, her judgment is essentially the same as the narrator-author's: "democracy" is becoming a "business" in which each voter tries to turn a profit. In Mrs. Baksh's humor the reader also hears a warning; she and the narrator agree that there is a new danger in town, a malaise. No one in Elvira seems particularly happy with the equation "democracy equals bribery," and this breaks through in the wit and sly humor about the campaign and election. Even Harbans the winner, glumly totaling his campaign expenses, complains: "This democracy is a strange thing. It does make the great poor and the poor great. It make me a beggar" (154). His sense that the equation of votes and money can lead to a topsy-turvy world is the narrator-author's attitude as well. Harbans's remark contains a suspicion that democracy may turn into a monster neither the candidates nor the voters can control. Other characters equate democracy with an erosion of the community's values and with an ironic inequality: "Everybody want something for nothing," Chittaranjan says. "I work for every penny I have, and now you have these people complaining that they is poor and behaving as though other people depriving them." Ramlogan concurs, adding sarcastically: "Everybody equal. People who ain't got brain to work and those who use their brain to work. Everybody equal" (141). Although lighthearted enough, these complaints also voice a deeper social dissatisfaction that foreshadows violence: the burning of Harbans's new Jaguar automobile. Everyone watches the car burning as if wondering how the campaign and election could possibly have led to this:

[Harbans] found the crowd standing in a wide silent circle around the burning Jaguar. . . . The firelight reddened unsmiling, almost contemplative, faces.

Harbans stopped too, to watch the car burn. . . . There was little smoke now; the flames burned pure. Behind the heat waves faces were distorted.

The people from the trace ran up in joyful agitation, flowed around the car, settled, and became silent. (205)

Thus, in the novel's ironic twist, democracy turns into destruction, and votes into violence. The end of the campaign, with its carnivalesque aspects, is this ritual burning.

The novel's double-voicedness, its counterplay between the narrator's and characters' voices and attitudes, makes it a book that can be easily misread. The narrator pokes fun at Elvirans, yet also shares with them a sense of social malaise. He satirizes their superstition, prejudice, and money-mindedness, yet also gives them a self-critical reflex. In answer to the question, does the novel do anything more than caricature politics in the colony, we must say yes, it does. Especially in its humor the novel partly conceals, partly reveals, an incipient social trauma; it shows a collision of forces shaping people's lives and the future of their society.

Like *Miguel Street, The Suffrage of Elvira* tells a double story. One story satirizes a campaign that turns on bribery; the second depicts the social trauma of a people partly confused by, partly critical of, the fusion of two new powers in their community: the power to vote and the power to buy and sell. In Elvira people have learned to live together, but in the con(fusion) of political and socioeconomic change, instead of becoming more democratic and open-minded, the village becomes less so, divided against itself. The final act in this "social comedy" is violent, a foreshadowing of a breakdown of old orders that Naipaul will scrutinize in later essays and novels.

## *The Mystic Masseur* (1957)

Recounting a healer and guru's rise to power in colonial Trinidad, *The Mystic Masseur* refers to a historical period extending from the 1920s or 1930s into the 1950s, beginning before the changes alluded to in *The Suffrage of Elvira* and continuing beyond them. Interestingly, Naipaul's early novels move in reverse chronological order from the 1940s and 1950s back to the turn of the century: *Miguel Street* treats three years that coincide with a period of the author's youth in Port of Spain and his departure for study in England; *The Suffrage of Elvira* covers the campaign and election of 1950 and shortly thereafter; *The Mystic Masseur* begins two or three decades earlier; and *A House for Mr Biswas* takes place a few decades before that in the late nineteenth or early twentieth century. After completing these novels, Naipaul wrote travel books/social studies/histories about the West Indies and South America and the land of his ancestors, India. Thus, he has moved forward in his career by turning to the past for his subject matter: his own past, the past of his family, the past of the West Indies and the Caribbean.

A variation of the double-voicedness and the double perspectives distinguishing *Miguel Street* and *The Suffrage of Elvira* also marks *The Mystic Masseur*, the most complex of the three 1950s novels. That complexity derives from the blurred relationship between the narrator as "knower" and as "sayer." His wit and humor, silences and absence of judgmental comments, make him hard to pin down; at times his evaluation of Ganesh, the mystic masseur, appears to be identical with the authorial evaluation, while at others it diverges from and conflicts with it. "A message can always be massaged" might be the appropriate motto of this novel, whose narrator becomes, like Ganesh, a masseur of words. Noting his mother's distrust of Trinidad doctors, the narrator recalls that, during his youth, people used to take their ills to unqualified masseurs or dentists, often with unhappy results:

My mother distrusted doctors and never took me to one. I am not blaming her for this because in those days people went by preference to the unqualified masseur or the quack dentist.

"I know the sort of doctors it have in Trinidad," my mother used to say. "They think nothing of killing two three people before breakfast."

This wasn't as bad as it sounds: in Trinidad the midday meal is called breakfast.[21]

The humor is delightful partly because it avoids any commentary—either on quackery or its victims, "two three" of whom lie before the reader's eyes. But the humor also conceals the narrator's attitudes: Does he intend only to describe his mother's exaggerated distrust of doctors? What is he suggesting about Ganesh? What is he saying about himself? Only through the cumulative effect of the narrator's commentary does his attitude show its slant, but even then, it is partly indeterminate. Indirection and equivocality, the open-endedness of the word: these seem to be the novel's narrative strategy and its subject. Both the narrator and Ganesh—for it is through the power of books that Ganesh promotes his "vision" and achieves renown—are masseurs of words. At one level of signification, the novel is self-reflexively about the power of the word and the problem of the word.

The narrator's attitude toward Ganesh ranges from nonjudgmental to sympathetic to distant and satiric. He begins the biography with his boyhood recollection of Ganesh, to whose house his mother takes him for treatment of an infected foot. The treatment is unscientific and ineffective, an early instance of Ganesh's quackery. But the narrator does not dwell on that: "In the end I went to a doctor in St. Vincent Street who took one look at my foot, 'Abscess. Will have to cut it.' And charged ten dollars" (17). Here the narrator allows the facts to speak for themselves, whether because he has adopted the stance of the "objective" biographer, or because the purpose of his biography is not to expose Ganesh's quackery but to show the cultural and social determinants of his life, or because Ganesh's story, in allegorical form, is the shadowy allegory of the author's own life and thus not to be judged so much as approached, through fiction, circumspectly.

The narrator sympathetically recounts the young Ganesh's restlessness and aspirations; these, in conjunction with a very limiting social milieu, are some of the same elements that drive the boy of *Miguel Street* to leave Trinidad for England. The narrator creates sympathy by describing Ganesh's sense of inferiority, awkwardness, and frustration with his social limitations. He was "so ashamed of his Indian name," the narrator notes, and so embarrassed by his thin hair that, while a student, he wears a khaki toupee to class (21). He describes Ganesh's sense of entrapment and painful difference between his life and the lives of others beyond his small island world: "[Ganesh] went for a walk along the wharves. It was early afternoon and gulls mewed amid the masts of sloops and schooners. Far out, he saw the ocean liners at anchor. He allowed the idea of travel to enter his mind and just as easily allowed it to go out again. He spent the rest of the afternoon in a cinema, but this was torture. He especially resented the credit titles. He thought, 'All these people with their name in big print on the screen have their bread butter. . . . They not like me'" (26). In this passage the reader sees Ganesh from the "inside," from the perspective of his awakening but as yet unfocused ambitions; we see him, in his naïveté, exaggerating the accomplishments of others, making the world beyond Trinidad bigger than it actually is. When the narrator describes Ganesh's feelings in this way, the character comes alive for the reader, and the distance between Ganesh and narrator diminishes. Similarly, the narrator writes sympathetically of Ganesh's discouraging experience as a teacher in a school where education is equated with discipline. "Form not inform" is the headmaster's directive, and this directive, although Ganesh rejects it initially and quits his job at the school, becomes the underlying principle of the empty medicine, empty spiritualism, empty business, and empty politics that he later engages in (24–25). From his experience as a teacher, Ganesh learns that success in the colony is a matter of masks and appearances, and he applies this lesson throughout his later life.

As Ganesh's story unfolds, the narrator looks at him less from the inside and increasingly from the outside, so much so that by the end of the biography, Ganesh no longer seems to have an inner world—only an exterior, an appearance, a set of masks. He has become an abstraction, a symbol of a cultural and social transformation in the colony and the colonial West Indies generally. He is no longer the Pundit Ganesh Ramsumair, for whom the narrator feels a certain sentimental attachment, but the formal, cold G. Ramsay Muir. The reader feels a sense of loss, just as the reader of *The Suffrage of Elvira* feels a sense of loss for a village world pulled apart.

The narrator defines his biography—the story of a villager who becomes author, entrepreneur, politician, and statesman—as a "history" of the times, meaning, among other things, the story of a successful East Indian who sums up in his career the forces of change during a particular period of the colony and the Caribbean. Ganesh's story constitutes a history in that he shapes and is shaped by socioeconomic forces that turn the villages of Trinidad from a communal to an individualist, commercialist order of society.[22] He represents a new entrepreneurship dressed in old customs and traditions, a marriage of marketing and mysticism. In the Fourways and Fuente Grove, where East Indian traditions are breaking down, he creates a spectacular image of himself as a man both of the past and of the future. Combining his education with the Hindu tradition of the masseur (following in his father's footsteps), he transforms that tradition into an enterprise.

He relies on his wits, the prestige of his education, and the quasimagical power of the written word to make his impact in villages where people do not read or write and thus look upon education and books as manifestations of special powers. "Education, sahib, is one hell of a thing," Ramlogan, Ganesh's father-in-law, says, showing him the recently purchased booklets, "The Art of Salesmanship" (42–43). Ramlogan cannot read and has been tricked into buying the booklets by Bissoon, a clever book salesman, but he is still proud to possess these talismans. In this context, any publication is special, and even slim volumes on a mundane subject partake of the aura of the almighty printed word. Thus, Ganesh's announcement that he is going to write a book is greeted as extraordinary: "Going to write a book . . . Big book," he declares. He naively dashes off a letter to the Street and Smith publishers telling them that he is "thinking of writing books," and proudly frames the reply that his family also greets with jubilation: "Ramlogan came all the way from Fourways and when he gazed on the framed letter his eyes filled with tears. 'Sahib, this is something else for the papers. Yes, man, sahib, write the books for them'" (75). The satire is harmless yet significantly pointed. Through the power associated with books, Ganesh creates an aura that enables him to play the guru in villages in transition from an oral to a print culture and from communalism to capitalism.

*The Mystic Masseur*, itself a play on words, is about the play of words—words and their power to captivate, hallow, manipulate, deceive. The printed word is a multiple symbol in the novel; it is a synecdoche for education, knowledge, success, and civilization, and it is a point of contrast between the oral culture of Fourways and Fuente Grove and the written cultures of the United States and Europe. Books signify Ganesh's (partly sham) knowledge, conferring on him credibility and power in the villages. The narrator, recalling his first meeting with Ganesh, notes that the Pundit did not look holy and wise except for the "big book" he was holding; the stacks of books in Ganesh's hut seal the impression: "As soon as we entered my mother winked at me, and I could see that even the taxi-driver was fighting to control his astonishment. There were books, books, here, there, everywhere; books piled crazily on the table, books rising in mounds in the corners, books covering the floor. I had never before seen so many books in one place" (13–15). The narrator comments that "after seeing all those books," he was "ready to believe in [Ganesh] and quite prepared to take his mixture" (16). The stacks of books—which in the Trinidad of *Miguel Street* are bought and sold by the dime, as in "Hat bought twenty cents' worth of book"—are Ganesh's equivalent to prestigious diplomas hanging on a physician's wall; they lend an appearance of professional qualifications and an aura of knowledge (96). Ganesh uses the mystique of books to bedazzle clients and townspeople, but because he is himself bedazzled by the printed word, it is uncertain where his manipulation of others through words begins and ends.

To be a reader, a collector of books confers a certain amount of power; to be an author, a hundred times more. That, at least, is partly the idea behind Ganesh's determination to write a book; he seeks the magical power of authorship for his self-image and for the impact that the printed word has on the villagers. The publication of his first book, *101 Questions and Answers on the Hindu Religion*, represents a great moment in his life, even though the thirty-page text, with a spine too thin for the title, looks disappointing. Nevertheless, the book affirms what was uncertain and only imagined, his credentials as an intellectual and his identity as an author, a person with special powers. At the same time this new identity mystifies him; caught between the romance of authorship and the actuality of his book, Ganesh says with wonder to his wife Leela: "I write a book. . . . look here at these words I write with my own hand. They print now, but you know I just sit down at the table in the front-room and write them on ordinary paper with a ordinary pencil." Leela responds with equal amazement: "Oh, man! Oh man! Oh, man, you really write the book" (99). There is a warmth in these portraits of Ganesh and Leela as well as traces of Seepersad Naipaul's and his son's romance with books and the idea of becoming a writer. In the Foreword to *The Adventures of Gurudeva*, the son recalls his father's excitement at the publication of short stories: "The printing was done, slowly by the Guardian Commercial Printery; my father brought the proofs home bit by bit in his jacket pocket; and I shared his hysteria when the linotypists, falling into everyday ways, set—permanently, as it turned out—two of the stories in narrow newspaper-style columns."[23]

Although the narrator treats Ganesh's aspirations with a certain affection, he satirizes his deception and his manipulation of others. Through the printed word Ganesh acquires a new identity, yet that identity is partly a fantasy. Like the "romancers" of Miguel Street and the carnival-spirited campaigners of Elvira, he inhabits a double reality; unlike them, he succeeds spectacularly at maintaining and marketing his fantasy. He uses the printed word to promote himself and milk others. His travel book, *The Guide to Trinidad*, recommends to American military personnel and other foreigners such attractions as his own hut, the "Fuente Grove Hindu temple" (159). To undermine a political rival, he founds a sensationalist, self-serving newspaper, *The Dharma*, which runs specious stories and carries bogus ads promising "superlative bargains in fictitious shops in unknown villages" (181).[24] Ganesh makes good as a politician because he has learned, by writing books like *What God Told Me* and *The Soul As I See It*, to be a "masseur" of words, to tell people what they want to hear.[25]

Ganesh's story is both biography and history, each with two sides, with a double meaning. As biography, it tells the story of a struggling East Indian who becomes successful in a limiting colonial society through his intelligence and his understanding of others; yet it also tells a story of a quack and con man who succeeds by hook or by crook and thus uses others. Through the account of his struggles, his wit, and style, Ganesh is depicted as an individual with a complex inner world; but in his manipulation of others and his transformation into a calculating, shifty politician and statesman, he is depicted instead as superficial, an abstraction, a final anglicization of the spirit of the West Indian colony. Ganesh turns into his titles, a new name, a false, English-sounding collection of words: "G. Ramsay Muir, Esq., M.B.E." In that new name the old Hindu world of Trinidad begins to expire, and the imperial English world triumphs, penetrating still farther into alien places. At the end of the novel Ganesh has become a symbol of a shift in the consciousness and cultural identity of East Indians and Trinidadians generally. To what degree his mimicry is imprisoning, and/or to what degree liberating, probably cannot be unequivocably determined, for one can never know for sure what goes on underneath a mask.

The narrator views Ganesh as both the shaper of and someone shaped by the forces of his day. He explains that his life is determined by historical attitudes and circumstances, such as the 1920s' and 1930s' East Indian attitude toward education, changes in the East Indian villages, the flow of new ideas from England and the United States, and the picaroon (every-man-for-himself) nature of colonial society at its worst. Had Ganesh been born "ten years earlier," the narrator speculates, he might not have been educated; had he been born "ten years later," he might have been sent abroad for his education. Given the former circumstances, he would have remained a villager; given the latter, he might have become "an unsuccessful lawyer or a dangerous doctor," the narrator says drolly. Similarly, had Ganesh taken work at a military base or become a taxi driver, the "mystic path would have been closed to him for ever" (205). He becomes a "mystic masseur" because he is born at the right time; he achieves success because he is adept at interpreting the old in the context of the new in a period of cultural and socioeconomic transition in the colony. In the footsteps of his father and in keeping with his East Indian cultural heritage, Ganesh chooses to become a masseur; sensitive to the cultural and economic influences from England and the United States, he learns to get on in the world and to sell the mystic. He represents, then, the meeting of the old East Indian world and the new, Euro-American world, combining the spiritualism of the former and the materialism of the latter. Above all, he molds and is molded by his commodity-oriented, client-oriented colonial society. He acts and reacts according to the pressures of earning a living and the possibilities of establishing a career in a society with few professions and few outlets for intellectuals. From beyond the colony, new ideas about the printed word, models of salesmanship and entrepreneurship, press upon him, but the colony has long been a land of commodities and clients and Ganesh's story is but another chapter in that history prepared for by previous chapters. In him twentieth-century marketing comes to Trinidad, but it comes to a colony that already knows the mechanism of commodities and the reflex of survival on any terms.

The Trinidad of these 1950s novels combines an exile's distanced evaluation with a colonial's old uncertainties and fears. Through the novels' double-voicedness and double perspectives, the author can write affectionately about the colony as well as satirize it. "To condemn the picaroon [colonial] society out of hand is to ignore its important quality," he writes in *The Middle Passage*. "And this is not only its ability to beguile and enchant. For if such a society breeds cynicism, it also breeds tolerance . . . tolerance for every human activity and affection for every demonstration of wit and style" (*MP*77). Of all of his works, the 1950s novels are perhaps most touched by the "wit and style" of a unique multicultural society whose predominant symbol is carnival, with its celebration of difference yet community. These novels are touched by the theatricality of the Trinidad carnival, with gaiety, outlandish creativity, masks, inversions. At the same time, though, they show the author's fear of a loss of identity through a carnivalistic immersion in the folk; they show an exile's distancing of himself from a society that he has left and must now justify having left. Through the masks of double-voicedness and double perspectives, he expresses both his affection for people and things of the colony and his sense of the colony's limitations and imprisonment.

Carnival can serve as a metaphor for this fictional world. As in carnival, where gaiety rules, the 1950s novels feature an inverting wit and humor, and folk characters who are often aware that they live in an epoch that is overturning an old social order. They wear masks to survive in a repressive colonial world and to assert a personal freedom that eludes its psychological and socioeconomic traps and trammels. Beneath and beyond the masks, however, lies another actuality, the "futility" of the colony as Naipaul perceives and constructs it. Trinidad carnival celebrates a liberation, but in these novels the author also looks at the patterns of the colony as they imprison rather than liberate.

# 2

# A House for Mr Biswas

> "A man that is born falls into a dream like a man who falls into the sea."
> —Joseph Conrad, *Lord Jim*
>
> History is . . . the experience of Necessity. . . . History is what hurts . . . what refuses desire and sets inexorable limits to individual as well as collective praxis.
> —Fredric Jameson, *The Political Unconscious*

Like Naipaul's 1950s novels, *A House for Mr Biswas* (1961) depicts communities being reshaped by larger cultural and social forces; moving from East Indian villages to Port of Spain city life, it records a colony's transition from a rural to an urban, industrialized society. Through the story of Biswas, whose life is a struggle between desire and necessity—or dream and history—*A House for Mr Biswas* tells a personal story and an ethnic, social history. At the same time, however, it also tells a story informed by the author's exile, and the ethnic communities and society of the novel are constructed out of that exile and a need to justify it. As Kenneth Ramchand has observed insightfully: "One suspects that the world of *A House for Mr Biswas* is one modelled upon a society from which the author has himself wished to escape, and that this attitude is the source of some of the over-emphasis in the fictional construct."[1]

Although similar in certain respects, *Mr Biswas* differs from Naipaul's previous novels in some important ways: first, in its detailed depiction of an East Indian family order and one individual's acculturation in Trinidad society and his acquisition of a social identity; second, in its directness and its balance of empathetic and evaluative views of its main character and his milieus; and third, in its creation of Biswas's inner world, as contrasted with the character sketches of previous novels. (The exceptions here are the boy of *Miguel Street* and Ganesh of *The Mystic Masseur*, but still we know much less of their feelings and views than we do of Biswas's.) The "distance" between the novel's third-person narrator and Biswas is less than that between the narrators and characters of previous novels such as *The Suffrage of Elvira* and *The Mystic Masseur*. The indirection of those novels, through which the narrator or author says one thing but often means something quite different, is largely replaced in *A House for Mr Biswas* by a directness and judiciousness that balance sympathetic, "inside" views and evaluative, "outside" views of the main character. Through this balance between sympathy and judgment, the novel renders Biswas's complexity and provisionally resolves the tension within the author between his Trinidad Indian heritage and his metropolitan experiences and attitudes. The author achieves this balance and resolution through an intimacy with his father's esprit and through the distanced perspective of exile. The experience of exile also has a different, countereffect, however: it works to devalue the society that the author has left. There is a sense in which the novel is about Naipaul's fear of what would have happened to him had he remained in Trinidad; thus, Biswas's unfinished manuscript, "Escape," signifies not only that character's unrealized dream of becoming an author, but also a son's apprehensive vision of what might have become of his own career had he stayed on the West Indian island.

*A House for Mr Biswas* is a collaborative creation between a son and his father's life and writings.[2] In "Prologue to an Autobiography" (1984), Naipaul writes that *Mr Biswas* was his "father's book. . . . written out of his journalism and stories, out of . . . knowledge he had got from the way of looking MacGowan [former managing editor at the *Trinidad Guardian*] had trained him in. It was written out of his writing."[3] This is not to say that the novel is a biography, that Mohun Biswas and Seepersad Naipaul are one and the same, but that the fictional creation emerges from the son's forging into art of the father's life and writings and his transformation of their voices by filtering them through his own. The son inherits the father's dream of becoming a writer, and by becoming a writer he in turn creates a fiction of his father and his father's dreams. Biswas emerges, as well, from the experience of alienation within Naipaul's exile: in Biswas's not-belonging is Naipaul's; his sense of being an outsider is also Naipaul's.

Through the interplay between Biswas's desires and his story's or history's modifications and ironic reversals of them, *A House for Mr Biswas* depicts the making of an individual's and family's cultural and social identity. Biswas undergoes a process of acculturation and socialization, but his story is equally about his alienation, about belonging to a particular society yet living in "exile" from it in his unrealized ambitions. In writing the novel Naipaul turns to his father's life and writings, but he also draws from his own experience of exile to create Biswas's sense of alienation and estrangement in the colony that he could not leave but which the author did.

Just as *The Enigma of Arrival* (1987) honors a deceased brother and sister, so too *A House for Mr Biswas* honors the author's father through the act of the novel's composition and through the fictional personage of Biswas. The novel begins with a reflection, a eulogy of sorts, on the life of Mohun Biswas, whose first name means, significantly, "beloved," the "name given by the milkmaids to Lord Krishna.' "[4] The Prologue touches on the themes of his life, such as his dreams of a profession and a house of his own, cherished objects like his yellow typewriter, his disappointments and successes, and it then recounts his life's story from birth to death. The novel divides that story into two parts: Part One traces his familial origins and childhood through the years of dependency on his uncle Bhandat and later on the Tulsi family to his desperate departure for Port of Spain and the beginning of his career as a reporter for the Trinidad *Sentinel*. Part Two follows his career at the *Sentinel*, his changes of jobs and residences, his son's rising expectations contrasting with his own waning ambitions and sense of waste, his failing health and dismissal from the *Sentinel*, and finally his death of a heart attack. Within Parts One and Two, the chapters divide according to the major fluctuations in his life, particularly changes of jobs and residence. The determinants behind these changes are the basic needs for food and shelter and his human need for identity and dignity. The novel's chapter divisions thus suggest that his life is largely shaped by basic necessities, which are a constant pressure on him and his family, reversing his intentions and undermining his dreams.

Part One delineates Biswas's limiting circumstances and the conflict between his desires and his modifying, "wounding" milieus. From infancy Mohun seems born only to feel the pain of living. His body is left unwashed, becoming "dusty" and "muddy"; malnutrition stunts his growth, causes "eczema and sores that [swell] and burst," and gives him a shallow chest, thin limbs, and a "rising belly" (22). His infant years are "pastoral"—the ironic title of the first chapter—only in the sense that the setting is rural. Life in rural Trinidad is hard, and *Mr Biswas*, like Naipaul's previous novels, can be read as an unromantic portrait of the colonial West Indies.

This first chapter sets the social and historical context of Mohun's life and of the East Indian villages that came into being through the migration of indentured workers in the nineteenth and twentieth centuries. In *From Columbus to Castro: The History of the Caribbean*, Eric Williams discusses the economic impetus behind and the scope of this migration to the Caribbean, explaining that with the abolition of the slave trade in 1807 planters turned to East Indians as a source of labor on the sugarcane estates. Nearly half a million East Indians immigrated to the Caribbean as indentured workers between 1838 and 1924.[5] Indians first came to Trinidad in 1845, and by 1917, nearly 150,000 had immigrated here.[6] Mohun's grandfather, like Naipaul's maternal grandfather, was one such indentured worker on a Trinidad sugar estate. Mohun's father is also a laborer, and apparently only slightly better off than the grandfather. Thus, Mohun and his brothers inherit the social identity of worker-laborer and socioeconomic limitations only marginally less constraining than indenture. After the death of their father, Mohun's brothers are in fact sent to work on a sugar estate, while Mohun, because he has attended school, is spared and sent to tend his uncle's shop instead.[7]

Throughout much of his life Mohun must depend on others for his food and shelter, first on his uncle Bhandat and later on the Tulsi family.[8] After leaving Bhandat's store, the young Mohun finds a job painting signs at the Tulsi store in Arwacas; there he meets Shama, a Tulsi daughter, whom he marries chiefly because he is pressured by the domineering Mrs. Tulsi. Biswas and Shama live at Hanuman House with the other Tulsis' sons and daughters and their families, but conflict between Biswas and the Tulsis eventually forces him to leave and work as a shopkeeper at a Tulsi store in a village called The Chase, "a long, straggling settlement of mud huts in the heart of the sugarcane area" (141).[9] After six years of "boredom and futility" at the Bonne Esperance (Good Hope) Grocery, Biswas abandons the indebted shop and reluctantly takes a job as a driver on the Tulsi sugar estate in Green Vale, while his wife and children remain behind at Hanuman House. Although he is an overseer (a supervisor), Biswas must humiliatingly live with workers in the estate's barracks;[10] in an effort to escape his depressing living quarters and his inherited identity as the "son of a labourer," he hires a carpenter to build him a house away from the workers' huts (49). The final product is a folly, not the fulfillment of a dream as he had hoped. Disappointed, tired of being a driver, exhausted by his life away from his family, Biswas falls ill, and Seth, a brother-in-law and the Tulsi family's business manager, takes him to Hanuman House to recuperate. In his absence from Green Vale, angry workers burn down his jerry-built house. With a wife and two children to support, Biswas finds himself with neither house, job, nor occupation; although he dreams of being independent, he is at the mercy of the Tulsis for his and his family's sustenance. After recovering his health, he has little choice but to leave his family again and look for a job in the city, Port of Spain.

In Part Two Biswas acquires a profession and moves into a house of his own, though each of these accomplishments has its qualifying, ironic side. Initially he finds work as a sign writer at the Trinidad *Sentinel* and later gets a chance to be a reporter for the newspaper. The editor, Mr. Burnett, tells Biswas that he can have a job as reporter if he can give him "one good fright."[11] Biswas responds with stories with sensational headlines like "FOUR CHILDREN ROASTED IN HUT BLAZE" and "DADDY COMES HOME IN A COFFIN" (323–27). He becomes the *Sentinel*'s star reporter. Unfortunately, his glory comes to an end when Mr. Burnett, his mentor and protector, is fired, and he himself is transferred to "court cases, funerals and cricket matches," where reporting is drudgery and where he works in constant fear of being "sacked."

Biswas's status as a reporter improves his standing among the Tulsis, and his wife and children rejoin him in Port of Spain. They live in a house owned by Mrs. Tulsi and then move to other houses both in and on the outskirts of the city. Biswas acquires a professional identity and achieves a certain independence from the Tulsis, but these accomplishments fail to measure up to his dreams. At the flush of his ambition as a writer Biswas begins a short story appropriately entitled "Escape," but after several attempts is unable to complete it. His reportorial work growing increasingly tedious, he quits his job at the *Sentinel* and takes a higher paying one at the Welfare Department. As he grows older, his thoughts turn less to his professional and literary ambitions and more to his son Anand's education and future. He is delighted when Anand wins a scholarship to college and then to a university in England: "Third in the island!" he proclaims ecstatically. "Only two boys more intelligent!" (486–87). Through the purchase of the house on Sikkim Street, Biswas realizes one of his lifelong ambitions; he soon comprehends, however, that he has been tricked into the deal by an unscrupulous agent and by his very dream of a house of his own. Deteriorating health and a heart attack leave him unable to work, and he is laid off. Shortly before he dies, he imagines a gallant, half-mocking, un-self-pitying headline for his obituary—"ROVING REPORTER PASSES ON"—but the actual notice reads, "JOURNALIST DIES SUDDENLY" (589). The difference between the two headlines— the one fanciful, the other matter-of-fact—encapsulates Biswas's life story: fantasy rejected or revised by history. His dreams and history's modification of them sum up the struggles of his life and concentrate the various forces shaping him, his community and society.

The social conflicts of Biswas's life derive chiefly from his caste and class designations as they predetermine others' judgment of him and as they grate against or affirm his own self-image and ideal. He will spend all of his life trying on the one hand to confirm that he is a Brahmin, and on the other hand to prove that he is not just the "son of a labourer" (i.e., someone fit for only the meanest kind of work) (49). Although his father, Raghu, was a laborer who owned his own land, his accidental drowning and the villagers' subsequent theft of the family property leave Mohun homeless and landless. As a boy he is already a kind of indentured worker in that he is sent by his mother to tend his uncle Bhandat's shop in order to earn his room and board. His perilous, powerless position in Bhandat's household—and symbolically in the East Indian community—is illustrated by the incident in which he is falsely accused of stealing money from Bhandat's till and then lashed on the face with a belt. Mohun is bruised into an early recognition of his dependency, and his lifelong goal becomes an escape from a powerlessness that his subservient relationship to Bhandat exemplifies. After being beaten by his uncle, he returns to his sister Bipti and says to her angrily: "I am going to get a job on my own. And I am going to get my own house too. I am finished with this" (67). A job and a house constitute two key elements of his dream because he seeks to escape from the battering and humiliation, the dependence and stigmatic identity of his inherited lower class.

His conflicts with the Tulsis also derive in part from caste and class designations. The Tulsis represent "Old India"; their patriarch, Pundit Tulsi, occupied a high caste there and has transferred the respect due to that caste to his family in Trinidad, a "pious, conservative, landowning family" (81). As a Brahmin, Biswas is also of a high caste, although the Tulsis do not treat him accordingly, assigning him instead to a low rung in the family hierarchy because he is the "son of a labourer" and because he does not contribute financially to the family enterprise. The hierarchy of people and space at Hanuman House, the Tulsi store-residence in Arwacas, reflects the lingering caste attitudes of the rural East Indian community. In that community the Tulsis are "haves" and Biswas is a "have-not"; their position gives them dignity, whereas his designation as laborer, his landlessness and joblessness make him a nobody. The Tulsis' image of Biswas conflicts with his self-image as an important-person-to-be whose "real" life of achievements has not yet begun. For their part, the Tulsis are infuriated by Biswas's refusal to work, either in the store or on the sugarcane estate; for his part, he is wounded by the family's insensitivity to his Brahmin status and their seeming refusal to treat him as an educated, intelligent person.

To Biswas the Tulsis become the enemy, and he revels in imaginatively overturning the family hierarchy by mocking it and satirically renaming its members: Mrs. Tulsi becomes, variously, the "old cow," the "old hen," the "old queen"; Seth, the elder brother-in-law and business manager, the

"Big Boss"; Mrs. Tulsi's pampered sons, Owad and Vidiadhar, the "young gods." Through his support of the iconoclastic Punkaj Rai and the Arwacas Aryan Association, Biswas challenges the Tulsis' beliefs such as parentally arranged marriages (that "cat-in-bag business"), idol worship, and, above all, the caste system. With his own stigma of "laborer" in mind, Biswas agrees with Punkaj Rai: "birth was unimportant; a man's caste should be determined only by his actions" (116). Biswas's obstinacy and mockery lead to his expulsion from Hanuman House. "This is gratitude," Seth berates him. "You come here penniless, a stranger. We take you in, we give you one of our daughters, we feed you, we give you a place to sleep in. You refuse to help in the store, you refuse to help on the estate. All right! But then to turn around and insult us!" (109). It seems that Biswas wants, contradictorily, both to be treated as a Brahmin and to shatter the caste and class system; driven by his caste and class designations, his humiliation by and dependency on the Tulsis, and his romantic image of himself, he becomes the iconoclast, right in standing up for his dignity yet a bit ridiculous in his vexing behavior toward the family on whom he and his wife depend.

Biswas's conflict with the Tulsis illustrates the novel's key conflict between desire and necessity. In part, Biswas lives in a fantasy; in his own eyes, he is not exactly who he is but the somebody he would like to be, and that the Tulsis do not share his great expectations for himself leads to his humiliation. Like the "romancers" of *Miguel Street* he lives a double life: his dream of future importance contrasts with the actuality of his jobs as storekeeper and plantation driver. He tries to escape vicariously, through the popular romances of Hall Caine, Marie Corelli, and Samuel Smiles, which intoxicate him with "worlds" beyond Trinidad. These exotic stories both fuel his fantasy and make him "despair of finding romance in his own dull green land" (78). They contrast with his inherited class identity and the limitations of Hanuman House, his rural community and colonial society. Given what he is and the agricultural colony in which he lives, what can he expect or even hope for? Especially at Hanuman House "there c[an] be no romance"—no hope of a new identity—he reflects with anxiety before marrying Shama and becoming a Tulsi (93). He joins the family out of necessity, yet once a member, he goes into an exile of sorts, turning to a fantasy of his future importance in order to convince himself and assert to the Tulsis that he does not truly belong to their enterprise. He clings to the belief that "[r]eal life was to begin . . . soon, and elsewhere" (147).

Biswas's search for a profession and his dream of a house of his own express the same desire for a sense of identity and belonging, and they meet the same obstacles and frustrations. Just as Biswas never really owns his own house, so too he never feels "at home" in his work or in any group within Trinidad society. Above all, he does not want to work as an agricultural laborer, as his brothers, father, and grandfather have had to do—as 70 percent of Trinidad's East Indian population did in 1917[12]—and he does everything in his power to escape this inherited class identity. Yet at the Tulsi sugar estate in Green Vale, where Biswas ends up after his six-year failure as a shopkeeper in The Chase, he must do what is equally abhorrent: oversee, push, and prod laborers—laborers not unlike his brothers, father, grandfather, or himself. His attitude toward and relationship with the estate laborers reverses his relationship of assigned subservience within the Tulsi hierarchy; at Hanuman House he is subject to their orders, while as a driver on their estate he oversees and subjects others. At first, he empathizes with the laborers, understanding their awe of the "blue and green moneybags" from which their wages are dispensed; he reflects that his brothers, Prasad and Pratap, are probably no different (208). In time, though, he becomes unsympathetic, tyrannical; he imaginatively identifies with plantation "overseers of legend who rode on horseback and lashed labourers on either side." The Green Vale laborers seem "brutish," and Biswas wonders why they are paid as much as they are, a mere three dollars a week (208–9). He becomes to the laborers what Seth, the eldest Tulsi son-in-law, has been to him: the "enemy," someone and something to be plotted against as an agent of repression. The ironies of Biswas's situation wear him out eventually. He spends sleepless nights worrying that he will be attacked and that his recently built house will be burned down.

As a driver, Biswas's dream of becoming a somebody recedes, becoming even more unreal. His attitude toward the Green Vale workers reflects his shame at his own class designation and his dependency on the Tulsis, who force him to work as a driver of men with whom he wants no connection but to whom he is connected by inheritance and circumstance. In nineteenth- and early twentieth-century Trinidad, East Indians were assigned to the lowest rung of the socioeconomic ladder,[13] and it is from this degradation of the agricultural laborer that Biswas seeks to escape. Throughout his life he remains sensitive to his caste and class designation, and this sensitivity is closely linked to his dream of a house of his own yet the painful reality of his "crowded, shabby room":

> In Tara's house [Biswas] was respected as a Brahmin and pampered; yet as soon as the ceremony was over and he had taken his gift of money and cloth and left, he became once more only a labourer's child—*father's occupation: labourer* was the entry in the birth certificate . . .—living with a penniless mother in one room of a mud hut. And throughout life his position was like that. As one of the Tulsi sons-in-law and as a journalist he found himself among people with money and sometimes with graces; with them his manner was unforcedly easy and he could summon up luxurious instincts; but always, at the end, he returned to his crowded, shabby room. (49)

In this passage caste, class, house, profession, self-esteem, and belonging or not-belonging are all linked. The "crowded, shabby room" to which Biswas returns signifies his class designation, dependency, lack of accomplishment, and inner "exile" or sense of not-belonging.

As a reporter-journalist Biswas not only acquires a semblance of a professional identity, but also finds an outlet for his creativity and through writing takes control of his world, seeing and defining it in his own peculiar way. As a feature-story writer, he uses his wit and a genius for the sensational in articles like "I Am Trinidad's Most Evil Man," part of a series on superlatives about the island's "richest," "poorest," "tallest," "fastest," "strongest" persons. As if imaginatively playing out dark possibilities of his own life, he writes articles about "unusual callings" such as thief, beggar, night-soil remover, mosquito killer, undertaker, birth-certificate searcher, and lunatic-asylum warden, and a series about handicaps of "one" such as "one-armed, one-legged, one-eyed men" (352). The power and romance of writing lead to his purchase of a typewriter, enrollment in a London Ideal School of Journalism correspondence course, and the beginning of a short story, "Escape." His typewriter, bought during the flush of his expectations as journalist and writer, and his short story "Escape" signify his partially realized dream of another identity and life. Of "Escape" and Biswas's other unfinished stories, the narrator elaborates: "their theme was always the same. The hero, trapped into marriage, burdened with a family, his youth gone, meets a young girl. She is slim . . . and dressed in white. She is fresh, tender, unkissed; and she is unable to bear children. Beyond the meeting the stories never went" (344–45). The wish fulfillment of these unfinished stories is transparent: the young girl is Biswas's fantasy life; slim and pristine, she is not weighed down by necessity, burdened with a lower-class designation or the responsibilities of a family; she exists outside of history.

If "Escape" is the dream, the Deserving Destitutes are the nightmare. As reporter for the *Sentinel*'s Deserving Destitutes' fund, Biswas travels to Port of Spain slums and sees and talks with people who have realized his worst fears. The urban landscape of his investigations is grim indeed:

Day after day he visited the mutilated, the defeated, the futile and the insane living in conditions not far removed from his own: in suffocating rotting wooden kennels, in sheds of box-board, canvas and tin, in dark and sweating concrete caverns. Day after day he visited the eastern sections of the city where the narrow houses pressed their scabbed and blistered facades together and hid the horrors that lay behind: the constricted, undrained back-yards, coated with green slime, in the perpetual shadow of adjacent houses and the tall rubble-stone fences against which additional sheds had been built . . . smell upon smell, but none overcoming the stench of cesspits and overloaded septic tanks: horror increased by the litters of children, most of them illegitimate, with navels projecting inches out of their bellies. (441)

Among the destitutes Biswas encounters his uncle Bhandat, now deaf and having nothing better to do than try to get lucky and win the slogan contest for Lux Toilet Soap; he listens patiently to Bhandat's story—"a familiar story of jobs acquired and lost, great enterprises that had failed" (450). Would Biswas end his life like his uncle Bhandat? Would the journalist and aspiring short-story writer end up writing soap slogans? In his uncle Bhandat and among the destitutes, Biswas brushes against all the shadowy possibilities of his life and the grim actualities of the colony.

Above all, houses are the meeting ground for the clash between dreams and harsh actuality in Biswas's life. The idea of having a house of his own functions as a container of desires holding the same feelings invested in his search for a profession and his efforts to become a short-story writer. As a boy, he loses his home after his father's drowning and the family's property is taken; his dream of a house of his own is, among other things, a longing for the lost father and lost security of his childhood. Except for brief periods of residency in houses he builds in Green Vale and Shorthills and in the house he buys on Sikkim Street, Biswas lives his life in others' houses. His dreams of independence are thus enclosed in a shell of those material dependencies. A history of humiliation, migrancy, and not-belonging is the context of the planning and construction of Biswas's house at Green Vale, a process exemplifying what the narrator of *Mr Stone and the Knights Companion* calls the betrayal of feeling through action, or what I have called the modification of the dream by necessity or history.[14] Biswas brings a romantic, pastoral vision to the plans for the house; he thinks of its site as a "bower," an enchanting word in a Wordsworth poem (238). But the house's construction—with all the necessary compromises in scope and materials, and the disappointing unfinished product—mocks his dream. Because he does not have enough money to build the kind of house he envisions, each step of the construction meets qualification. Instead of concrete, as he desires, the house is built on wooden pillars; instead of pitchpine, a cedar floor is laid down; instead of boards separating the ceiling and roof, branches are put in place; instead of a new roof, a bent, rusty, hole-ridden one is installed. When the house is completed, its roof, patched with pitch tar, drips black "snakes" that snap and fall to the floor like tormenting demons. To make matters worse, the estate workers' children drive nails into the floors and pillars and make mud marks on the floor and the crossbars. The house turns into an embarrassment—and a target, when in Biswas's absence, disgruntled workers burn it down. Like the difference between the beautiful word *jasmine* and the dull vegetation,[15] the romantic word *bower* creates a feeling within Biswas that the actuality of his house and its location seem to betray.

The Shorthills house constitutes Biswas's second attempt to realize his pastoral vision; although this time he can afford the preferred building materials and erects his home on a site "as wild and out-of-the-way as he could have wished," its location dooms the enterprise. Shama, Biswas's wife, has to walk a mile to the village for shopping, water has to be toted up a hill from a spring in the woods, the children must ride to school in the Tulsi family car, and Biswas must bicycle long distances to work every day (424). Like its predecessor in Green Vale, the Shorthills house goes up in smoke almost as soon as it is completed, though this time it is Biswas who accidently sets it afire while clearing bush and forest—it is as if the dream house is too fragile and impractical to exist for very long amid the necessities of the workaday world.

The house on Sikkim Street, the only one that Biswas considers "his house," is purchased as impulsively as the Green Vale and Shorthills houses are constructed (13). He buys it without noticing its considerable flaws, having in his mind "only a picture of a house cosy in the rain, with a polished floor, and an old lady who baked cakes in the kitchen" (566). Although taken advantage of by a dishonest agent-owner, Biswas is deceived chiefly by his own desire for independence and belonging. His final life achievement, the Sikkim Street house, is thus a qualified one; he spends his final years burdened with a debt that he cannot pay back and that his family will inherit. But still, the narrator explains, the house means something more: "How terrible it would have been . . . to be without it: to have died among the Tulsis, amid the squalor of that large, disintegrating and indifferent family; to have left Shama and the children among them, in one room; worse, to have lived without even attempting to lay claim to one's portion of the earth; to have lived and died as one had been born, unnecessary and unaccommodated" (13–14). In solemn phrases and cadences this passage transforms Biswas's story from a biography to a history of an ethnic group and dispossessed people of the world.

We can read Biswas's story from two critical perspectives: as history informed by fiction, or as fiction informed by history. From the first, Biswas's story tells a specifically Trinidad Indian story. His struggles to educate himself—in 1917, 97 percent of the island's Indians were illiterate—and to secure a profession and a house of his own were largely the struggles of his fellow East Indians in the colony. Bridget Brereton elaborates on their hard progress from indentureship to middle-class independence: "In general, right up to the end of the indentureship period Indians remained low-paid manual labourers in agriculture or poor smallholders. . . . In the towns, where they flocked from 1884 on in response to worsening conditions on the estates, they filled miserably paid, generally despised jobs as scavengers and porters, 'coolies' in the true sense of that term. Very few Indians, up to 1917, occupied any of the positions that society defined as prestigious; in 1921 only 187 Indians were classified as 'officials and professionals.' "[16] Although referring to a slightly later period, the 1930s and 1940s, Biswas's story reflects the stories of other East Indians in their progress from despised agricultural laborers to respected members of middle-class society.

Biswas's story also tells a colonial, Trinidadian story about a struggle to survive in what Naipaul describes as a "picaroon society." Because of its history of slavery, "mixed population," and "closed colonial system," the island "recreated attitudes of the Spanish picaroon world," he writes; in this society "the weak were humiliated . . . the powerful never appeared and were beyond reach . . . no one was allowed any dignity . . . and everyone had to impose himself" (*MP* 73). The individual had to depend on his wits, boldness, and endurance to get by. By "picaroon" Naipaul seems particularly to have in mind the tough, lower-class neighborhoods of Port of Spain, where conditions were like those Biswas describes in his encounters with the "deserving destitutes." In *A History of Modern Trinidad: 1783–1962* Bridget Brereton elaborates on those conditions during a period prior to the time frame of the novel:

One editor, writing of Port of Spain in 1885, described "hordes of destitute and suffering creatures, more or less ill-fed, their diseases unattended to and their abodes the scene of squalor and every unwholesomeness." The wretched housing conditions worsened after about 1860, as continued immigration into the city put increasing pressure on totally inadequate lower-income housing in the slum sections of the capital.

These harsh physical conditions of life gave rise to characteristic urban social problems. Juvenile crime and vagrancy were widespread; if the newspapers can be believed, there were hundreds of children on the streets who lived on errands, casual jobs and petty crime. . . . after 1880 there was a serious unemployment problem in the city . . . and the press was full of complaints about the lawless behaviour of the urban vagrants. . . .

The harsh conditions of lower-class life inevitably bred crimes, and the courts usually proceeded on the assumption that a black or Indian labourer was guilty unless he could prove himself innocent; the whole machinery of law enforcement was directed against the lower classes.[17]

Although we might consider Naipaul's picaroon society as primarily an exile's construct, there is a historical actuality of tough, lower-class urban life in the colony that the concept seems to have grown out of.

More generally, the picaroon society is a society of limitations, of a paucity of traditions and institutions where the individual carries the burden of making meaning and making his way; it is a society on the margins of others' power and prosperity, and for this reason its people may feel, as Biswas often does, an unreality and futility about their lives. It is a society of individuals in search of whatever identity they can make for themselves, not one of institutions conferring identity through educational and professional accomplishment. Individuals' identity in the picaroon society may be both more fixed and more fluid than in societies with well-defined professions and institutions. A laborer is a laborer, and a shopkeeper is a shopkeeper; but beyond such basics, there is a certain fluidity because in the colony professions and institutions have not yet developed elaborate and fixed rules.

In Biswas's career we see aspects of the individual's struggle to acquire a professional identity in a colonial society with aspects of the picaroon world. About that society's limited opportunities, Naipaul has written: "I had been born in a static colonial time; and in Trinidad, where I spent my first eighteen years, I had known the poverty and spiritual limitations of an agricultural colony where, as was once computed, there were only eighty kinds of job."[18] In *The Middle Passage* and *The Overcrowded Barracoon* he elaborates further: "The only professions [in Trinidad] were those of law and medicine, because there was no need for any other; and the most successful people were commission agents, bank managers and members of the distributive trades."[19] In such a society, acquiring a profession can often be, as for Biswas, a matter of ingenuity and luck. Thus, without having any specialized education or work experience, Biswas gets a job as a reporter and later becomes a celebrity through his masquerade for the newspaper's Scarlet Pimpernel contest. The flush and fame are short-lived, though, for his identity as a professional is always insecure and fragile. It has not been conferred by an institution or a professional society, and therefore can disappear just as suddenly as it appeared. Throughout his working life, Biswas constantly fears being "sacked" not only because there is no network on which he can depend to find another job but also because he feels at times that he is masquerading as a journalist-writer. His idle typewriter and unfinished short story convey something of this insecurity; like others in the colony, he worries that he is not who he seems to be and is disappointed that he is not what he would like to have been.

In Biswas's sense of inverted reality we see an effect of his enclaved ethnic community and his colonial society. He believes that his "real life" is always about to begin and that reality lies somewhere far beyond Trinidad (147). As a youth he turns to Samuel Smiles's romances to find out about that world and lives in frustration that his own life cannot compare with the lives of the heroes of those romances. And just as Edward of *Miguel Street* looks to the United States as a land of greatness beyond the littleness and insignificance of the colony, so too even as an adult Biswas looks up to British-educated Owad Tulsi as an extraordinary person who has been "where life was to be found" (540). Unable to go "there," Biswas turns instead within: "He sank into despair as into the void which, in his imagining, had always stood for the life he had yet to live" (494–95). His despair is the feeling of futility produced by the colony, a feeling whose inverse is fantasy.

The second critical perspective on the novel, that of fiction informed by history, emphasizes Biswas's story as construct—it is a fictionalized biography of a father, overwritten by the son's own story of exile. Of course, the struggles of Seepersad Naipaul, which the author describes in detail in "Prologue to an Autobiography" (1984), are reflected in Biswas's story. For example, like Biswas the sign writer (and Ganesh of *The Mystic Masseur*), Seepersad Naipaul had a special feeling for lettering and the printed word; as a journalist he wrote about sensational topics such as "village feuds, family vendettas, murders, bitter election battles" and "strange characters" such as a Negro hermit, "once rich and pleasure-seeking, now living alone with a dog in a hut in the swamplands." The father's obstinacy and iconoclasm inform Biswas's rejection of the Tulsis and his satire of Hindu practices such as parentally arranged marriages and the tradition of not educating female children. Like Biswas, Seepersad Naipaul remained an outsider, even within his own family: "my father had always been on the other side. The family, with all its pundits, were defenders of the orthodox Hindu faith. My father wasn't." He belonged to a Hindu reformist movement called Arya Samaj (see Punkaj Rai and the Arwacas Aryan Association of the novel), which was against "caste, pundits, animistic ritual," and "child marriage," and for the "education of girls."[20] In one notorious incident, Seepersad Naipaul refused to make a ceremonial sacrifice to the mother-goddess Kali and thus angered the traditionalist Hindu community, just as Biswas's iconoclasm angers the traditionalist Tulsi family.[21] At the *Trinidad Guardian* the father knew uncertainty and "daily humiliation," just as Biswas does at the *Sentinel*; he felt a "fear of extinction . . . combatted only by the exercise of the vocation [of writing]."[22] Above all, it is the father's two-sided temperament that informs Biswas: "[He] had a prodigious sense of irony," Naipaul writes, "a way of turning all disaster into comedy, which he transmitted to his children. I always felt a tremendous tenderness towards him. . . . he was unhappy much of the time. But he had a tremendous gift for joy which I share."[23] Certainly we find these qualities in Biswas—the dark humor, the spontaneity, the brooding unhappiness.

The effect of the author's exile in England shows in the narrator's attitude toward Biswas: the distanced, "exotopic" perspective of exile—a recollecting, from the margins, of his family, community, and society—enables him to write sympathetically yet unsentimentally. At the same time, the experience of the author's exile overwrites Biswas's story of alienation, charging it with an intensity and perhaps exaggerating certain negative aspects of that community and society. For Biswas's colony is also the colony that the author has "escaped" from; his exile must be justified. In this context, one wonders, is the "tragedy" of Biswas's life that, unlike the author, he did not pull off his "escape," symbolized by the unfinished manuscript of the same name?

In *West Indian Literature* Bruce King writes that *A House for Mr Biswas* "has a reputation as a New World epic celebrating the struggles of an immigrant towards acculturisation and success."[24] Indeed, the narrative shows Biswas's successes and defends his desires, which sustain him and give him the ambition to be somebody other than a laborer and the courage to strike out into the unknown beyond his rural East Indian community. A less dreamy, more malleable Biswas would not have resisted the pressures to be incorporated in the Tulsi family enterprise as a lifelong worker in the shops and fields; a less adventurous and resourceful Biswas would not have boarded the bus for Port of Spain and talked and written his way into a job as a reporter at the city newspaper. Yet the narrative also shows the fragility of Biswas's successes and his illusions. A careful, less impulsive Biswas would not have wasted his money building the Green Vale and Shorthills houses and would not have looked so cursorily at the house on Sikkim Street before purchasing it. His dreams also betray him and isolate him from others.

His ambitions to be a professional, to educate his children, and to have a house of his own are realized more fully than seemed possible for the homeless son of a laborer and the grandson of an indentured worker; but to celebrate that success is to celebrate in the shadow of Biswas's mortgaged house, idle typewriter, unfinished short stories, and his sense of not belonging to any group or community. Selwyn Cudjoe, in *V. S. Naipaul: A Materialist Reading*, calls the novel a "prose-tragedy," explaining: "the tragedy of Mr. Biswas is that because he has not fulfilled his *dharma* (the duty and morality that befits his caste) and his own *dharma* (his personal morality and duty) toward his mother and his kind, his *karma* becomes predictable and inevitable. . . . Mr. Biswas, the contemporary anti-hero, is destined to wander in an alien land, unable to realize himself."[25] Cudjoe is right that Biswas never really belongs within his family, community, or society; he always remains the iconoclast, the outsider, the man on the margins. Informing Biswas's wandering in the wilderness is not only the character's experience of unfulfilled *dharma*, but also the author's own experience of exile. For Biswas is a fictional representation informed by the life of the author's iconoclastic, alienated father, as well as the son's experience of exile. That exile overwrites the fictionalized biography of the father, superimposing one story of wandering on another. In this sense, it is Naipaul the exile who is Mr. Biswas, the author creating a character in the spirit of his father yet also infusing that character with his own exile's alienation and wandering. Without suggesting that Naipaul's work is a "seamless whole"—it is not, it has its fissures and contradictions—we can say that Biswas, Ralph Singh, Salim, and the narrator of

*The Enigma of Arrival* are each shaped by a spirit of estrangement and exile, and it is of course the author's own experience of exile that forms these different yet similar characters.

In sum, the novel tells a two-sided story: it is about a third-generation immigrant from an enclaved, rural, ethnic community who succeeds in making his way in an industrializing, urbanizing colony; but it is also about his unfulfillment and not-belonging in that colony, about a sense of shipwreck that author as exile infuses into the fictionalized story of his father. "Life ha[s] to be lived," the novel's narrator remarks matter-of-factly, and indeed Biswas lives his life with courage, resourcefulness, and dignity. Yet, at the same time, his life is charged with disappointment and not-belonging; he is always somewhat of a "wanderer with no place . . . [to] call his own," retiring to a "crowded, shabby room" (40, 49). His life's wanderings leave behind a typewriter, unfinished manuscripts, and a mortgaged house—themselves two-sided symbols of his material achievement and the ironies of his unfulfilled dreams. *A House for Mr Biswas* at once honors a real father, hallowing his life's struggles and ironies, and overwrites his fictionalized story with the life of the son, whose exile shapes the fictionalized father's alienation in the colony he will never fit into and never escape from.

# 3

# Metahistory and Marginality

[The colonies] are yet Babes that cannot live without sucking the breasts of the Mother Cities, but such as I mistake when they come to age they do not wean themselves.
—James Harrington, *Oceana* (1656)

Myth does not hide anything nor does it display anything: it distorts; [it] is neither a lie nor an admission: it is an inflection. . . . it transforms history into nature.
—Roland Barthes, *Mythologies*

*The Middle Passage* and *The Loss of El Dorado* look back to the author's early fiction about the colony and forward to later essays and fiction about developing countries in the postcolonial world. These works seek to bring to light the history of a region and to diagnose the cultural and social maladies that derive from colonialism and imperialism. The former work writes history through commentary on five colonial societies of the West Indies and Caribbean; the latter focuses specifically on Trinidad and environs, isolating the myths that have rendered six centuries of the imperial enterprise in the New World "natural" and "commonsensical." Both works consider the effects on the region of mercantilism and imperialism in the mid-twentieth century.

*The Middle Passage* and *The Loss of El Dorado* contain a mix of autobiographical and historical elements, that is, the author's probing of his own identity through reflections on the problems of colonial societies and the history and metahistory of the West Indies and Caribbean. As its subtitle, *Impressions of Five Societies—British, French and Dutch—in the West Indies and South America*, states, *The Middle Passage* records "impressions," and these impressions sometimes reveal the split within the author between a colonial and a metropolitan sensibility. In its hypercritical loathing of aspects of colonial Trinidad and Caribbean culture and society, *The Middle Passage* expresses self-reflexively a malady of colonialism and marginality that it simultaneously diagnoses. Through an emphasis chiefly on those debilitating characteristics of Caribbean societies, it constructs the author's self-justification of exile. Both works grow out of that exile, written from a dual insider's-outsider's perspective that at times reveals new insights yet at others estranges the author from his subjects. History, social study, and autobiography mix and are superimposed on one another; by researching the history of Trinidad and the region, Naipaul also reflects on and constructs a new understanding of the forces and contexts that have played a role in shaping his identity. From the epochal perspective of *The Loss of El Dorado*, the colonization of the Americas raises the question of the self's relationships with culturally different others, a question that the author as exile poses in his daily life in England and in his travels and encounters with other peoples of the world. Part of his interest in the history of the Americas—the travel book and history *A Turn in the South* (1989) is another instance of that interest—has to do with the question of the Other. The experience of exile focuses that question, for exile begins with an estrangement, a breaking of bonds with one's community and society. But exile also holds the possibility of new bonding and a deepening understanding of self and others. In *The Middle Passage*, the controversial account of the author's return to the Caribbean, the latter is a possibility that Naipaul sometimes accepts but more often withdraws from.

## *The Middle Passage* (1962)

Five centuries ago the voyages of Columbus brought the history of Europe to the Americas, but at the time Naipaul wrote this study, the lines of a truly Caribbean history were still sketchy or absent. "The history of the islands can never be satisfactorily told," he laments. "Brutality is not the only difficulty. History is built around achievement and creation; and nothing was created in the West Indies."[2] That, at least, is the controversial slant of *The Middle Passage*, which treats the lasting effects of Caribbean societies' histories of imperial depredation and depletion and colonial marginality.

The Caribbean has been described as Europe's other sea, the Mediterranean of the New World. It was a Mediterranean which summoned up every dark instinct without the complementary impulses towards nobility and beauty of older lands, a Mediterranean where civilization turned satanic, perverting those it attracted. And if one considers this sea, which the tourist enlivens in his fantastic uniform, as a wasteful consumer of men through more than three centuries—the aboriginal population of some millions wiped out; the insatiable plantations: 300,000 slaves taken to Surinam, which today has a Negro population of 90,000; the interminable wars: 40,000 British soldiers dead between 1794 and 1796 alone, and another 40,000 discharged as unfit—it would seem that simply to have survived in the West Indies is to have triumphed. (169)

*The Middle Passage* is about clients and consumers, and what has been consumed are chiefly precious metals, sugarcane, and human beings—Amerindians, African slaves, Asian indentured workers, and European colonists, soldiers, and missionaries. In European history, the West Indies or Caribbean came into being as a landfall for a hunt for treasure, developed into mines and plantations, and continues as such in new forms today. In the words of Trinidad economist Lloyd Best, the West Indies have gone from "pure plantation" to "modified plantation" to "plantation even further modified."[3]

Naipaul's book is divided into six chapters whose subjects are five colonial West Indian and Caribbean societies: Trinidad, British Guiana (Guyana), Surinam (Suriname), Martinique, and Jamaica. From a personal, even idiosyncratic perspective each chapter considers the cultural, psychological, and socioeconomic ills of the respective colonies and relates the region's history of colonialism to its problems in the late 1950s and early 1960s. The titular "middle passage" can be read as alluding to at least five kinds of voyages: primarily to the infamous freighting of slaves between Africa and the Americas, but also to the voyages of Columbus and other explorers, *conquistadores*, and colonists from Old World to New;

to Naipaul's homecoming voyage from England to Trinidad; to the emigration of West Indians to England; and finally to the cruises of tourists to the Caribbean. These various "passages" link Old World to New World and suggest that the problems of the West Indies and Caribbean are connected with the problems of Europe and the North American continent.

Since the voyages of Columbus, who on reaching the Gulf of Paria between what is now Trinidad and Venezuela expected to find a "terrestrial paradise," the West Indies have been objects in a quest for power and symbols of a romance of new beginnings, of leisure and pleasure, of an Eden by whatever name. Chapter 1 of *Middle Passage* considers the other side of paradise, which has led to a passage in reverse from New World to Old, from the West Indies to England and to other European countries. Twentieth-century West Indian emigrants also seek a "promised land," but in the metropolis not the colony, and one from which, ironically, even upon their arrival in England, they find that they are already barred by the color of their skin (12). Racial tensions both in the colonies and in the metropolis are lasting effects of empire; one of Naipaul's fellow passengers on the *Francisco Bobadilla* speaks in disgust of the "orang-outangs" who disembark in Southampton at the end of the Old World leg of the ship's crisscross voyage between England and the Caribbean. Similarly, a mulatto, West Indian tourist says haughtily of blacks getting on the ship at St. Kitts: *"The wild cows are coming on board"* (24, 27). Quoting a writer of 1805, Naipaul notes that racial gradations and attitudes like these go back hundreds of years in West Indian history: "'The creole slaves . . . looked upon the newly imported Africans with scorn, and sustained in their turn that of the mulattoes, whose complexions were browner; all were kept at a distance from the intercourse of the whites" (27).

Chapter 2, "Trinidad," diagnoses the maladies of Naipaul's native island. An epigraph from Tacitus's *Agricola* inscribes the chapter's argument: "And so the Britons were gradually led to the amenities that make vice agreeable—arcades, baths and sumptuous banquets. They spoke of such novelties as 'civilization', when really they were only a feature of enslavement" (40). More than 150 years after the end of the middle passage, Trinidadians are still slaves, the author contends, in that they are chiefly clients and consumers in a distant colony; like Britons of the

Roman empire, Trinidadians are enslaved by the Euro-American "civilization" that they purchase and grow to value. The very "modernity" on which colonial Trinidadians pride themselves, he argues, only shows their dependence on foreign economies and their attachment to foreign models of cultural identity (46).

Naipaul bemoans an equally enslaving attachment to values projected by the American and British media. In a recurrent theme in this and other books, particularly *The Mimic Men,* he criticizes West Indian "mimicry": Trinidad society is remaking itself in the image of "the Hollywood B-man," he writes (61). Its modernity is the "extreme susceptibility of people . . . unsure of themselves," without a "taste or style" of their own (47). Like other colonials, Trinidadians have been forced to sell cheaply and buy dearly, to accept and to imitate. Furthermore, as a colonial people on the margins of empires, Trinidadians have learned to live in ignorance of their own history, he argues, and in a fantasy of the world beyond the island: "we could never be convinced of the value of reading the history of [Trinidad] which was, as everyone said, only a dot on the map of the world. Our interest was all in the world outside. . . . Our own past was buried and no one cared to dig it up" (43).

Chapter 3, "British Guiana," takes its point of departure from Anthony Trollope's embellishment of what is today Guyana as "the Elysium of the tropics—the West Indian happy valley of Rasselas—the one true and actual Utopia of the Caribbean Seas—the Transatlantic Eden" (86). Naipaul trashes this mythopoeia, and British Guiana, with descriptions of the dirt, pathos, and dilapidation of the stops on his Guyanese-Brazilian itinerary. In Boa Vista, a border town that he locates "somewhere behind the back of beyond," life is nasty, brutish, and short: "The smell of dog-dirt was inescapable, as was the sight of starved mongrels locked in copulation, their faces blank and foolish. Few of the thin children I saw were without some skin disease; one or two were deformed. We went to the primitive printery which produced the ragged government gazette; most of the people there appeared to be doing nothing. We went to a small insanitary market in which everything apart from some Amerindian straw fans had been imported" (111). Such descriptions typify the stylized disgust of this chapter, which on the one hand contrasts a South American country's plans for development and the actuality of undevelopment, and on the other hand shows the unbridgeable gap between Naipaul as observer and the people and sights he observes. In particular in Guyana he sees vestiges of the country's three-hundred-year slave era, of such "exceptional brutality" that it created a people who want only "to be left alone" (118). "Slavery, the land, the latifundia, Bookers, indenture, the colonial system, malaria" have made the Guyanese "at once revolutionary and intensely reactionary" (119).

Chapters 4 and 5, "Surinam" and "Martinique," critique two seemingly different responses to colonialism in the Caribbean: nationalism and assimilation. Nationalists seek independence, considering anything less "a permanent inferiority" (165). But the nationalist movement in colonial Suriname is troubled by a split identity deriving from its history as European colony and landfall for the slave market and Asian immigration: on principle, nationalists reject European culture for Asian and African culture, yet in actuality they feel Europe in their "bones" and thus find Africa and Asia "contemptible and ridiculous" (165). Pulled in opposite directions, the Surinamese nationalist movement demonstrates "how imprisoning for the West Indian his colonial culture is," the author contends (165).

An alternative to nationalism, assimilation would seem to deny identity to the colonized people. Assimilation has been ironically so successful in colonial Suriname, Naipaul writes, that the country resembles "a tropical, tulip-less extension of Holland," with the people referring to themselves as "Holland's twelfth province" (164). Indeed, a majority have visited the "mother country," and as of 1980, twenty years after the writing of *The Middle Passage*, 40 percent of the Surinamese population were actually residing in Holland.[4]

Just as Naipaul considers Paramaribo, the capital of Suriname, a tropical, imitation Holland, so he views life in Martinique as a "French colonial monkey-game" (210). Through assimilation the island has been "reduced . . . to a helpless colony where now more than ever the commission agent is king" (199). All goods except sugar, rum, and bananas are imported from France, he points out. And even commodities like coconut oil and milk come from abroad because, although Martinique has plenty of coconuts, it does not have the factories to extract, process, and bottle the oil. Assimilation has hampered rather than boosted Martinican development, which is stifled by island attitudes and an inability to compete with French industry (199). (Significant inequalities persist, thirty years after publication of the *The Middle Passage,* between France and its Caribbean overseas department, Martinique and Guadeloupe, whose level of unemployment, for example, is three times as high as in the metropolis.[5] A third of the population is out of work and four out of ten of those who do work are employed in a top-heavy public sector. According to one Martinican high official, "France is a country that for various reasons lives beyond its means. Here, it's a caricature."[6])

Chapter 6 ponders futility and extravagance in Jamaica, an island paradise for some but a land of poverty for many more others. The author visits the Kingston slums, reputedly some of the worst in the Caribbean:

Hovels of board and cardboard and canvas and tin lie choked together on damp rubbish dumps behind which the sun sets in mocking splendour. . . . Filth and rubbish are disgorged everywhere. . . . Pigs and goats wander as freely as the people and seem as individual and important. . . . And wherever you look you see the surrounding Kingston hills, one of the beauties of the island. . . . Against such a view lay a dead mule, its teeth bared, its belly swollen and taut. It had been there for two days; a broomstick had been playfully stuck in its anus. (216)

In contrast to the slums, at Frenchman's Cove, a 1960s version of Club Med, the author encounters the "West Indies of the tourist's ideal" (227). His sojourn there resembles an episode from the "Twilight Zone": weary man enters luxury island resort that promises to gratify his every desire, but man loses his desire and falls into lethargy. "Everything was at the end of the telephone, and it was my duty to have exactly what I wanted. . . . the struggle between duty, to indulge, and inclination, which was not to bother, was unequal. I fell into a torpor. The whisky remained untouched beyond the first day's sampling; and at the end of my stay I had drunk only half the bottle of brandy . . . I couldn't be a tourist in the West Indies, not after the journey I had made" (230).

Naipaul calls tourism an "unavoidable degradation" and a "new slavery" for the poor countries of the region (191). In "Escapism, Penetration and Response: Industrial Tourism and the Caribbean," Herbert Hiller discusses the relationship between the tourist's fantasy and its requirements on the islander; he questions the charade of Caribbean tourism, with its forced *larbinisme*, to use a term of Aimé Césaire (i.e., islanders' adoption of the flunkey's mentality [*larbin*] in their identities as waiters, maids, valets, and other service personnel): "It is completely unacceptable that the poor of the world are ordered to put on their Donald Duck suits and smile mindlessly at their own reduced condition." Hiller adds: "The problem with international tourism in the Caribbean is that it demands an image of paradise, and the fiction has become too costly to maintain."[7] *The Middle Passage*'s critique of tourism and its description of "the other side of paradise" is just as relevant today as it was in the early 1960s, for not only has the traffic to the Caribbean increased but also tourists now spend their vacations far away from urban centers like Kingston and Port of Spain, either in sequestered resorts like Frenchman's Cove or on "Love Boat" cruises whose object is to conceal reality and create fantasy. In the words of the authors of *The Other Side of Paradise*, "tourists like the security of the ships and the isolation they offer from the stark realities of Caribbean poverty. At nightfall the gaily lit ship, like a floating carnival, weighs anchor and heads out to sea, with snatches of party music drifting back to the darkening island."[8] The object of *The Middle Passage*, conversely, is to shine light—though a stark light—on the islands, to remember the history of a region where centuries ago the ships plying the Caribbean were loaded with a different human cargo. Today there are tourists, yesterday there were slaves. What percentage of today's tourists would even know?

Although Naipaul occasionally notes the beauty of the region and remarks on the virtues of its people—the tolerance and cosmopolitanism of Trinidadians, for example—his primary intent is to deromanticize the "Land of the Calypso" by focusing on the harsh realities and uncertain identity of the colonial societies. Citing Graham Greene's statement that a writer needs to empathize but not to identify with the attitudes of the society he observes and interprets, Naipaul states that the West Indian writer cannot be "blamed for reflecting his society," but should be blamed for "promoting . . . unimpressive race-and-colour values" and for failing to "diagnose the sickness" of the society (70). The sickness that Naipaul seeks to diagnose derives from colonialism and imperialism: slavery, the plantation system, the immigration of indentured workers, and the treatment of the Caribbean and West Indies only as a resource to be exploited have created an unstable amalgam of peoples uncertain of their identity and the ways to develop their societies. In the Foreword to the 1981 edition of *The Middle Passage* the author calls the West Indies a "client culture" and a "client economy" (5). He quotes the English historian James Anthony Froude: "[The West Indies] were valued only for the wealth which they yielded, and society there has never assumed any particularly noble aspect" (9). Or, as Eric Williams explains: "The West Indies were ideal colonies"; they "provided a market, directly as well as indirectly, through the slave trade, for British manufactures and foodstuffs, whilst they supplied sugar and other tropical commodities that would otherwise have had to be imported from foreigners or dispensed with entirely."[9] The colony and metropolis are related through an exchange that enriches the latter and depletes the former; the colonialist "earns more and spends less," Albert Memmi writes.[10] The Eurocentered view or system of the colony as a one-sided exchange in which the metropolitan country takes as much as possible and returns as little as possible determined the nature of the colonies and produced a constellation of problems that can be lumped under the broad term *underdevelopment*. Echoing Froude again, Naipaul states that "nothing was created" in the British West Indies, a situation attributable to the one-sided colony-metropolis relationship: "There were only plantations, prosperity, decline, [and] neglect" (27). The "degrading fact" about colonial society is that "it never required efficiency" or "quality"; not only were these values unnecessary, but also they became "undesirable" (58). "I knew Trinidad to be unimportant, uncreative, cynical," he recalls. "The only professions were those of law and medicine, because there was no need for any other. . . . It was a place where the stories were never stories of success but of failure" (41). For the colony as plantation, skills did not matter; only the client-consumer relationship mattered, and this created a "money-minded" society (42, 82).

Naipaul argues that West Indian colonies are plagued by a sense of marginality. The colonial-metropolitan relationship has rendered the colonies unknown to themselves and ignored or unseen by others; thus colonial Trinidadians, although perhaps fascinated by the world far beyond and knowing something of the history of the metropolis, do not know their own island's history: "Our interest was all in the world outside, the remoter the better; Australia was more important than Venezuela, which we could see on a clear day. . . . The England of 1914 was the England of yesterday; the Trinidad of 1914 belonged to the dark ages" (43). Colonials believe that they have an identity only in relation to the metropolitan country, and thus they think of themselves as marginal and unimportant.

Imperialism and marginality foster West Indian imitation of Europe and North America. Naipaul dwells on the deleterious effects of the Western media, especially cinema, whose influence in the colony is "incalculable." Like Bogart and Hat of *Miguel Street*, colonial Trinidadians mimic the attitudes and behavior presented in films: "In the immigrant colonial society, with no standards of its own, subjected for years to the second-rate in newspapers, radio and cinema, minds are rigidly closed; and Trinidadians of all races and classes are remaking themselves in the image of the Hollywood B-man" (61). Naipaul is certainly exaggerating here, constructing a caricature of a culture in order to comprehend his own exile. Yet other writers have noted this particularly colonial or neocolonial phenomenon. In "The Bartered Bride," Ian Buruma discusses a neocolonial imitation of America by Filipinos, "for whom culture had been reduced to being knowing about the world contained between Hollywood and Manhattan." Buruma finds a resemblance between Filipino cities and East Los Angeles, with their "minimarts, discos, hamburger joints, and honky-tonks"; the sign above a Filipino funeral parlor reads drolly, "Funeraria Rosaria: Home of the Superior Casket."[11] What Naipaul apparently does not consider in his critique of West Indian mimicry is the possibility that he is misreading colonial behavior; perhaps, after all, "mimicry" may be an intentional holding of the Euro-American civilization at bay, a game of masks played to survive among alien powers. In "Of Mimicry and Man: The Ambivalence of Colonial Discourse," Homi Bhabha argues that mimicry and parody can be read as the colonial's or former colonial's method of subverting authority.[12] Citing Aimé Césaire, James Clifford contends that mimicry can also turn into syncretism, a construction of a new identity: "The Caribbean history from which Césaire derives an inventive and tactical 'negritude' is a history of degradation, mimicry, violence, and blocked possibilities. [Yet] it is also rebellious, syncretistic, and creative. This kind of ambiguity keeps the planet's local futures uncertain and open. There is no master narrative that can reconcile the tragic and comic plots of global cultural history."[13] In his readings of the colony, does Naipaul overlook the possibilities of ambiguity? In *The Middle Passage* and *The Loss of El Dorado* he focuses on the tragic aspects of the history of Caribbean colonial societies in order to strip away distorting romantic-mythic views; in keeping with that, he sees the phenomenon of mimicry within this tragedy. In his earlier 1950s novels such as *Miguel Street* and *The Mystic Masseur*, characters' mimicry does show comic and subversive aspects as well, however. Behavior in the colony has an ambiguity that Naipaul the novelist has captured, but which the ethnologist and sociologist ignores.

Mimicry, feelings of inferiority, self-contempt—Naipaul's treatment of these maladies of the colony goes to the heart of problematic elements of *The Middle Passage*. Can a writer diagnose the ills of colonial societies and purge the traces of those ills from himself as colonial without taking a devaluing attitude and echoing the pejorative tone of European colonial discourse? Albert Memmi explains that a pattern of European devaluation and negation "extends . . . to everything that touches the colony and the colonized: to his country, which is ugly, too hot . . . smelly; to the vicious climate, to the geography so hopeless that it condemns him to contempt and poverty, to dependence for eternity."[14] Not unlike this devaluation, *The Middle Passage* echoes the negativity of European colonial discourse: Naipaul states that "nothing was created in the British West Indies," that "modernity" in Trinidad is "flawed," that Trinidadians have "no taste or style of their own," that they live in an "unimportant, uncreative" society without "scientists, engineers, explorers, soldiers, poets," or "heroes" (27, 41–42). The book's pejorative commentary sometimes conveys disgust and contempt. Thus, folkloric dance in Martinique is a "mincing mimicry" of African dancing; the enchanting sound of the steel drum in Trinidad is detestable (41, 209). Certain impressions come off like mean-spirited gibes: Amerindians are "emotional parasites," and the Guyanese are *"inhospitable, reactionary and lethargic except when predatory"* (102, 117). There is an emphasis throughout on dirt and the failure of the colonial peoples of the region—as in European colonial discourse, as a metropolitan traveler with little sensibility for the region might observe and comment on. However, there is an important difference between the self-other relationship in European colonial discourse and in Naipaul's discourse on the West Indies and the Caribbean. In the former, the European self reduces the colonial other to an object, an entity devoid of an "I"; because colonial subjectivity has been denied, there can only be a hollow colonial mimicry of the European self.[15] In the latter discourse, the author as exile who returns temporarily to the Caribbean is torn between conflicting aspects of his own identity; the colonial subject cannot be made to disappear because, in a sense, Naipaul is himself the subject of his own travels and critique. Not wanting to be again a colonial, though unable to deny the colonial self, he wrestles with his malaise, which sometimes enhances his vision while at other times interferes with his social critique.

In the process of diagnosing colonial maladies and bringing to light the region's forgotten history, *The Middle Passage* also records Naipaul's inner turmoil. It shows an exile's alienation from his society and the Caribbean and an attempted justification of that exile through caricature and devaluation of colonial others. It shows a troubled search for an understanding of a divided self. More than twenty-five years after the writing of *The Middle Passage*, Naipaul put such a recognition or confession in the chapter of *The Enigma of Arrival* entitled "The Journey," in which the novel's narrator-writer reflects on his first travel book, one much like *The Middle Passage*. He explains that when he began the book in 1960, he started "psychologically and physically" from his "little colonial island." He writes that he was "glamoured by the idea of the metropolitan traveler, the man starting from Europe," but that "as a colonial among colonials" he "could not be that kind of traveler." The absence of "a metropolitan audience to 'report back' to" and the conflict between his "idea of . . . the traveler-writer" and his identity "as a colonial traveling among colonials . . . made for difficult writing." He "took refuge in humor," "comedy," and the "satirical reflex" as a means of "covering up for confusion."[16]

Travel in the Caribbean and the writing of *The Middle Passage* widen the split within the author between colony and metropolis. On the one hand, the very problems of colonial peoples that Naipaul diagnoses—uncertainty of identity, feelings of inferiority, contempt for one's own culture and society—are expressed reflexively in some of his critiques of the region, especially those stylized ones in which he sounds like other British satirists. On the other hand, Naipaul's diagnosis is a colonial exile's pained examination, inscribing a search for a new understanding of the society and region that he has left. It attempts to bring back history and break down Western, stereotyped images of the Caribbean as a tropical paradise, and thus, if read from this perspective, it has a positive, deromanticizing effect, even though from the perspective of West Indian and Caribbean readers the book echoes European colonial discourse and offends in its negativity. It is important to add, though, that the author as colonial is himself equally the subject of his study; on the surface a travel book, social study, and history, *The Middle Passage* is also a kind of autobiography of exile.

### *The Loss of El Dorado: A History* (1969)

Although in *The Middle Passage* Naipaul laments that a history of the West Indies "can never be satisfactorily told," he continues to write that history in one form or another in subsequent works (*MP* 28–29). *The Mimic Men* (1967) picks up the theme in its protagonist Ralph Singh, who has ambitions of writing a history of empire. By telling his story, Singh also writes a history of a West Indian struggle for independence and postindependence disillusionment. Two years after the publication of *The Mimic Men* and seven years after *The Middle Passage*, Naipaul returns to the writing of West Indian history in *The Loss of El Dorado*, which provides what the author calls "a peephole into the development of civilization over three centuries."[17] What does he mean by this metaphor? Here, a peephole is a symbolically charged cluster of events in the history of Trinidad and the region; through these clusters, Naipaul gives meaning to the panorama of history that spreads out before the reader's eyes.

*The Loss of El Dorado* springs from Naipaul's investigations into Trinidad and Caribbean history and his effort to bring back that history as a process of understanding self and society. In the opening and closing pages of the book he writes of his "wonder" as a Trinidadian youth at being seemingly "cut off from a past" and the rest of the world: "Then [the 1940s] . . . [Trinidad] felt like a place at the rim of the world. . . . Port of Spain was a place where things had happened and nothing showed. Only people remained, and their past had dropped out of all the history books" (11, 374–75). One intent of the author's research into documents at the British Museum and of the book that grew out of the research was to uncover that past. The absence of history is a colonial malady that Naipaul diagnoses in *The Middle Passage,* and this malady becomes a theme in several of his works. "We forget; we have no idea of our past; it is part of the trouble," he tells his fellow West Indians in the Introduction to *East Indians in the Caribbean: Colonialism and the Struggle for Identity.*[18]

In Trinidad and the West Indies the absence of a knowledge of history has resulted in a substituted myth or metahistory. Myth distorts not by "deny[ing] things," but rather, by simplifying and "purify[ing]" them, "rendering them innocent," and "founding them in nature and eternity." Myth gives to "things" the "clarity . . . of a report."[19] It is from this perspective that we can read Naipaul's remarks that history in Trinidad was "a fairytale about Columbus and a fairytale about the strange customs of the aboriginal Caribs and Arawaks." It was "the Trinidad five-cent stamp: Raleigh discovering the Pitch Lake"; it was "a fairytale not so much about slavery as about its abolition, the good defeating the bad" (375). *The Loss of El Dorado* deconstructs this Trinidadian metahistory and tells instead a factual story of wandering expeditions, genocide, the colonial plantation system, and failed revolutions in nearby South America. In this history, there are not so much good guys or bad guys, as people of a colony, recognizable in their motives, attitudes, and actions, shaped by and shapers of their milieu.

*The Loss of El Dorado* focuses on the myths and metahistory of three fields of events: Trinidad-based expeditions for gold into the South American jungle, the Spanish and British colonization of Trinidad, and British-sponsored attempts at revolution in South America (13). When Columbus sailed into the Antilles, J. M. G. Le Clézio notes, he sought not only a route to India and China, but also, like other Renaissance voyagers, the land of the Amazons, where female warriors were said to guard a fabulous throne room replete with gold and other riches.[20] The legend of *el dorado*—the Indian "chief who once a year rolled in turpentine, was covered with gold dust and then dived into a lake" (18)—and his city of gold would seem to be a variation of the myth of the Amazons, of fantastic riches in an exotic land. The quest for El Dorado symbolizes the imperial quest generally, which, though perhaps born of romance and an urge to extend the boundaries of knowing, leads to genocide of the Amerindians, slavery, and the beginning of the inequalities between the "First World" and "Third World" that continue today. Paradoxically, from Old World civilization came a barbarity in the New one.

Naipaul calls the legend of El Dorado "a Spanish delusion," the fevered product of Antonio de Berrio, an aging conquistador whose expeditions into the jungle of Guyana end in "kidnap, solitude, and lunacy." Berrio's own accounts of these expeditions, however, relate a different story; they inscribe a "dream of innocence, resource, and power," at once Berrio's and Spain's. Similarly, Walter Raleigh's account of his explorations, *The Discovery of the Large, Rich and Beautiful Empire of Guiana*, is a metahistory that casts the debacle of his expeditions in a heroic light and superimposes a classical, mythic landscape on the steamy jungles of South America: "a book about the discovery of Arcadia . . . it suggests mines and gold, spaciousness, enamelled forests." It is "part of the world's romance," Naipaul explains, capturing "the New World at that moment between the unseeing brutality of the discovery and conquest and the later brutality of colonization" (107). The brutality of the discovery and conquest was "unseeing" in that it was wrapped in a myth of the *New* World, the idea that this land did not belong to any people, was not part of any living, human fabric, and, therefore, could be named and possessed by Europeans for the very first time. It is the nature of myth, Barthes explains, to purify, to render innocent, to make attitudes and actions seem natural and commonsensical,[21] and the metaphor of the New World purifies and renders natural an Old World dispossession and silencing of civilizations.

Naipaul calls El Dorado a "New World romance" and a "dream of Shangri-la" (31). Essentially a wish to return to the Garden of Eden and to possess a "virgin" land, the legend of El Dorado and the story of Robinson Crusoe express "the two fantasies of the New World": "To be the first man on the earth, to see the first shoots of the first crop, to let off 'the first gun that had been fired there since the creation of the world'" (41). The myth bespeaks a mystical experience, but the history that the myth distorts is a record of obsessions and failures. De Berrio's expeditions into the South American jungle are little more than fevered wanderings. During the third of these, he "heroically" orders the expedition's two hundred horses slaughtered in order to keep his troops from deserting; after a death march during which many men died and the sick were abandoned, he and those of his ragged troops that remained returned to Trinidad, eighteen months later (17, 26–27). Similarly driven by heroic ideals and the legend of a gilded Indian, Raleigh embarked on two South American expeditions, the second of which resulted in the death of his son, Wat, the suicide of Raleigh's "lifelong friend" Laurence Keymis—whom Raleigh taunted by blaming him for Wat's death and the expedition's failure—and Raleigh's eventual imprisonment and beheading in London. With Raleigh's failures the "medieval romance" in the New World came to an end, turning into "a cynical extension of the developing old world, its commercial underside," Naipaul writes (108).

Beneath its idealistic trappings, the quest for El Dorado was a failed business (ad)venture, a preliminary foray in what Eric Williams has dubbed the "first gold-rush . . . of the modern world."[22] Looked at from this perspective, the metaphor of the quest ennobles greed and theft. As Conrad's Marlow exclaims of imperial explorers: "They grabbed what they could get for the sake of what was to be got."[23] But even today we normally do not talk about the great European explorers in this way; the myth of discovery and the metaphor of the quest still hold sway over us. The myth makes history disappear; it glorifies the European "discoverer" and renders invisible the indigenous peoples who are dispossessed. That other eyes saw the New World before Columbus, a hero in whose honor Americans have set aside a national holiday, that other peoples knew this world as their fabric of life for ages before his discovery, does not seem to matter in our metahistory of the Americas, our "home."[24]

In his recounting of Trinidad's colonization, Naipaul again contrasts myth and history. Spanish exploits in the Americas are still shrouded in glory, but theirs was a brutal settling in, typified, for example, by Domingo de Vera's founding of the Trinidad city of Saint Joseph de Oruña: after pacing off the plaza and taking possession of the land by "turf and twig," de Vera has a pillory and gallows built to impress Spanish power on the Indians (34–35). Paradoxically, in the midst of the European Renaissance, it was chiefly death that the Old World brought to the New. Within a hundred-year period the Indian population in Trinidad was reduced from forty thousand to four thousand (118). In other colonies a similar genocide took place: in Hispaniola, the Indian population dropped from an estimated 250,000 in 1492, to 60,000 in 1508, to 14,000 in 1514.[25] Todorov estimates that between 1500 and 1550 the Amerindian population dropped from 80 million to 10 million—a destruction of 90 percent of the population or 70 million human beings. "If the word genocide is ever applied with precision in a case, this is certainly the one," he comments.[26] Those Indians who survived, their culture shattered, resigned themselves to broken domestication; in Trinidad the Arawaks Indians "declined from Spanish allies into Spanish servants" (118). Some, like the "man-eating" Caribs, however, resisted and challenged authority. Naipaul describes one bloody incident involving the Carib Indians and Capuchin missionaries, and the subsequent retaliation. The Indians were driven to the sea, where many chose to drown themselves; of those who did not, some were shot while others were tortured, tried, and hanged, their "heads and hands . . . cut off, their bodies quartered and the pieces spiked on the public road" (118–20).

Genocide, the shattering of an other's world, constitutes an initial chapter of New World colonization, though that history has been refracted through the prism of metahistory. In *Le Rêve mexicain, ou la pensée interrompue* (The Mexican dream, or thought interrupted), J. M. G. Le Clézio writes movingly of the contradictions in the New World's conquest and colonization:

The silencing of the Indian world is without doubt one of the most infamous dramas of humanity. At the moment when the West was rediscovering the values of humanism and creating the foundation of a new republic based on justice and respect of life, it initiated, through the perversity of the New World conquerors, the era of a new barbarity based on injustice, dispossession, and murder. Never had Man seemed at the same moment so free and so cruel, discovering in the same instant the universality of law and the universality of violence. Discovering the generous ideas of humanism and the dangerous conviction of the inequality of races, the relativity of civilizations and a cultural tyranny. . . .

The silencing of the Indian world is a drama whose consequences we have not finished measuring. It is a double drama, for in exterminating the American Indian cultures, the conqueror destroyed a part of himself that he will never be able to retrieve.[27]

But the metahistory of Spanish soldiers and missionaries puts a different accent on the silencing of the Indian world, commemorating soldiers through a story of heroic conquest and glorifying missionaries through a tale of their "savage" martyrdom. Missionaries became "the new adventurers of the Spanish Empire," Naipaul writes, with "their martyrdoms . . . celebrated in . . . engravings" and "ecclesiastical histories." Thus a history of the New World was written with a Spanish inflection, as a "Spanish heroic cycle," with first *conquistadores* and later missionaries as the heroes: "Spanish blood now for Indian, the heroism of martyrdom for the heroism of conquest" (123). In their encounter with the Other, what the Spanish discover in the New World is the difference between the colony and the metropolis: the colony, far away, becomes the proper place for massacres, a not quite real place where brutality can be transformed into myth. The Spanish initiate "the civilization of the massacre" and transform it into a heroic cycle. They initiate the deception of the colonial era, during which "conquest" is written about as "pacification."[28]

As in his account of New World conquest and colonization, Naipaul reads a myth that supports slavery and the plantation system in Trinidad. An Arcadian-Christian myth casts the island's planters and landowners in the role of an ordained aristocracy who rule by a mixture of divine and natural rights and are served by various levels of workers and servants, indentured whites and Negro slaves. The planters view themselves as bearers of civilization to a savage land and peoples; the French planters in Trinidad, he notes, were fond of giving their slaves classical and biblical names such as Icare, Thisbe, Piram, and Goliah, a practice illustrating their "taste for pastoral" (213–14). The planters view Trinidadian governor Thomas Picton, known for his stern punishment of Negroes and his "impartial terror," as a "'saviour of the colony'" (158, 215). The Arcadian-Christian myth recasts the world in a shape that makes slavery and the colonial plantation system seem right and commonsensical: Greek and biblical names civilize African savages; "law and order" hold at bay a dark, pagan, chthonic chaos; jailings, torture, and capital punishment purge evil from the island-colony and make it ready for civilization and redemption.

Naipaul treats Picton, governor between 1797 and 1803, and his legendary jail with its *cachots brûlants* (hell holes) as central symbols of the inhumanity that slavery and the plantation system produced through three centuries in the West Indies. Picton "inherited . . . a slave island, where he alone was the law," and he was changed for the worse by that system. A military man by background, Picton, "like a convert to a cause," turns into the perfect colonialist, "vehement[ly]" defending slavery: "He had the vocabulary and could make the private jokes; he could describe the system as 'the assistance of Africans from the Coast' " (152, 182). Naipaul judges Picton as neither good nor evil, but as contaminated by the malady of slavery and colonialism. Of his trial in London, Naipaul writes that Picton was "a victim of people's conscience, of ideas of humanity and reason that were ahead of the reality"; he was tried less for what he did—the torture of Luisa Calderon—than for having been "governor of a slave colony" (156–57). Picton the victimizer is thus also the victim of contradictions within metropolitan society—about colonization as a noble, civilizing force, on the one hand, and about guilt over slavery on the other. He is a scapegoat for belatedly awakening metropolitan scruples over the colonial enterprise in general. Thus, as in *The Middle Passage,* Naipaul views slavery and the colonial system as a social malignancy that harms the colonizers as well as the people and the land they colonized. Vallot, the doddering jailer who goes about his business, whether it be flogging, cutting off an ear or nose, or trussing and hoisting a prisoner by rope and pulley, is another such victimizer and victim of the colony. He is portrayed as someone who does his job without thinking about it too much, the desensitizing world of the slave colony shaping his attitudes and actions.

The jail where Vallot labors is the dominant symbol of Picton's governorship. With its dark, windowless cells and withering temperatures—"never less than 100 degrees"—the *cachots brûlants* resembled a hell that fit within the Arcadian-Christian myth of the colony's planters. "[P]risoners there, chained flat on boards, quickly wasted away and became demented," Naipaul recounts (189). He draws a correlation between the abominable conditions of the *cachots* and the planters' fear of being overwhelmed by dark forces associated with the Negro: The jail was "a place of horror: it could not be otherwise: the planters . . . entering the jail faced the tortures, confessions and rotting bodies like the African darkness that might overwhelm them all: [visions of] powder turning to insects to ravage a plantation, charms killing the canes, money turning to dung, Negroes dying in convulsions, the world ending in blood and flames" (201). The Arcadian-Christian myth transforms the *cachots* into the hell to which rebellious Negroes must be condemned; it counteracts an "African darkness" with a Christian darkness. Slavery and the colonial plantation system thus interact in an imprisoning circle: slavery separates and imposes a dualistic ideology, whose products are the owners' fear and the slaves' rebellion, which in turn is viewed as a harbinger of an African darkness and is punished by imprisonment in the *cachots brûlants,* a Christian hell to counter an imagined, pagan chaos.

The third "theme" of *The Loss of El Dorado*—revolution and revolutionaries in nearby South America—parallels the book's other two themes. Naipaul is interested in the romance of revolution, in the myth of absolute change from injustice to justice, inequality to equality, evil to good. In particular, he focuses on nineteenth-century revolutionary Francisco Miranda, a victim of his colonial background, the age's romanticism, and the exile-induced gap between his Europeanized, nostalgic perception of Venezuelan society and the un-European frontier society that the country actually was. After thirty-five years' absence from Venezuela, Miranda "dealt in romance," Naipaul writes, a personal romance that included Amerindians but not Negroes. While in Trinidad, Miranda "preferred not to see . . . Negroes" because they "formed . . . no part of his vision of a world made classically pure and beautiful" (316). Naipaul portrays Miranda—" 'a would-be Inca-emperor with a private cause' "— and other South American revolutionaries like Manuel Gual and Manuel de España as seekers of personal glory whose vision, defined with "borrowed words," does not match a South American society where the "only cause was self and survival" (181, 310, 365). Like Berrio and Raleigh, Miranda and other would-be revolutionaries are victims of a myth.

In *The Middle Passage* Naipaul calls the history of the Caribbean a story of commodities and markets; in *The Loss of El Dorado* he links that story with the metahistory or myth supporting it. The titular loss about which he writes is the corruption of a vision and a rejection of a potential new understanding of other peoples. From the Old World quest for riches to the genocide of the Amerindians and theft of their land, the transport of a labor force from Africa and Asia and its exploitation, and the rivalry between European powers for lands, minerals, and markets, the history of Trinidad and the West Indies is not a history of "the good defeating the bad," but of a barbarity and dispossession of others that grew out of the competition between Old World powers in a geographic arena that became known as "the cockpit of Europe" (375).[29] *El dorado*, the fabled gilded Indian, eludes the European explorers, but to those whom they do find they respond as if to an enemy. "*Comprendre, prendre, détuire*"—get to know, take from, destroy—such was the nature of the Old World encounter with the New World others.[30] The explorers seek *el dorado* not to communicate with him as someone different from yet equal to them, but to learn his secrets and then dispose of him. *El dorado* is less a person (an "I") than a thing, the gold that covers a body. He is the first commodity in a continuing Caribbean history of commodities and markets.

To the Europeans El Dorado was something else as well, though: he was a dream of the eternally new. Explorers and colonists sought what Robinson Crusoé in Michel Tournier's *Vendredi* finds on his island, Speranza: "Each morning was . . . a new beginning, the first day in the history of the world. . . . [The island] vibrated in a perpetual present, without past or future."[31] El Dorado is about being in this "paroxysm of perfection." Through his encounter with Vendredi (the "savage," the Other), Tournier's Crusoé is changed and sees in a new way; he understands, to use words of Julia Kristeva, that "Strangely, the stranger lives within us; he is the hidden face of our identity."[32] The history that Naipaul has written is not about finding "the stranger within," but rather about a feeling of incompleteness, of something lost. In "the loss of El Dorado" lies a gap between myth and history, idea and action, that is linked with a sense of alienation and loss in Naipaul's own, reversed, New World to Old World encounter with European others. In the loss of El Dorado he finds, in displaced form, his own exile.

Both *The Middle Passage* and *The Loss of El Dorado* are stories about exile—a paradise lost, the forced migration of peoples, the colony as a distant, "unreal" world. These books show Naipaul as sociologist and as historian of the consciousness and mythologies of the West Indies and the Caribbean. He seeks to diagnose the region's problems by bringing back its history; but in order to do that, he must expose its metahistory, the myths that distort that history. His intention in both books is to show the effects of colonialism and imperialism in the West Indies and the Caribbean. These books link the journeys of explorers, *conquistadores*, colonizers, missionaries, slaves, indentured workers, emigrants, and tourists with the author's journeys to the region where he no longer lives. Autobiographically, these books record his malaise as a colonial and his disillusionment as an exile; but they also explore an epistemology of exile, an attempt to understand the self better through a knowledge of the history of one's own society and those of others.

# 4

# The Greater Shipwreck

> . . . for the colonial there can be no true return.
> —V. S. Naipaul, "East Indian"

> The drawback of exile consists in a renouncement of strong ties with others.
> —Tzvetan Todorov, *Ourselves and Others*

> . . . halfway between the abyss and the summit . . . abandoned to directionless days and sterile souvenirs. . . .
> They feel the profound suffering of all prisoners and all exiles—to live with a memory that serves nothing.
> —Albert Camus, *The Plague*

To be a colonial is already to be an exile, for by definition a colony is a satellite, something ancillary; the colonial lives his unnecessary life in an unnecessary land. But especially beyond the colony in the metropolis a colonial confronts his difference from others and his blatant or subtle exclusion: "To be a colonial is to be a little ridiculous and unlikely, especially in the eyes of someone from the metropolitan country," Naipaul has written.[1] The negative aspects of the colonial's experience of exile—his sense of his ridiculousness in the eyes of others, his severed ties with his colonial community and society, an absence of strong ties in the metropolitan society, his sense of "self-defilement"—inform Naipaul's novels of the mid-1960s, *The Mimic Men* and *Mr Stone and the Knights Companion*. These books, which grow out of the creative impulse of exile, express, conversely, exile as a division and an alienation: fragmentation and isolation, a sense of futility, and the absence of belonging to a meaning-giving community and society.

Even though exile and home are linked to places, they are more precisely experiences of absence and presence and phenomenological constructs of places. For characters in Naipaul's early novels about colonial Trinidad, exile is an experience of the colony's marginality, while home is a romance of life in faraway England or the United States. These experiences of exile and home thus take the form of a colonial deprivation and a colonial fantasy in which romance-minded, restless characters like Edward of *Miguel Street* and Mohun Biswas of *A House for Mr Biswas* believe that "reality," the center of the world, lies far away from the limiting, marginal West Indies. Edward dreams of leaving Trinidad and living in the United States, where there are "enormous houses" and the "biggest cars in the world" (*MS* 144). Mohun Biswas reads Samuel Smiles's novels set in northern countries and envies his brother-in-law Owad, who having studied in England has been, like a pilgrim, to the place "where life was to be found" (*HB* 540).

A defining element in Naipaul's early works is their characters' romantic desire for the "real world" beyond Trinidad. This real world, or imagined home, is not exactly England but a construct of it, a collective, colonial fantasy of the metropolis, the center to which all things from the colonies gravitate; it is the idealized, affluent, modern First World. As a Barbadian agent wrote in 1689, "By a kind of magnetic force, England draws to it all that is good. . . . It is the centre to which all things tend."[2] Hundreds of years later, this myth of the center still holds sway over the mentality of characters like Titus Hoyt, the boy-narrator of *Miguel Street*, Owad, and Biswas. According to this myth, the metropolis is home; it is the omphalos, the sacred navel of the world. In the famous words of Frantz Fanon, for the colonial the metropolis carries a highly charged, quasi-religious significance; of Martinicans who go to and return from the "mother country," France, Fanon writes: "The black who goes to France changes because for him the metropolis represents the Tabernacle; he changes not only because Montesquieu, Rousseau and Voltaire come from France, but also because it is from there that doctors, administrators, and innumerable petty potentates come. . . . There is a kind of distant enchantment, and someone who is leaving in a week for the Metropolis creates around himself a magic circle where words like Paris, Marseille, the Sorbonne, and Pigalle represent the keys of the spell."[3] Bewitched by his image of the metropolis as the omphalos of the world, the colonial is bound to be disenchanted and disillusioned after more than any brief stay in the "mother country."

Along with disillusionment comes a sense of exile as deracination and fragmentation, and the twentieth-century metropolis, once a magic center, becomes for the colonial a disenchanted margin, a place of outcasts and automatons. It is to this experience of exile and these colonial metropolitan-produced constructs of exile and home in Naipaul's 1950s essays and mid-1960s novels that I now turn. Informed by the author's experience of the destructive aspects of life in the metropolis, *The Mimic Men* and *Mr Stone and the Knights Companion* tell complementary stories of exile, alienation, and an absence of a meaningful community of others. Ralph Kripal Singh of *The Mimic Men* is a political exile from the Caribbean island of Isabella and an intellectual exile from his youthful, colonial vision of the metropolis as center of the world.[4] Conversely, the protagonist of *Mr Stone and the Knights Companion*, a middle-class London librarian and office worker, "a gentle, endearing man nearing retirement, of no particular consequence," is alienated in the impersonal city from nature, others, and meaningful work and achievement.[5] Above all, Stone and Singh experience exile or alienation as an internal state, as a division between ideas and experience. The novels convey the destructive aspects of the experience of exile partly through ironic allusions to literary and mythic structures: Robinson Crusoe for *The Mimic Men*, and King Arthur and the Knights of the Round Table for *Mr Stone and the Knights Companion*. The novels demythologize the colonial image of the metropolis, yet in its place they construct other complementary, dualistic images of exile and home. In the absence of a community of others and of alternatives for action, the protagonists of *The Mimic Men* and *Mr Stone and the Knights Companion* experience isolation, fragmentation, and withdrawal into aestheticism and fantasy.

### "An Unlikely Colonial" (1958–1965)

"An Unlikely Colonial," a group of essays in *The Overcrowded Barracoon* (1972), reflects on the incongruities of Naipaul's cultural and literary identity. Two essays in particular, "East Indian" and "London," illuminate the predicaments of the protagonists of Naipaul's 1960s metropolitan novels. "East Indian" describes the sense of instability and exile seemingly inherent in the author's ethnic, colonial identity, and "London" describes the English metropolis, with its disjunct privacy and absence of community, as a paradigm and construct of exile.

These essays reflect on the opposing cultural identities and literary traditions of Naipaul the colonial writer and his metropolitan, English readers. Certainly part of Naipaul's struggles as a writer to define himself, his subject matter, and his audience, and to be published and read, were influenced by the habits and attitudes of the 1950s and 1960s English readers and with the unpropitious publishing market for books about West Indians, circumstances that led, for instance, to the immediate rejection of *A House for Mr Biswas* by Alfred A. Knopf, one of Naipaul's later publishers. During a 1979 interview the author recalls the "anguish" of this period: "How was I to take the nature of my own life, which I couldn't refer to anything in my literary experience, and look for ways of entering the other life, a life led by people who would be strangers to one, people, say, living in London, with a history. It took me several years . . . to feel that I could do the job."[6]

"East Indian" (1965) ponders the sense of incongruity and fragmentation inherent in Naipaul's ethnic, colonial identity. A "muted mutual mistrust" exists between the colonial and citizens of the metropolis; each is a stranger to the other, and each is viewed from the perspective of the others' assumptions and apprehensions. But a sense of exile does not begin at the moment of the colonial's voyage to the metropolis, it begins in language and the history that a language both records and distorts. Naipaul's nominal, ethnic identity is doubly, triply incongruous: he is a "colonial," an "East" Indian in the "West" Indies, and a "West Indian" by a happenstance of history. "To be an Indian from Trinidad is to be unlikely," he writes. "It is, in addition to everything else, to be the embodiment of an old verbal ambiguity" (33). For the "East Indian-West Indian" like Naipaul, language inscribes a fragile, illusive identity; like "Indian" ink and "Indian" paper, which in fact come from China, the appellation "West Indies" derives from Columbus's mistaken belief that his ship had landed in Cathay, India. To be an East Indian in the West Indies (whose very name connotes mistaken identity, a European miscalculation) is to be half one thing, half another; the incongruous identity must always be explained to others. At the same time, though, this incongruity holds the potential for a new hybrid identity, a syncretistic fusion of Indian, West Indian, and English literary traditions.

Exile is a condition of absence that cannot be filled either by returning home or to a former identity, manner of perception, or way of thinking. The essay "East Indian" concludes that there can be "no true return," whether for the colonial in the metropolis going back to the colony, or the East Indian-West Indian going back to India. Referring to the experiences of Indians who immigrated to Trinidad and gradually lost their old identity and became Trinidadians, the author remarks that "the colonial . . . is a product of revolution" and that "the revolution takes place in the mind" (37). For the exile a similar "revolution in the mind" must take place to unify the self and construct a sense of society and home. This involves seeing in a new way. A new syncretistic identity must evolve, but that identity cannot evolve in isolation, without a new social context. Inhabiting a limbo between an old and new identity, the exile has cut himself loose from his old community, yet in absence of a bond with a new community of others, he lives in between, like the shipwrecked Robinson Crusoe. Naipaul speaks of the sense of "self-defilement" that pricks the consciences of Trinidad Indians who emigrate from the West Indies to Great Britain; if only as his sense of self-defilement, the colonial-exile carries with him the old society, which makes him uncomfortable in the new. The sense of exile ends only when there is no longer a barrier between one's "new" self and a new community of others; one belongs to a society through a "revolution . . . in the mind," a way of seeing anew and by creating a construct of a society in which one belongs (37). This is a syncretistic activity. In order to be at home, the exile must create a construct of home by "seeing" in a way that is both familiar and new.

In the essay "London" (1958) Naipaul creates an image of the metropolis that conveys the negative, destructive aspects of his exile. London is the limbo where the colonial self is cut off from a community of others; it is the site where the West Indian writer and his English readers live privately and look at the world differently. "The privacy of the big city depresses me," he writes. "There are no communal pleasures in London. Between the activity and the response there is always the barrier of self-consciousness" (15). London may be "the best place to write in," he states, but adds the qualifier that he must travel—to Trinidad, India, and elsewhere—to avoid "sterility." He paints a portrait of such sterility in *Mr Stone and the Knights Companion*, whose protagonist has been turned into stone, so to speak, through the routines and impersonality of the big city. London is a place of exile for Naipaul because there he lives without a sustaining community, on the margins of English society. Like Ralph Singh, an inverted Robinson Crusoe going from New World to Old World, he is shipwrecked on an island full of people with whom he shares no rooted connection.

## *The Mimic Men* (1967)

*The Mimic Men* is both fictional autobiography and colonial and postcolonial history, the former linking it to *The Enigma of Arrival* and the latter to *The Middle Passage*. The protagonist's story of "shipwreck," or exile, tells an early version of the narrator's "Mediterranean fantasy" in *The Enigma of Arrival:* the tale of a voyager suddenly recognizing his exile—the ship is gone, there can be no return—and coming to grips with a sense of wasted life, cast out from a community of others. The protagonist's story is also a history of the colonial and postcolonial disorder of a fictional West Indian island, Isabella;[7] it critiques colonial Isabella from the same perspectives that *The Middle Passage* critiques colonial Caribbean and West Indian societies. *The Mimic Men* resembles *The Mystic Masseur* in that both tell a "history of the times" by telling the story of one West Indian's life and career. Ranjit Kripalsingh becomes Ralph Singh just as Ganesh Ramsumair becomes G. Ramsay Muir.

Singh, a middle-aged, East Indian-West Indian businessman and politician, recounts the memoirs of his life on Isabella (a British colony), his career, and his exile in England. His memoirs begin with a recollection of post–World War II London, where he did university studies and later worked at the British Broadcasting Corporation. He recounts incidents from both his personal life and his successful entrepreneurship on Isabella, the memoirs including his childhood and his family history, Isabellan friendships, participation in the island's independence movement, and his brief political career. When Singh and others in his party fail to satisfy the expectations of the newly independent people, he is removed from his governmental position and put on a plane for London, carrying with him "sixty-six pounds of luggage and fifty thousand dollars."[8] Throughout his recollections, but especially in the novel's final pages, Singh contemplates his exile from the colony and bitter withdrawal from metropolitan English society, which he once eagerly looked to as the center of the "real world" beyond the shipwreck of his life on Isabella. Ironically, England becomes for Singh the "greater shipwreck"; there, without hope of going home, he lives in exile, cut off from others, his thoughts turning between the poles of fantasy and nihilism. Alternately, Singh looks with disgust at London and longs for a blank, cold, unpeopled world, or, as in his seduction by Lady Stella, "enter[s] a fairyland" (230, 232).

The greater shipwreck is an exile without alternatives, where memories are futile and where the future is a dead end; it creates a permanent division between self and others. For Singh, neither his former West Indian colony nor the English metropolis can be a home. He considers colonial West Indian societies, with Isabella the paradigm, as fundamentally flawed because they are "transitional or makeshift societies" that lack "order"; they are "fragmented" and "inorganic," with "no link between man and landscape" and no "common interests" unifying their multicultural populace (8). Real power lies "outside" the societies not within, in other countries or in First World–controlled economic corporations (206). Singh's critique of colonial societies is essentially the critique that Naipaul puts forward in *The Middle Passage:* the colony is inherently flawed. Neither is the metropolis a solution, though: London and England are "the greater disorder, the final emptiness" in Singh's fragmented life

(8). The negative aspects of his exile carry his memoirs toward two complementary states of mind: fantasy and nihilism. Like the people cordoned off in Oran in Camus's *The Plague*, Singh "float[s] rather than live[s]," suspended in memories, doubts, negations. Through him, *The Mimic Men* portrays the emptiness of the exile's shipwreck, of being without a society.

Singh's memoirs convey a stagnancy, directionlessness, and fragmentation of exile. He is "adrift" and incomplete: "a cell of perception" not a unified, feeling and acting being. He ceases to be a "whole person" (27). It is the same for other colonial exiles that Singh meets, who like him are "trapped into fixed, flat postures," their personalities "divided bewilderingly into compartments" (27). Singh first travels to England pursuing his vision of the center, of the "real world" beyond marginal Isabella. In the colony he is bent on escape; he dreams of a world of "bigger men," "bigger lands," "journeys that t[ake] two days and a night," "continents with mountains five miles high and rivers so wide you couldn't see the other bank" (179). Yet once in the metropolis, he becomes disillusioned and restless, torn between past and present and constructs of exile and home: "I thought of escape," he confesses, "and it was escape to what I had so recently sought to escape from" (31). He rejects the metropolis; in his mind the marginal colony now becomes the center, home, and he eventually returns to Isabella with his bride.

Singh's relationships illustrate the exile's isolation, his split or fragmented identity. He describes his distaste for intimacy yet his fetish for fondling and being fondled: "Intimacy: the word holds the horror. I could have stayed for ever at a woman's breasts, if they were full and had a hint of weight that required support. . . . [As for sex] I was capable of the act required, but frequently it was in the way that I was capable of getting drunk or eating two dinners" (25). For Singh, breasts signify the center, home, the time before the shipwreck of his exile's life. He is initially attracted to his future wife, Sandra, because her breasts seem to match this ideal. In a dream he imagines himself a baby suckling at his mother's breast. "What joy!" he exclaims. "The breast on my cheek and mouth: a consoling weight, the closeness of soft, smooth flesh" (116). By way of these symbols, Singh's dream expresses a dependency that is an analogy of the dependency of the colony on the "mother country." We think of

James Harrington's words in *Oceana:* "[The colonies] are yet Babes that cannot live without sucking the breasts of the Mother Cities, but such as I mistake when they come to age they do not wean themselves."⁹ Figuratively, Singh and his colony have come of age, yet they are not yet independent.

Singh's life in London inverts his dream of nurture and security. Impressions of his fragmentation and disgust blend into a commentary on the emptiness of urban life. Of London and its imprisoning, isolating effects on him and others, he laments:

> We seek the physical city and find only a conglomeration of private cells. In the city as nowhere else we are reminded that we are individuals, units. . . .
>
> So quickly had London gone sour on me. The great city, centre of the world, in which, fleeing disorder, I had hoped to find the beginning of order. . . . But the god of the city was elusive. The tram was filled with individuals, each man returning to his own cell. The factories and warehouses . . . were empty and fraudulent. . . . In the great city, so solid in its light . . . life was two-dimensional. (18–19)

London, the "two-dimensional" city, is not exactly a place, but a construct that grows out of and symbolizes Singh's exile; the separate "cells" of activity in a mass of people express the barriers between his exiled self and others. Singh cannot find the "god" of the city; he cannot create, from his experience in the city, a construct of home, a community of others. For him, London has an inhuman quality; he calls it a city "made by man but [now] passed out of his control," pushing its inhabitants either toward "breakdown" or fevered, automaton-like "activity." He describes London as a "dying mechanized city," and imagines himself magically escaping from it to the city of centuries ago, a time of "sheep . . . in Soho Square" (52, 81).

Singh experiences an exile's disjunction between ideas and actions, constructs and actuality. In his dualistic perception, he associates ideas with purity, and actions with failure and decay. "I no longer dream of ideal landscapes or seek to attach myself to them," he writes. "All landscapes eventually turn to land, the gold of the imagination to the lead of the reality" (10).[10] As exile he is like the voyager of Cavafy's "The City," who carries with him a complementary longing and dissatisfaction that he cannot escape:

> You will find no new lands, you will find no other seas.
> The city will follow you. You will roam the same
> streets. And you will age in the same neighborhoods;
> and you will grow gray in these same houses.
> Always you will arrive in this city.[11]

Singh's exile is not just in a physical place; it is a place in his mind as well. He maps this latter, "inner" place of exile onto London, the city of ruin at which he always arrives.

Before his departure from the colony for the English metropolis, Singh infuses the world beyond the tiny island with a specialness. He is particularly fascinated by the thought of snow: "on the snow slopes of the Laurentians [in Canada], was the true, pure world" (146). His images reflect a colonial and neocolonial dualism, which considers the metropolis or First World as central and true and the colony as marginal and false. A product of his colonial background, his romantic, quasi-religious images of the metropolis and the world beyond the colony assure his disappointment and eventual disillusionment on his arrival there. His memoirs convey that surprise and disillusionment; he is particularly struck, for example, by the difference between the glamorous, regal image of the BBC imparted to international listeners and the plainness of its operations and facilities: "there in the canteen of a radio service which, when picked up in remote countries, was the very voice of metropolitan authority and romance, bringing to mind images, from the cinema and magazines, of canyons of concrete, brick and glass, motorcars in streams, lines of lights, busyness, crowded theatre foyers, the world where everything was possible; there now, at the heart of that metropolis, we sat, at a plastic-topped table, before thick cups of cooling tea and plates with yellow crumbs" (46). In its inner sanctum, the BBC, the voice of metropolis and empire, loses its quasi-magical quality and becomes ordinary; like the radio station, the metropolis quickly loses its aura as well. The "gold of the imagination" always turns into the "lead of the reality," Singh laments. Incorporated into the routine of the metropolis, he loses any special feeling about where he is or what he is doing.

In exile, with an identity divided between colony and metropolis, Singh, just as he has idealized the "real world" beyond Isabella, constructs a counterweight romance of the Arcadian island world he has left behind. He falls into a reverie of his retirement on a cocoa plantation in Isabella, with its "old timber estate house," dark and shiny floors, "wide low-eaved verandas," and "cooling ferns." "Everywhere," he imagines, "the eye would have found pleasure" (32–33). In the fields, laborers "of the olden time" work at "undemanding tasks" such as cutting down pods with "gullets, hand-shaped knives" like "weapons of medieval knights"; in the "shade," "arcadian figures" stand by the "multicoloured heap of pods" (33–34). Through reverie Singh fashions a home that is the reverse of his exile, but there is little that is factual about his cocoa plantation. The authors of *The Other Side of Paradise* provide this description of plantation work—a reality quite different from Singh's reverie:

> Men are paid not by the hour or by the piece, but by each ton of sugarcane they cut. They live by the strength of their arms, the blade of their machetes, and their ability to endure a way of life that has hardly changed for hundreds of years. They trudge into the forests of ten-foot cane, repeatedly bending down to swing their machetes; at the end of the day, they load their two or four tons of sugarcane into a waiting bin. . . . [They] work seven days a week during the six-month sugar harvest and receive about $1.50 for each ton cut. They cut about two tons in a day that lasts from four o'clock in the morning to six o'clock in the evening.[12]

There is a discrepancy between Singh's vision and actuality: hardly "arcadian figures," West Indian field-workers are often shackled to a livelihood that is another form of slavery. His cocoa plantation is a false paradise, a dream of a false home.

In London, Singh lives like a man in a cage. In contrast with the spacious plantation of his reverie, his hotel room is prisonlike and characterless with its "regulation hotel furniture" (34). It is tawdry: "Nothing . . . has been fashioned with love or even skill; there is as a result nothing on which the eye rests with pleasure" (33). As nondescript and limiting as the hotel room is, though, Singh prefers it to the city beyond, for at least the room provides "decorum and calm," an escape from the perceived vulgarity and rabble of the metropolis. Singh the exile, the alienated man, observes of the Londoners and London beyond his hotel room: "I do not believe that there is communication between these people any more than I believe in the hilarity of the advertisements by which they are surrounded: those irritating drawings in which the mouths of funny men are too wide open . . . those beer-mats whose circular legends I know by heart. *Who comes here? A Grenadier. What does he want? A pot of beer"* (35). Singh is separated from the metropolis and its denizens by his background, task at hand (to write a history of empire), and sensibility. Everyone and everything he notices is irritating. Looking out of his hotel window he regards "middle-aged ladies, mutton dressed as lamb," who tan themselves by a putting green; he is buffeted by a "ceaseless roar of traffic" and assaulted by the "tainted air." In contrast to the tropical landscape of his reverie, life in the metropolis seems a negation, an absence as exile itself is a collection of absences: "No cocoa trees! No orange-yellow *immortelle* flowers! No woodland springs running over white sand in which dead golden leaves and fresh red flowers have become embedded! No morning rides!" (33–35). Singh lives in a world of negations.

His reverie of the cocoa estate and description of the hotel room and the surrounding city are products of his divided consciousness. In Singh the negative aspect of exile and the colonial malady of marginality take the form of a desire for what is absent or out of grasp, not for what is present and realizable. Like his fetish for women's breasts, his reverie of the cocoa estate expresses his need for nurturing and security and creates a construct of home in contrast with his constructs of exile (i.e., London the mechanical, godless city). From one perspective, his reverie romanticizes the West Indies in contrast with the impersonal city, thus inverting the usual colonial-metropolis dualism in which the metropolis is viewed as the center of the real world. Singh longs for a paradise lost. From another perspective, his reverie, coupled with images of the hotel room and metropolis, critiques twentieth-century urban society, which has conquered nature and ordered the world but has in the process enslaved itself in a cheapness and an anesthetizing sameness.

In the novel's allegory, the story of Singh and his former colony, Isabella, are interrelated: the turmoil of his exile matches that of Isabella's decolonization; his story is partly Isabella's history, and vice versa. Like a hypertext, autobiography and history are set within and comment on each other; the movement is two-directional—the story of a particular colonial businessman and exiled politician grows out of the history of decolonization in a West Indian colony, and that history is interpreted and understood through the lens of Singh's perspectives and constructs. His

# The Greater Shipwreck 99

life and career manifest the "restlessness" and "disorder" that have come about through imperialism and decolonization because they and his career interpenetrate; different manifestations of the same cultural and socioeconomic forces, his failed career and failed decolonization comment upon each other, are understood one through the other. Singh's restlessness is a Caribbean or West Indian restlessness, and Singh's malaise is a Caribbean or West Indian malaise. And it is partly through exile, its exotopy, that Singh (and Naipaul) can make these connections between self and society.

As a commentary on decolonization in a Caribbean or West Indian colony, the novel develops three themes: the damaging effect of an absence of a regional, historical consciousness; an entrapment in a preindependence rhetoric and mentality; and a reliance on or belief in First World solutions to Third World problems—a belief that the industrialized nations have all the answers, when, in fact, they may have very little to offer that will work in the context of a developing island nation. First, through mechanisms of colonialism, the peoples of the Caribbean and West Indies have been rendered invisible to themselves. At the root of problems of decolonization, an absence of a regional, historical consciousness prevents formerly colonial peoples from understanding their past and imagining their future identities. Second, politicians of newly independent colonies get trapped by absolutist rhetoric and thinking; coming into power through the struggle for independence, they have become accustomed to making their appeals in terms of absolute change and cannot put into action a limited step-by-step amelioration of their society. Third, given the First World's economic clout and its dominance of technical knowledge and expertise, former Caribbean and West Indian colonies, with no alternative pattern of development to guide them, continue to imitate Europe and the United States, which prevents finding solutions to problems in the islands' own regional contexts.

In Isabella, decolonization turns into a shout for everything. Of the exaggerated promises of his own political party, Singh complains: "the wild men . . . promised to abolish poverty in twelve months. . . . They promised farmers higher prices for sugar cane and cocoa. They promised to renegotiate the bauxite royalties and to nationalize every foriegn-owned estate. . . . They promised; they promised; and they generated the frenzy of the street-corner preacher who thrills his hearers with a vision of the unattainable rich world going up in a ball of fire" (198–99). Here and elsewhere, Naipaul contends that political change in the colonies preceded a change in the colonial self; ideologies took the place of an understanding of self, society, and the relation of one's society to others. He also ascribes failures of decolonization to a cumulative, colonial deficit of skills and knowledge and former colonies' relative powerlessness in a competitive, Euro-American–controlled market. Singh describes, for example, Isabella's failed attempt to establish a plastics industry on the island. He and his party hire a foreign entrepreneur to build a factory that eventually produces flawed bowls and combs unsalable in the world market. Isabellans pay for their technical dependency; they are the victims of a deficit of skills and knowledge, not just of a shady deal. Nor will a we-versus-them attitude—"tell me who the enemy is"— yield positive results in a global market controlled by First World corporations, for no West Indian or Caribbean nation can by itself, without the support of other nations in the region, successfully challenge a tightly controlled First World–owned industry. A case in point is Singh's failed attempts to pressure the foreign-owned bauxite companies to increase royalty payments. The problem is not exactly that Singh is unskilled at negotiation, but that there is nothing to negotiate because the company can shut down its operations in Isabella and mine and process its product in another country. Isabella needs the bauxite company more than it needs Isabella. The company can thus play one developing country against another and thereby obtain the most lucrative mining agreement from the most malleable, most desperate client. Bauxite company officials humiliate Singh and put tiny Isabella in its place by pointing out that there are always alternatives for bauxite extraction; they explain that the company can always leave the island when it chooses: "and then the natives could play as long as they pleased with the red dust, as they had done before 1935" (217).

In this plight, Isabella faces an economic predicament analogous to those of today's Caribbean basin countries, which depend on industries controlled by large transnational corporations. The aluminum industry in the Caribbean and South America, for example, is controlled by six transnational corporations (i.e., Alcoa, Alcan, Kaiser Aluminum and

Chemical, Reynolds Metal, Pechiney Ugine Kulman of France, and Swiss Aluminum), which have great power in determining the terms of contracts with individual, bauxite-rich countries. Seventy-five percent of bauxite sales and 87 percent of aluminum sales are made by the affiliates of these corporations. Caribbean countries are tiny, and the transnational corporations are huge: the sales and assets of some are many times larger than the gross national product of the countries in which they operate; in 1981, for example, Shell had forty-six times more in annual sales than Suriname's annual exports.[13]

Singh's negotiations with bauxite company officials illustrate the economic realities of decolonization: Caribbean islands, like the fictitious Isabella, remain just as dependent today on imperial power or First World–controlled markets as before, because decolonization has not altered the fundamental economic structure of the colony-metropolis relationship. After two decades, Caribbean nations like Isabella are no less, and in many cases more, dependent than they were prior to political independence. The authors of *The Other Side of Paradise: Foreign Control in the Caribbean* (1984) state: "The Caribbean . . . has little to show for 20 years of attempted economic development. Two of the six poorest nations in the hemisphere are Caribbean countries, including Haiti, one of the most destitute places in the world. The Gross National Product . . . of most Caribbean nations has either stayed the same or declined in relation to that of the world's largest capitalist nations. The region is hopelessly in debt to the developed world, unemployment has grown to depression levels, the cost of imports is rising much more rapidly than the value of exports, and no signs herald an economic turnaround in this decade."[14] This is not only a Caribbean plight, but a Third World calamity: "according to the U.S. Agency for International Development (AID), 70 of the world's 95 least developed countries are economically behind where they were 10 years ago."[15]

Naipaul describes well the dependency and relative economic powerlessness of Caribbean basin countries, but his dominant focus in the analysis of woes of decolonization is the state of mind of former colonial peoples. As the title of the novel indicates, he focuses on mimicry as the chief cause of Caribbean dependency on the First World. Underlying this cause, however, is the deeper cause of the former colonial society's lack of knowledge of its history, which produces confused, divided identities, fantasy and myth, and racial antipathies. Isabellan society is "fragmented" and "inorganic," without "common interests" to unite it (206); in place of the bond of reality and shared backgrounds and interests that Caribbean history would provide, Isabellans are divided by racist attitudes and racial myths like that of Deschampsneufs, which classifies nations and peoples into the categories of "short-visioned," "medium-visioned," and "long-visioned." Orientals are long-visioned, Africans short-visioned, and Europeans, especially the French, medium-visioned. "I can't see our Afric brethern coming to much," Deschampsneufs philosophizes. "Lot of noise and so on, but short-visioned. . . . You know those fellows in the South American bush, when they kill something, say a deer or something like that, you know they just sit down and eat out the whole damn thing" (172). In the makeshift multicultural colony, myth sometimes fills the vacuum of cultural and historical knowledge. "We [former colonials] have all learned that political independence is unimportant without economic independence," Naipaul remarks in his introduction to *East Indians in the Caribbean*, "but I don't think we have yet learned that true creativity comes from a sound intellectual life as much as it might come from a sound political life. Societies . . . have continually to create themselves; and this act of creation requires the highest kind of intellectual endeavour."[16] Racial myths like Deschampneufs's block this endeavor and keep the former colony divided against itself.

Likewise divided, Singh bears the wounds of his colonial background and metropolitan exile. His own envisioned "intellectual endeavour," a history of modern imperialism, does not come to fruition, and his energies spill out unchanneled in reveries and fantasies. Bearing his colonial wounds, isolated in his metropolitan exile, Singh can find no alternative to the fragmentation and disorder of the colony and the fragmentation and orderly emptiness of the metropolis; his mind turns to myths of ordering and building and pastoral withdrawal. Just as life in the colony produces an escapism, so too life in the mechanized city produces a counterescapism, a nursery-rhyme pastoralism. While reading *The Oxford Nursery Rhyme Book* and *The House at Pooh Corner*—books that Lady Stella, a confused soul of the great city has loaned to him—Singh's thoughts fill with sadness and an overwhelming sense of decay and loss in the "roaring red city" for the London of old: "of village greens and riders on horseback and milkmaids and fairs and eggs in baskets and journeys by country folk to . . . town." He wishes that he could exist in that former time, within "that limpid, direct vision of the world . . . of order" (230). Whether to Merry Old England, the Isabellan cocoa plantation, or the house at Pooh Corner, Singh the would-be historian's thoughts lead, ironically, into aesthetic withdrawal and a romance of history. The milkmaids, the fairs, the quaint image of eggs carried in baskets: this vision of England, like a stylized painting, depicts an imagined past; it depicts a place of rest, an aesthetic withdrawal, not a historical moment. Like the protagonist of *The Enigma of Arrival*, Singh through this vision creates a construct of a safe home somewhere on the other side of his exile. Conversely, his thoughts also range to images of sublime emptiness—"snow," he notes, is his favorite element—as in his reverie of a horseman in the steppes of Central Asia, "riding below a sky threatening snow to the very end of an empty world" (82). Singh's escape from the colony does not lead to involvement in a new community or society, but rather into the bondage of aloneness and nihilism from which he seeks to extract himself if only through the self-examination of autobiography. In works written in this period, Naipaul depicts the destructive quality of "freedom from." Singh is incapable of transforming his freedom into meaningful action or commitment to a community of others; only by writing his memoirs does he begin to put himself back in the world of men and accept the challenge of "freedom to."[17]

*The Mimic Men*, as its title suggests, tells the story of a false relationship between self and others in which the identity of the self is masked or distorted or rendered invisible by imitation. The mimic men of the colony have a divided sensibility and a divided social identity, and Singh the colonial in exile in the metropolis is doubly divided in his relation to other colonials and to the citizens of the metropolis. Divided by his attraction to and repulsion from both the colony and the metropolis, and by aestheticism on the one hand and nihilism on the other, Singh is paralyzed. He arrives at a dead end. For Naipaul, the way out can be found only through a new way of looking; the possible solution to the problems of decolonization requires, among other things, a change in the mind of former colonial peoples. If in nothing else, by writing his memoirs, Singh begins a long reflection on self and society that is the prerequisite for this.

## Mr Stone and the Knights Companion (1963)

The opening pages of *The Mimic Men* allude to the themes of *Mr Stone and the Knights Companion:* "The pacific society has its cruelties," Singh explains. "Once a man is stripped of his dignities he is required, not to die or to run away, but to find his level" (8). In this context he then wonders what has become of a former colonial acquaintance who is, like him, in exile in England: "Was he pining away tamely in some office job?" (9). This "pining away," a draining of vitality and creative energy, a metaphorical turning into stone, is the subject of *Mr Stone and the Knights Companion*, a novel about the routine life of a librarian-office worker and the pacifically cruel metropolitan world as a place of alienation and exile.

Whereas *The Mimic Men* laments the absence of a New World order, *Mr Stone* laments a numbing, Old World orderliness. An appropriate subtitle for this novel would be "The Hollow Men" or "The Wasteland," for the novel presents an urban landscape where the natural world, surviving only as alley cats and apartment gardens, has been largely replaced by the inanimate and the mechanical, where people live in "separate cells," where action is routinized, and meaning derives from parody—in Stone's case, a parody of Arthurian romance or a mimicry of a romantic past.[18] Singh is a mimic man of the New World; Mr. Stone is a mimic man of the Old.

A dark, ironic novel of middle-class life in the metropolis, *Mr Stone* grows out of the author's experience of double exile, in London the metropolis and in India "the motherland," where he traveled for the first time while writing this novel and collecting materials for *An Area of Darkness* (1964). The qualities of Stone's "exile" are conveyed in the novel's opening pages by an incident symbolizing the rift between the modern, city-dwelling, solitary, bureaucratic man and the natural world. While Stone is fumbling for his front-door key, he is startled by a cat that leaps down the stairway. Upon entering the apartment, Stone reaches for a poker to protect himself, prepares a trap, and retreats exhaustedly to the bathroom to calm himself: "sitting on the cover of the lavatory bowl, still in his hat and overcoat, he waited. . . . Often, walking down the cat-infested street, he had been surprised by a cat sitting sedately on a fence post at the level of his head, and he had always made as if to shield his face. . . . He feared the creatures; and there were all those stories of cornered cats, of cats growing wild and attacking men" (6). A division exists between Stone and other living things, whether cats or people. His phobia signifies an urban-induced division between self and others— between human beings, who live in separate units of concrete, brick, and steel, and between the human and still slightly untamed natural world. A solitary bachelor in his sixties, Stone has become through the years a man of a routine and orderliness, which stifle any wayward aspirations and produce in him a fear of anything outside the ordinary. The cat is not only frightening, it is upsetting as well because it disrupts the sameness of Stone's day, filled with habits that have been in place for years: he always shaves the right side of his face first, always puts on his right shoe first, always reads only the first page of the *Telegraph* during breakfast (16). The meaning of his life comes from these domestic rituals.

"The English bourgeoisie are mimicking their former roles," Naipaul has remarked. "They express their soul by the color of their walls."[19] Mr. Stone is this mimicry, or more precisely, a personification of bourgeois ritual. He embodies the "three quasi-theological virtues" of the bourgeoisie: "the art of detail, self-control, and the ritualization of the quotidian."[20] Stone stands for a bureaucratic rather than a natural order, that is, an order of meticulous classification and quantification: "Mr Stone liked to think in numbers. He liked to think, 'I have been with Excal [his employer] for thirty years.' . . . 'I have been living in this house for twenty-four years.'" Stone paints his life according to numbers; he is carefully counting time. He keeps track of the changing of the seasons, for example, according to the alternation of his secretary's business suits: "All around [Stone] were such reminders of solidity, continuity and flow. . . . In the office Miss Menzies . . . had exactly eighteen 'business' outfits . . . a number which in the end had formed part of the soothing pattern of his existence. Individual outfits faded and were replaced, but the number remained constant, one outfit for each day of the week until three weeks had passed and the cycle began again. . . . Their passing away . . . were like the shedding of the leaves of his tree; her new garments were like the leaves of spring" (15, 17). Stone lives within a synthetic, bourgeois orderliness; what is pleasing to him, or so he has been patterned by the metropolis, is not life as an experience, but as epitaph: "Life was something to be moved through. Experiences were not to be enjoyed at the actual moment; pleasure in them came only when they had been . . . docketed and put away. . . . It was only then that they acquired colour, just as colour came truly to Nature only in a coloured snapshot or a painting, which annihilated colourless, distorting space" (15). Stone separates act from experience, the present from the past; what counts for him is not the living but the last will and testament of having lived. Stone is an artist of sorts, but he is a bourgeois artist of numbers, with the notch, or the docket, his bourgeois art form.

In the *The Mimic Men* Ralph Singh goes to London with great expectations, seeking the "flowering" of his self (*MM* 26); in *Mr Stone* the protagonist is portrayed as a typical, ironic product of the great city that Singh has sought. Viewed from the perspective of Naipaul's exile, the metropolis (the disappointing center of a decadent world) produces Stones, not flowers. And it is significant that the novel begins not in Stone's childhood or youth, but in his advanced middle age, with his approaching retirement. His world is a world in decay. The prior sixty-two years of his life are rendered in scattered phrases as if to emphasize that those earlier years are of little or no interest and that they are more or less identical to the childhood, youth, and maturity of thousands of other inhabitants of the metropolis, each the same in their separate cells. The novel is not about how Stone became who he is, but about what he has become—a routinized, almost inanimate man partially awakening to a sense of a wasted life. As is Mr. Stone, so too are London and English bourgeois society by a metonymic extension: the novel portrays a busy but barren urban world; it portrays Naipaul the exile's vision of a decadent English bourgeoisie.

The flat, uneventful narrative and the novel's untitled chapters emphasize that little of consequence takes place in Stone's life. The peaks of the narrative are like tiny eruptions on an otherwise smooth surface: a cat springs down a stairwell; Stone wins the affection of Margaret, his future wife, by telling her the story of the cat springing down the stairwell and his feeble attempt to trap it using cheese as bait; during their marriage, Margaret burns a piece of cake on the coil of an electric heater, which leads to raised voices and hurt feelings; while on a vacation in Cornwall, she and "Doggie" (her term of endearment for her husband) are frightened by the smoke from a burning field; Stone conceives the idea of the Knights Companion, a program to reach out to retired clients of Excal; upon his own retirement, Stone is made a Knight Companion. There are brief exchanges, silences, misunderstandings, clipped celebrations, replays of it all, an underlying frustration and emptiness.

The narrative's flatness emphasizes the banal life of Stone and other city dwellers like him; this banality, and its dulling of perceptions and sapping of creative energies, is the "sterility" that Naipaul alludes to in the essay "London" and that he seeks to elude through travel. Stone also tries to escape the city's humdrum; his fantasy of magical flight responds to a sense of blockage and imprisonment: "He ignored traffic lights; he flew from pavement to pavement over people and cars and buses (the people flown over looked up in wonder while he floated serenely past, indifferent to their stupefaction)" (8). In his fantasy Stone soars out of his prison of dulled sensations and sapped energies, above the pavement of the imprisoning city. He becomes a genius of the air, like fliers of kites in short stories by Gabriel García Márquez, and Vendredi in Michel Tournier's *Vendredi ou les limbes du Pacifique* (Friday or the margins of the Pacific).[21] In flight Stone takes a bird's eye view of things; he breaks away to where he can see the routines of the city.

A genius of the air, creation, a new way of seeing—this is what Stone secretly desires and expresses mutedly in his concept, the Knights Companion, an attempt to brighten up the lives of company retirees. He conceives of the Knights Companion in response to his own approaching retirement and his sense of having accomplished nothing distinctive in life. According to his idea, retired employees of Excal company will visit retired employees of Excal clients, presenting them with a token gift; the retirees will thus be given something to do with their time, and Excal will improve its public image. Stone considers the Knights Companion a practical and noble idea: "He rescued men from inactivity; he protected them from cruelty. He preserved for men the comradeship of the office, which released them from the confinement of family relationships. He kept alive loyalty to the company" (66). But Whymper, a young colleague of Stone's at Excal, mocks the sentimental aspects of the Knights Companion, calling it, deflatingly, a "society . . . for the protection of the impotent male"; he emphasizes instead the project's public relations value to the company. Whymper adds theatrical touches that catch the media's attention: each Knight Companion is issued a "scroll of appointment" and a lapel button showing a knight "armoured and visored, charging at full gallop." Knights Companions are honored at the "Christmas Round Table dinner," with the Knight Companion of the Year receiving a sword *Excal*ibur (95). Thus, at Excal Company, chivalry and commerce become, in parody, in mimicry, one and the same.

Stone resents Whymper's tinkering and theft of his idea—it is Whymper whom the media credits with the concept of the Knights Companion—and Stone withdraws into a quietism: "Nothing that was pure ought to be exposed. And now he saw that in that project of the Knights Companion which had contributed to his restlessness, the only pure moments, the only true moments were those he had spent in the study, writing out of a feeling whose depth he realized only as he wrote. . . . All action, all creation was a betrayal of feeling and truth" (118).[22] Stone is not just dispirited, he is a man in an exile of sorts. In his divisions between action and feeling, creation and truth, he forsakes the workaday world and withdraws into his own contemplative constructs. One could say that Stone and Singh meet in the isolation of Stone's study or in Singh's hotel room, in their sense of division between the pure and the impure, the self and others. Singh's fantasy of a return to an England where sheep graze in Soho Square, and Stone's fantasy of flight and his idea of the Knights Companion express a sense of exile from the "true" self, from others, and imprisonment in a decayed world. Stone and Singh share a division of the world between pure and impure, between what they perceive as falsifying action and truth sustaining aesthetic withdrawal. As alienated men, as exiles, they guard what is "pure" within themselves from the "impure," threatening world of others that surrounds them. It is interesting to note again that Naipaul composed *Mr Stone* primarily during his first sojourn in India; Stone's withdrawal is infused with the sense of illusion and negation conveyed in the final paragraph of Naipaul's first book about India, *An Area of Darkness:* "The world is illusion, the Hindus say. We talk of despair, but true despair lies too deep for formulation. It was only now, as my experience in India defined itself more properly against my homelessness, that I saw how close in the past year I had been to the total Indian negation, how much it had become the basis of feeling and thought."[23] Stone personifies the English bourgeoisie, but his sensibility is also partly Hindu. Just as Naipaul's own exile infuses the story of Mohun Biswas, so too it infuses Stone's disappointments and alienation.

*The Mimic Men* and *Mr Stone* conclude with negations. The former ends with disgust and repulsion, a symbolically violent breaking-off of Singh's discourse: "I pulled my face behind the pillar and studied Garbage bringing his two-pronged knife down on the struggling cheese. *Dixi*" (250). The "two-pronged knife" and the "struggling cheese" convey Singh's sense of the vulgarity of the English world of his exile; they convey as well his perception of a world divided between the destroyers and the destroyed. (Life is about who will clean up the shit, one of Paul Bowles's characters explains in *Up Above the World*.)[24] *Mr Stone* also ends bleakly: "It was not by creation that man demonstrated his power and defied this hostile order, but by destruction. By damming the river, by destroying the mountain, by . . . scarring the face of the earth" (125–26). Though Stone imagines himself capable of being such a man of power, he retreats into his study, resigned like other city dwellers to doing "a little work" until his spouse returns for dinner. Stone is a product of the metropolis, taking from it his purpose and identity, his life used up in its routines and busyness. In Stone Naipaul forecasts the dark vision that overcomes Salim of *A Bend in the River* during a walk in London: a vision of "men lost in space and time, but dreadfully, pointlessly busy."[25]

*Mr Stone* can be read as a portrait of a decadent England, as a critique of bourgeois mentality, and as a parody of Arthurian romance, all of which are informed by Naipaul-the-colonial's exile in the metropolis. In London, no longer do the issues of empire dominate the public forum, but instead conundrums such as the proper number of pins in new shirts, matches in matchboxes, and the quality of paper in omnibus tickets. The energy that Sir Harry, head of the Excal company, expends on these items signifies a national fall from imperial might to bureaucratic blight. In a letter to the *Times* Sir Harry complains: "The smudged curling scrap of paper with which I am presented neither looks nor feels like an omnibus ticket. . . . It is scarcely suitable for tucking into the hatband, like any respectable ticket" (60–61). Harry's letters spring from a curmudgeon's brain; they are also symptomatic of an imperial power in decline.

The novel casts disconcerting glances at other classes and cultures, for example when Stone is shocked by the sight of a waifish child with deformed teeth ("fangs") and Whymper is driven "to fury" by the sight of blacks walking down a London street (90). But the novel's critique of narrow-mindedness and middle-class values centers on the function of work in the metropolis. Stone's career as librarian and office worker deadens him rather than channels his energies in a creative way; for him, as for thousands of others in the metropolis, numbing work is the chief "pacific cruelty" of the modern, urban society. The novel portrays the world of the city dweller, with its petty jobs and "petty gardens of petty houses" where people seek "to accommodate themselves to life" (125–26). This portrait of the city and its Stones is infused with an exile's disillusionment. The narrator of the semiautobiographical *Enigma of Arrival* confesses: "For years, in that far-off island . . . I had dreamed of coming to England. But my life in England had been savorless, and much of it mean."[26]

With Stone the knight-errant and Excal the king's court, *Mr Stone* can be read as a parody of Arthurian romance that diminishes the urban, bureaucratic world. In another sense, however, the romance functions as a projection of Stone's idea of home and meaningfulness. At work, in the city, at his home, Stone is a man apart; the idea of knights carrying out meaningful action and a community of men united for a common purpose project Stone's concept of the ideal society from which he is exiled. He is in the wilderness as Singh is in the wilderness.

## Exile and Home as Constructs

In *The Mimic Men* Singh compares his life on colonial Isabella to a shipwreck, and his life in England to "the greater shipwreck" (180). This figurative wreck is a loss of close ties to others, to one's community and society; it is a loss of a sense of belonging or home. Singh and Stone are both Robinson Crusoe figures in that, in different ways, they are shipwrecked men who have lost a sense of belonging.

Exile and home are not exactly places, though; they are ways of looking at places. As alienation, exile is an inability to look at the world in new ways; it is a figurative shipwreck, a breaking apart of connections between self and others. As exploration, exile can be the making of new connections, of seeing things anew through the lens of others. For some, home is a given, like one's very skin; but for the exile, a new home can only be a difficult creation, a new way of seeing. Homecoming for the exile is the entry into a perception of belonging, of seeing one's belonging within the normal and everyday as if seeing with new eyes. This is depicted beautifully in Michel Tournier's *Vendredi ou les limbes du Pacifique* at the moment when Robinson Crusoé, after a long period of habitually thinking of Vendredi the Arwacan as only a savage and servant, glimpses in his eye something "brilliant," "pure," "delicate," a possibility in him heretofore hidden to Crusoé's own eyes:

Robinson is fascinated by this organ so finely composed, so perfectly new and brilliant as well. . . . And if in this precise instant he discovers by chance the stupefying anatomical beauty of Vendredi's eye, must he not truly wonder if the Arwacan is not completely an addition of things equally admirable and that he has ignored this only through his blindness?

Robinson turns over this question in his mind. For the first time he clearly sees beneath the gross and stupid native that irritates him the possible existence of another *Vendredi*—as he had suspected another island, hidden under the administrative island long before discovering the grotto and the valley.[27]

After discovering this vision of the hidden island and of another, completely different Vendredi, Crusoé grows at home on the island because he has in a sense rediscovered the world, which becomes new to him with each day. The island ceases to be a place of exile and becomes a home. At the end of the novel, Crusoé chooses not to leave the island because he fears losing the perception, the insight that he has gained there.

Singh and Stone are still on the other side of Crusoé's insight, for they have not yet realized that the city in which they live is partly the city of their own making and that their alienation is also partly of their own making. They are exiles without the new vision that can come from the radical changes of exile, the vision that comes in part to Crusoé and to the narrator of *The Enigma of Arrival*, who learns to look at Waldenshaw and Port of Spain in new ways.

In *Mr Stone* and *The Mimic Men* Naipaul examines exile's *déchirement*. Through these novels he confronts his *étrangeté* (his sense of foreignness) as a West Indian colonial exile in the English metropolis and expresses his fear of being used up creatively and becoming like a silent Singh or Stone. "Unless I am able to refresh myself by travel—to Trinidad, to India—I fear that living here will eventually lead to my own sterility," he reflects in the essay "London."[28] It will be twenty years—with *The Enigma of Arrival* (1987)—before Naipaul publishes another novel set in England. And then that setting will not be London but a countryside that resembles Singh's reverie of the "Old England." The narrator of *The Enigma of Arrival* learns what Singh and Stone do not; like Robinson Crusoé, he learns to see things anew, syncretistically, and comprehends that exile and home are not exactly places but constructs.

# 5

## An Exile in the Motherland

> Nowhere do I see the India I know.
> —*An Area of Darkness*
>
> Perhaps India is only a word.
> —"In the Middle of the Journey"

That Vidiadhar Surajprasad Naipaul has written a book about India is hardly surprising; what is, is that he has written almost four books about the country and a long chapter of a fifth about neighboring Pakistan, part of prepartition India. The motivation behind his travel to the subcontinent and the writing of these books derives from his ethnic heritage, colonial identity, and exile. The encounter between Naipaul and "motherland" generates controversial works in which, on the one hand, he seeks a connection with, a rootedness in India, while on the other, he emphasizes his difference from Indians and his repulsion at the "decay" of the country.

In "A Resting-Place for the Imagination," the first chapter of *An Area of Darkness* (1964), he remarks that an idea of India informed his youth "in a special way."[1] (His maternal grandfather immigrated to Trinidad from a village in India in the nineteenth century,[2] like 145,000 Indians who came to Trinidad and Tobago between 1845 and 1924, most of whom worked as indentured laborers on the island's sugarcane plantations.)[3] As a child he equated India with his grandfather and with common objects such as string beds, plaited straw mats, and wooden printing blocks. But as a land India remained "featureless" in his imagination:

> I thought of the time [of my grandfather's journey] . . . as a period of darkness . . . which also extended to the land, as darkness surrounds a hut at evening, though for a little way around the hut there is still light. The light was the area of my experience, in time and place. And even now, though time has widened, though space has contracted and I have travelled lucidly over that area which was to me the area of darkness, something of darkness remains, in those attitudes, those ways of thinking and seeing, which are no longer mine. (32)

As an adult Naipaul travels to India to discover something of his ancestral past and to experience, if only partially, a manner of "thinking and seeing" that are "no longer" his. His journey is a discovery of places and peoples and a discovery of aspects of self.

As a British colonial Naipaul is interested in India as a former British colony. Thus, in these essays and books—*An Area of Darkness*, "India," and *India: A Wounded Civilization*—he compares and contrasts the effects of colonialism in India with its effects in Trinidad and the West Indies; as in *The Middle Passage*, his book about former Caribbean colonies, he examines problems that derive from a long history of colonialism and imperialism. Ironically, though, what he often examines is his own "malady," his own "wound" of colonialism and exile; in hindsight, some twenty-five years after the writing of his first book about India, the author has confessed: "The poverty of the Indian streets and the countryside was an affront and a threat, a scratching at my old neurosis. Two generations separated me from that kind of poverty; but I felt closer to it than most of the Indians I met."[4] These aspects of India carry him back to the colony—the place from which he has escaped though still has nightmares about.[5]

As an exile Naipaul is drawn to India as an antithesis of modern, private, materialistic London, the "godless" city of *Mr Stone and the Knights Companion* and later of *The Mimic Men*. He travels to India in response to the *déchirement* of exile, a sense of loss and alienation. In leaving Trinidad for England more than a decade before, he realized a dream of all colonials—to live in the glamorous metropolis[6]—and an ambition of young West Indian writers.[7] But the dream changed to disillusionment: "I came to London. It had become the centre of my world and I had worked hard to come to it. And I was lost. London was not the centre of my world. I had been misled; but there was nowhere else to go" (*AD* 45). If only from a distance, India signifies a "clear world beyond the brick and asphalt" (45). The image of a snow-capped peak of the Himalayas surrounded by a perfectly blue sky, "India" is a mystical presence within his exile's sense of loss; it stands for a purity and truth beyond the vulgarity and disillusionment of London (44). With this India in mind, he travels to the land of his ancestors only to realize that idea and actuality are different and that he is also "an exile in the Motherland."[8]

In India he is an exile in a double sense. First, he is an outsider, yet in his not-belonging he sometimes sees insightfully from that "exotopic" perspective.[9] As a traveler and someone who is neither completely of the East nor of the West, he can read the signs of India's "texts"—its images, words, actions, traditions—and perceive a significance not evident or hidden to the insider who sees only from a caste perspective or an "Indian" point of view. He is an exile in a second sense as well. He carries a "secret wound," to use Kristeva's phrase, attributable in part to aspects of his heritage as a Trinidad Indian, as a member of an ethnic group that has experienced poverty and relegation to the lower rungs of that society; and as an exile, just as his ancestors carried with them something of India to Trinidad, he carries with him something from Trinidad that resembles too closely what he finds in India. As colonial, as metropolitan writer, as Hindu, as a specifically Trinidad Indian, as "exile in the Motherland," Naipaul views India from potentially illuminating yet also tangled contexts. Is the "wound" that he examines his or India's? In the encounters between Naipaul and his Indian others, who is he and who are they? What are the results of those encounters? As we read these books about India, we need to be alert to their tangling of ethnography and autobiography.

## *An Area of Darkness* (1964)

During the 1960s and 1970s Naipaul spent more than sixteen months in India, visiting provincial states and big cities such as Bombay, Delhi, and Calcutta. He records his first visit in *An Area of Darkness,* a second in essays entitled "India" collected in *The Overcrowded Barracoon,* and a third in *India: A Wounded Civilization*. In 1990 he published a fourth book, *India: A Million Mutinies Now*. *An Area of Darkness* mixes autobiography and ethnography, interweaving impressions of the author's personal journey in his ancestral land and observations on Indian culture and society. The "inner" movement of the journey consists of a dialectic of thesis, to antithesis, to synthesis, or of a mystical idea or myth of India, to disillusionment, to negation of the disillusionment in a new understanding. The "thesis"—India as spiritual land—is symbolized by Naipaul's memory of snow-capped mountains in religious pictures at his grandmother's house: "a special joy had been with me. . . . It was the joy of being among mountains; it was the special joy of being among the Himalayas. I felt linked to them; I liked speaking the name. India, the Himalayas: they went together. In so many of the brightly coloured religious pictures in my grandmother's house I had seen these mountains, cones of white against simple, cold blue. They had become part of the India of my fantasy" (176). Like Ralph Singh of *The Mimic Men*, the author feels a fascination for mountains, snow, and cold, and the idea of purity that they convey; it is part of a Hindu fascination that he alludes to in a review of Nirad Chaudhuri's *The Continent of Circe:* the snow-capped Himalayas are "objects of pilgrimage" for Hindus, and some, "in their hysteria, look beyond that to the North Pole, of which modern mapmakers have made them aware."[10]

This India collides with the actuality. Landing in Bombay, Naipaul reflects: "Perhaps all lands of myth were like this: dazzling with light, familiar to drabness, the margin of the sea unremarkably littered" (45). The "cones of snow" in his idea of India contrast with the Bombay shoreline litter; in the dialectic of his personal journey, thesis is countered by antithesis, a process that repeats from beginning to end in *An Area of Darkness*. Naipaul's "fantasy" of India is negated by a disgusted interest in scatological India, in excrement and degradation. In his description of Dal Lake, he contrasts these two Indias: "Shankaracharya Hill . . . is one of the beauty spots of Srinagar. It has to be climbed with care, for large areas of its lower slopes are used as latrines by Indian tourists. If you surprise a group of three women, companionably defecating, they will giggle: the shame is yours, for exposing yourself to such a scene. . . . Indians defecate everywhere. They defecate, mostly, beside the railway tracks. But they also defecate on the beaches; they defecate on the hills; they defecate on the river banks; they defecate on the streets" (73–74). It is not exactly the marred picturesque landscape or the excrement itself that annoys Naipaul, with his lingering Hindu sense of "the unclean," but the cultural attitude expressed by the casual defecation in public. Throughout *An Area of Darkness* he struggles with the epistemological difference between his way of seeing and that of Indian others: "I had learned to see; I could not deny what I saw. They remained in that other world. They did not see the defecating squatters beside the railroad in the mornings; more, they denied their existence. And why should these squatters be noticed anyway? Had I seen the beggars of Cairo or the negro slums of Rio?" (225). The ethnographic reflection is two-directional; by looking at India Naipaul also looks at aspects of his own background. For him, the Indian disregard of public defecation goes to the center of caste-system attitudes and Hindu philosophy, yet that disregard also engenders a questioning of his own attitudes and assumptions. Each observation has the potential to occasion both a cross-cultural and self-reflection—though sometimes neither occurs, and the author can seem only to be venting his disgust or "scratching" an "old neurosis" (*IMMN* 8).

Spiritual journeys parallel physical journeys, tracing Naipaul's inner movement from empathy with things Indian to repulsion and antipathy. During a nighttime train journey the author is befriended by a Sikh who draws out Naipaul's darkest feelings. He writes that he feels a bond with the Sikh because the minority Sikhs seem "closest" to Trinidad Indians in their sense of difference from the larger society (235). The author and his Sikh traveling companion strike a bond in their disgust and cynicism: "He grew more perceptibly bitter as the journey went on, but this answered my own mood. . . . he became my irrational self" (238–39). Through the Sikh he can express his most embarrassing, antipathetic feelings; the night journey turns into an excursion into the wounds of India and his own wound of exile:

It was nearly midnight. . . . The platforms were like mortuaries. In the dim light prostrate men showed as shrunken white bundles out of which protruded bony

Indian arms, shining stringy legs, collapsed grey-stubbled faces. Men slept; dogs slept; and among them, like emanations risen from the senseless bodies, over which they appeared to trample, other men and other dogs moved. . . . From everywhere dogs howled. One hobbled off into the darkness at the end of the platform; its foreleg had been freshly torn off; a raw bloody stump remained. (239)

Naipaul feels a "hysteria" induced by his exchange with the Sikh and by the surreal "deformity" and "degradation" of this night:

The Sikh's anger was feeding on everything he saw, and I longed for the land and the people to change. . . . I tried to transmit compensating love to every starved man and woman I saw on the road. But I was failing. . . . Love turned into a self-lacerating hysteria in which I was longing for greater and greater decay, more rags and filth, more bones, men more starved and grotesque, more spectacularly deformed. I wished to extend myself, to see the limits of human degradation, to take it all in at that moment. For me this was the end, my private failure; even as I wished I knew I would carry the taint of that moment. (243)

There is a confessional element that lifts this passage out of the ethnographic realm. It is not exactly about a place but about a negation of a "myth" within the author, about the collision between his sense of spirituality and a sense of decay, degradation, and absurdity. Naipaul is the focus of the encounter between self and Indian others—what he depicts in this passage is less India than his "private failure."

A visit to his grandfather's village in Uttar Pradesh and his return to England complete this dialectic and the book. During the visit to the village he temporarily shakes off the disgust that has marked much of his journey and experiences wonder at being in his ancestor's village. The visit "provided such an unlikely adventure," he reflects. "It distorted time; again and again I came back, with wonder, to my presence in that town, in that hotel, at that hour. . . . The act of writing released not isolated memories but a whole forgotten mood" (271). This mood stirs in him a belonging, a connection with his Hindu past, but the mood is broken by a villager's persistent requests for money (purportedly to pay for litigation related to Naipaul's grandfather's land). Naipaul feels imposed upon, refuses the requests, and leaves abruptly: "We drove off. I did not wave. . . . So it ended, in futility and impatience, a gratuitous act of cruelty, self-reproach and flight" (277). Again, the focus in this passage is more autobiographic than ethnographic; Naipaul is perplexed by his responses to India and Indians. He finds, again, exile, not home.

His return to England occasions a reflection on his journey and an attempted synthesizing of tangled ideas and feelings. He left England pursuing an idea of India; but during much of his journey, he has contrasted the West, its rationalism and drive toward amelioration of material existence, with India, its irrationality, passiveness, and acceptance of decay and degradation. Once back in Europe, he reconsiders this evaluation and reexperiences those negative aspects of Western life that, in part, motivated his flight from London a year earlier. In the Rome airport he observes a fashionably dressed woman who symbolizes to him shallow Western materialism (in contrast with impoverished Indian spiritualism). "She was extravagantly made up: she required to be noticed. How could I explain, how could I admit as reasonable, even to myself, my distaste, my sense of the insubstantiality and wrongness of the new world to which I had been so swiftly transported. This life confirmed that other death; yet that death rendered this fraudulent" (279). In interpreting India from a Western perspective, Naipaul has privileged Western thinking only to be confronted, when once again back in Europe, by a kind of confidence trick. He can be at home in neither East nor West: Eastern spirituality leads to a passiveness in the face of problems, while Western materialism leads to a perversion.

His sense of not-belonging produces a culminating withdrawal into a territorylessness: "The world is illusion, the Hindus say. . . . It was only now, as my experience of India defined itself more properly against my own homelessness, that I saw how close in the past year I had been to the total Indian negation, how much it had become the basis of thought and feeling. And already, with this awareness, in a world where illusion could only be a concept and not something felt in the bones, it was slipping away from me. I felt it as something true which I could never adequately express and never seize again" (280–81). Exile for Naipaul is not just a not-belonging, but also a perception and experience, one of whose consequences is the duality of construct and experience. The exile is haunted by a sense of fraudulence, falsehood, and illusion. The personal journey to India begins and ends in a rift between concepts and actualities, in territorylessness and wordlessness.

## "India" (1972)

As ethnography, *An Area of Darkness* diagnoses "maladies" of Indian culture and society. One focus is the caste system, with its thousands of divisions, at whose "centre . . . l[ies] the degradation of the latrine-cleaner" (36).[11] Naipaul notes signs of the caste system in bodily marks, clothing, street scenes, and offices, and analyzes its effects on Indians' mentality and behavior. It creates "degrees of degradation," he explains, because it reduces Indians to ever narrower functions, identities, and ranges of perception and understanding. It constitutes not only a set of "relationships of servitude," but also a myopia and culturally conditioned incapacity.[12] "Indians have been known to go on picnicking on a river bank while a stranger drowned," he comments, because they did not consider it their responsibility to come to his aid. The caste mentality fosters a disregard for others and a callousness; because it is based on categorical differences, it can promote inequality, xenophobia, prejudice, and racism.

Like the caste system, colonialism has shaped Indian mentality and behavior. In "Jamshed into Jimmy," from the essay collection "India" in *The Overcrowded Barracoon*, the author treats a familiar theme in his writings: colonial or Third World mimicry of the West. Here he satirizes the changes of identity that the upper-class Indian undergoes to move into the realm of Englishness—such as emulation of a British accent, an acquired fondness for golf, and, above all, an Anglicized name: "The Indian name of Anand . . . might become Andy; Dhandeva will become Danny, Firdaus Freddy, Jamshed Jimmy. Where the Indian name cannot be adapted, the box-wallah will most usually be known as Bunty."[13] In the anglicization of names Naipaul reads the over-dependence of upper-class Indian society on foreign attitudes and values: "It is the special mimicry of an old country which has been without a native aristocracy for a thousand years. . . . Yesterday the mimicry was Mogul; tomorrow it might be Russian or American; today it is English" (60). Through castes and colonization, the Indian psyche has been fragmented, Naipaul contends, and now looks to foreign models to unify itself. In mimicry, he reads India's divided self: "Mimicry conceals the Indian schizophrenia" (225).[14]

In "A Second Visit" (1967), he extends this critique, arguing: "Every discipline, skill and proclaimed ideal of the modern Indian state is a copy of something which is known to exist in its true form somewhere else."[15] Such an extremist critique might be dismissed as crankish—and empty? What, after all, is a "true form"? But what Naipaul seems to mean is that Indians' England derives partly from fantasy, from a "fairytale land of Anglo-India," as if upper-class society "has fallen for a casual confidence trickster" (61). The latter metaphor sums up Naipaul's critique of colonialism's effect on Indians; the problem is one of perception, of seeing and not-seeing, and Indians are deceived or blinded by myths and beliefs rooted in English colonialism and Indian religion and philosophy.[16]

"A Second Visit" presents a caustic attack that responds to the fad for things Indian that characterized the Western countercultural movement of the late 1950s and the 1960s. Allen Ginsberg and the Beatles traveled to India to sit under the bodhi tree, and a generation of Western intellectuals took to the road as "dharma bums." Here Naipaul attacks both Western seekers and Eastern "seers and sages." He describes the beatniks he encounters along the way as uniformly dressed, fuzzy creatures—"papa beatnik, mama beatnik, baby beatnik"—who step out of the Goldilocks fairy tale; they are scraggly figures marring the Indian landscape and putting a further burden on the impoverished society (80). He writes that Western seekers and Eastern gurus discover one another like the "maimed" meeting the "maimed" (80). And thus he stands on its head the notion of India as land of enlightenment. Western seekers in their spiritual quests discover nothing profound because India "lies all on the surface," he contends; the decay that they see is exactly what there is (80). At the end of the seeker's journey is hoax, exemplified by the "holy man" of Hyderabad who "pull[s] a prick . . . out of his mouth" (80).

Naipaul reads signs of India's "intellectual failure" in government speeches, newspaper articles, and autobiographies (86). The inspirational themes of an Indian minister-designate's speech to a group of college students consist of platitudes such as "a clever man never smiles" and "some people can not get over the loss of even a small amount of money"—which reduce thought to "folk-wisdom" and "old fairy-tale" (87). Naipaul finds Indian journalistic discourse equally platitudinous, citing postelection headlines such as "PAST MISTAKES RESPONSIBLE FOR CURRENT PROBLEMS" and "MASSES MUST BE EDUCATED TO MAKE DEMOCRACY A SUCCESS" (87). Examining autobiographies of Gandhi, Prakash Lal Tandon, and Mirza Ismail, he concludes that all were "written by the same incomplete person" (90). They illustrate "the Indian habit of exclusion, denial, non-seeing" (55–56). Above all, the Indian intellect lacks a "sense of tragedy," he concludes, a responsiveness to decay and degradation; no matter what the changes are that may come to the country, it will remain the same until it sees the world differently: "It is what appals about India. The palace crumbles into the dust. . . . But . . . there is no loss. The palace might arise again; but, without a revolution in the mind, that would not be renewal" (86).

Naipaul's trenchant critique depends on an implicit juxtaposition of East and West. In the final pages of "A Second Visit" he explicitly contrasts the two: "The gap between India and the West is not only the increasing gap in wealth, technology and knowledge. It is, more alarmingly, the increasing gap in sensibility and wisdom. The West is alert, many-featured and ever-changing; its writers and philosophers respond to complexity by continually seeking to alter and extend sensibility; no art or attitude stands still. India possesses only its unexamined past and its pathetic sensibility . . . India is simple; the West grows wiser" (96). Here, as elsewhere in these essays, Naipaul weakens his critique by looking at the world categorically and dualistically.[17] In stating the differences between India and the West extremely, Naipaul seems to echo a stereotypical, Orientalist discourse.[18] There are some differences, however, between Naipaul's position and that of the Westerner critiquing the East: first, as a (Trinidad) Indian, he shares an ethnic connection with the people he critiques and therefore his critique can, but does not necessarily, reflect back on him as an autocritique of sorts; second, he writes as an exile, as someone who belongs completely to neither East nor West; and third, he is usually aware of his critique's limitations—his position in these writings is almost intentionally problematic, as if he wishes to draw attention to the contradictions with which he is wrestling. He hammers Indian religion and philosophy, but in *An Area of Darkness*, for example, he explains that he shares with Indians an "ability to retreat": "It is only now, as the impatience of the observer is dissipated in the processes of writing and self-inquiry, that I see how much this philosophy had also been mine. It had enabled me, through the stresses of a long residence in England, to withdraw completely from nationality and loyalties except to persons; it had made me content to be myself alone, my work, my name . . . it had convinced me that every man was an island, and taught me to shield all that I knew to be good and pure within myself from the corruption of causes" (*AD* 198). Not only does he recognize aspects of India within himself, but also he understands that what he knows—about himself, about India—is a construct. As he points out in "The Middle of the Journey," the "despair" that the traveler in India feels is often only his own: it "lies more with the observer than the people" (42).

What Naipaul should be taken to task for is neither his trenchancy nor his Orientalism, but rather for a lack of dialogue with the people he observes. At least he does not bring that dialogue sufficiently into the essays and books about India, and consequently we rarely have the feeling that the author knows the people he writes about at close range— the big exception here is *India: A Million Mutinies Now* (1990). The self-other encounters depicted in the 1960s and 1970s texts do not evolve toward an appreciation of difference and an acknowledgment of equality.[19] That is, Naipaul does not find value in the Indian otherness; he therefore cannot enact a bond, a sharing, with those others, because they are never acknowledged as his equals. Without such a bond, or "ideological bridge," to use M. M. Bakhtin's and P. N. Medvedev's phrase, there can be no communication.[20] The crux of the matter is Naipaul's exile: on the one hand, its outsideness, its exotopy, allows him to see what Indians themselves sometimes do not see about their country; yet on the other hand, his sense of not-belonging, coupled with his fear of belonging, prevents him from getting to know the people he is writing about. He is "an exile in the Motherland," a self whose contradictory positions in relation to Indians frustrates communication.

## *India: A Wounded Civilization* (1977)

This collection of essays continues Naipaul's diagnosis of a "devitalized" Indian mentality. The book's titular metaphor refers to a psychic, not a physical wound; its argument runs as follows: because of its particular religious and philosophic attitudes and its lack of a historical sense, India is unequipped to compete in the twentieth century. Indians prefer to withdraw into the self and into a myth of the "Old India." The argument contains various overlapping subpoints whose treatment corresponds to the eight chapters of the book, their evocative titles expressing the argument in miniature: "An Old Equilibrium," "The Shattered World," "The Skyscrapers and the Chawls," "The House of Grain," "A Defect of Vision," "Synthesis and Mimicry," "Paradise Lost," and "Renaissance or Continuity?"

In "An Old Equilibrium" the author focuses on a contradiction symbolized by India's allegiance to the sacred cow on the one hand and its acquisition of a nuclear arsenal on the other. The country's attempts to move forward economically and socially clash with its religion and philosophy and postindependence identity; that identity, tied to the ideas of Gandhi, involves looking backward to the village past rather than forward to the urban future. "In the British time . . . Indian nationalism proclaimed the Indian past; and religion was inextricably mixed with political awakening. But independent India, with its five-year plans, its industrialization, its practice of democracy, has invested in change. There always was a contradiction between the archaism of national pride and the promise of the new; and the contradiction has at last cracked the civilization open."[21] The larger source of the crisis, however, lies in India's fatalism and focus on the self; the "old equilibrium" refers to the response of retreat and quietism in the face of distress and failure: from the quietist's viewpoint, because life and the world are "passing," because "the perfect and the imperfect are all the same," there is no reason to "bother about anything'" (14).

In "An Old Equilibrium" and "The Shattered World" the author reads two contemporary Indian novels, R. K. Narayan's *Mr Sampath* and *The Vendor of Sweets*, as illustrations of the confrontation between old and new that has "cracked the civilization open." Before Naipaul's visit to India in 1961, Narayan remarked to him, somewhat cryptically: "India will go on." Narayan's words seem to affirm his belief in the permanence and profundity of Indian civilization; ironically, the protagonists of *Mr Sampath* and *The Vendor of Sweets* fail because of their belief in and attachment to an unchanging India—or so Naipaul reads these novels (10). He reads them allegorically; *Mr Sampath* is at once a novel about modern India and a fable "intensely Hindu" (13). In Srinivas, the protagonist who fails to come to the aid of a desperate friend, Naipaul reads the inadequacy of Indian religion and philosophy and the sickness of its civilization. Of Srinivas's motivation he explains: "out of the sentimental conviction that India is eternal and forever revives, there comes not a fear of further defeat and destruction, but an indifference to it. India will somehow look after itself; the individual is freed of all responsibility. And within this larger indifference there is the indifference to the fate of a friend" (17). In Srinivas's passivity, Naipaul reads the paralyzing effects of a belief in *"karma,"* "nonviolence," and a "vision of history as . . . religious fable." Passiveness on a personal level extends to the social and economic levels, to a parasitic dependence on (especially "foreign") others to provide services and supports, in short to do the dirty work of keeping the world running. Srinivas's non-doing, Naipaul writes, "needs the world, but it surrenders the organization of the world to others. It is a religious response to worldly defeat" (17–18). In Srinivas Naipaul sees a reflection of the larger Indian psychological, sociopolitical predicament—"a foreshadowing of the tensions that had to come to India, philosophically prepared for defeat and withdrawal (each man an island) rather than independence and action, and torn now between the wish to preserve and be psychologically secure, and the need to undo" (19).

Like *Mr Sampath*, Narayan's *Vendor of Sweets* presents a "fable' whose plot is "a venture into the world of doing, and at the end . . . a withdrawal" (33). Jagan, the protagonist, abandons his Westernized son who, having studied and married in the States, returns to India with his half-Korean, half-American wife and attempts to set up a factory there with American collaboration. This in itself is difficult for Jagan the devout Hindu to accept; but embarrassment follows further embarrassment, culminating in the crisis of the son's arrest when a bottle of liquor is found in his car. Faced with new demands on his Hindu worldview, Jagan feels his world begin to crack; rather than aid his son, he retreats into Hindu religion with its "sweet rituals of the . . . ordered past." Naipaul reads Jagan's responses to his son's plight as an allegory of the inability of Indian religion and philosophy to respond to change in any way other than withdrawal: "Jagan seeks only to maintain the stability of the world; he is capable of nothing else. To be pure in the midst of 'the grime of this earth,' secure in the midst of distress: that is all he asks. When his world shatters, he cannot fight back; he has nothing to offer" (38). Jagan's nondoing is "the ultimate Hindu retreat . . . not a return to a purer Aryan past . . . but a retreat from civilization and creativity, from rebirth and growth, to magic and incantation, a retrogression to an almost African night, the enduring primitivism of a place like the Congo. . . . It is the death of a civilization, the final corruption of Hinduism" (38–39). Jagan and Sampath symbolize the emptiness of a religion and philosophy that have "diminished" the Indian intellect and left Indians ill-equipped to meet the challenges of a changing world. Allegorically, Jagan's and Sampath's stories play out the recurrent themes of Indian history: "vulnerability, defeat, withdrawal" (50).

In "The Skyscrapers and the Chawls" Naipaul describes his experience of teeming Bombay, a city into which fifteen hundred new inhabitants pour each day and where more than 100,000 people sleep on the pavement at night—a situation that will certainly worsen in the future; by the year 2000, 75 percent of Bombay's projected population of sixteen million will live in huts or on the city's pavement (56).[22] People press upon people, buildings crowd upon buildings; "the warm air," Naipaul writes, "always feels overbreathed." Bombay is a city of contrasts: glittering hotels and skyscrapers are juxtaposed with industrial mills and their adjacent slums. Naipaul implicitly critiques the complementary relationship of privilege and exploitation. Evoking the mentality of wealth and privilege, he quotes from the *Bombay Handbook*, a tourist publication of the American Women's Association: "'Here you are . . . QUEEN FOR YOUR STAY. . . . Your dream of having servants is about to come true'" (58). He points out that although Bombay cannot shelter and feed its poor, "they are always needed, and forever called in"; the *Bombay Handbook* treats this exploitation naively, as a feature of the Indian landscape like the River Ganges or the Taj Mahal. While the Western tourists amuse themselves at the luxury hotels, Indians work in the mills and eat and sleep in the chawls ("barracks" or "substandard housing for factory labor"). Naipaul contrasts "the metropolitan glamour" and "towers of light" of the skyscrapers with "the central nightmare of the mill area" (58–59). The chawls are products of economic exploitation, but so too is the chawls' inner world a product of caste attitudes and a religious reflex. In Naipaul's view, Indian religion and philosophy teach surrender—to one's fate, to dehumanizing living conditions, to the socioeconomic mechanism of the mills and chawls—and for that reason religion and philosophy can be imprisoning.

In "The House of Grain" he critiques the idea of "Old India," equated variously with "beliefs," "rituals," the "gods," a "code" of behavior, a return to a "golden age." "Old India" expresses a nostalgic longing "for Gandhian days" and extols Indian village life (71). But that village life had its features of exploitation and imprisonment, Naipaul points out: it "was not a community of peasant farmers," but "was divided into people who had land and people who hadn't; and the people who had land were divided into those who were Masters and those who weren't" (89). The village rhythms were an impediment to intellectual development: "Twelve hours of darkness followed by twelve hours of light; people rose at dawn and retired at dusk; every day, as from time immemorial, darkness fell on the village like a kind of stultification" (88). "Old India" distorts this actuality with a myth of changelessness and purity.

In "A Defect of Vision" Naipaul considers the legacy of Mahatma Gandhi, the figure with whom Indians associate the "Old India." Like the essay "Indian Autobiographies" in *The Overcrowded Barracoon*, this chapter contends that Indians' "self-absorption" impedes their ability to respond to a changing world. Naipaul finds evidence of this "defect of vision" in the writings of Nehru and, surprisingly, Gandhi, the latter praised in *An Area of Darkness* for his ability to stand outside of Indian experience and thus evaluate it with perspicuity. In their autobiographies the world "is reduced to a succession of stimuli, and the reacting organism reports codified pleasure and pain; the expression of an egoism so excluding that the world, so far from being something to be explored, at times disappears, and the writers themselves appear maimed and incomplete" ("SV" 90). Although Gandhi spends three years in England, he "drops not one descriptive word about London in the 1880s"; he never writes about Africans, even though he spends twenty years in South Africa ("SV" 90). No matter the place, Gandhi looks inward, not outward. The autobiography "declines into . . . an obsession with vows, food experiments, recurring illness, an obsession with the self."[23] An examination of Gandhi's writings shows that Naipaul's claims here are misleading; Sudha Rai, in *V. S. Naipaul: A Study in Expatriate Sensibility*, states that "Naipaul makes out a bad case for Gandhi's 'defects' by placing his bets too squarely on Gandhi's *Autobiography*. He distorts Gandhi to suit his own theory."[24]

Naipaul digs up support for his claim of an Indian "defect of vision" in Nirad Chaudhuri's *Autobiography of an Unknown Indian*, which contends that Indian self-absorption is "encouraged by a religious view of life . . . [which] emphasizes our lone coming into the world and our lone exit from it" ("IA" 57). Naipaul discusses this "self-absorption" with a psychotherapist from Jawaharlal Nehru University: "Indians are immersed in their experiences in a way that Western people can seldom be. It is less easy for Indians to . . . analyze. The difference between the Indian and the Western ways of perceiving comes out most clearly in the sex act. Western man can describe the sex act; even at the moment of orgasm he can observe himself. Kakar says that his Indian patients, men and women, do not have this gift, cannot describe the sex act, are capable only of saying, 'It happened' " (108). This kind of categorization, which occurs to a lesser degree throughout his writings on India, seems a low point in Naipaul's encounter with the country and its people; an extraordinary writer can certainly offer us more than a *National Enquirer* superficiality.

The final chapters—"Synthesis and Mimicry," "Paradise Lost," and "Renaissance or Continuity?"—draw together topics and themes treated previously in this book or others: colonial and postcolonial dependence, self-absorption, and myth and metahistory as causes of India's decline. Turning again to the link between Gandhi and the "Old India," Naipaul argues that Gandhi's "very success" ensured Indian "tyranny and political sterility" because his politics have led to "obsessional" protest and engendered a backward-looking vision (158). Naipaul meets Gandhi's ironic heritage in political leaders who, in their advocation of a reestablished village system, substitute "clamor and religious excitation" for programs of action (159). Gandhianism has been perverted into a myth of a golden age, of a time of innocence and purity. Again Naipaul quotes an Indian psychotherapist: "The Indian intellectual's struggle is on two fronts—inner and outer—for it has been our developmental fate that . . . earliest childhood . . . was seen to be the golden period of individual life, just as the remotest past is considered to be the golden age of Indian history" (162). Indians live out a debilitating myth of "paradise lost" and an attempted paradise regained: "in all the distress . . . protest looks back to the past, to what is thought to have been violated, what is known to be lost. Like childhood, this golden Indian past is not to be possessed by inquiry; it is only to be ecstatically contemplated. The past is a religious idea, clouding intellect and painful perception, numbing distress in bad times. And it is into this past . . . that Gandhi has been absorbed. . . . To possess him, or to act in his name, is to have the illusion of regaining purity and the past; and in order to possess him, men have only to look inward" (162).[25] For Naipaul India's only hope lies in further decay: "The past has to be seen to be dead; or the past will kill" (191). Its crisis, he concludes, is not only economic and political; it is also cultural, in the religion and philosophy and habits of mind of its people; it is the crisis of a "decaying civilization" (191).

But is that the final judgment? By its very title, *India: A Million Mutinies Now* (1990) would seem to be still another study of the sinking Indian ship, yet it is, surprisingly, a breakthrough book for Naipaul that reveals what had only been called "decay" before as partly a postcolonial remaking, a movement toward a new order. Although the book does describe large-scale social decay, in Dharavi and Calcutta, it also observes a reversal of that decay in certain instances. Touring the Karnataka countryside, Naipaul sees signs of improvement: "There was nothing like the destitution I had seen 26 years before, when I had travelled through on a slow, stopping bus. There were none of the walking skeletons, with their deranged eyes. The agricultural revolution was a reality here; the increased supply of food showed" (149). In *India: A Million Mutinies Now* one has the sense that the author, after nearly thirty years of travel to and writing about India, has begun to look at the country and its peoples through others' eyes as well as his own, and with a largeness of spirit absent in earlier accounts.


India is different things to different travelers. As Indians themselves remark, there is nothing one can say that is not true somewhere, in some part of their country: it is beautiful and ugly, rich and poor, ancient and modern, spiritual and materialistic, dignified and dehumanizing. The "world's second largest country, it is by far the most complex, the most variegated," Dilop Hiro writes. "This variety pertains not only to physical geography . . . but also to language, religion, art and architecture, social customs, race, and, most importantly, different states of economic development—from prehistoric shift cultivation to modern atomic power plants." In India, one can encounter "the entire spectrum of pastoral life, feudalism, mercantilist behaviour, unbridled capitalism, and blotches of socialist earnestness."[26] What India is depends on what the traveler takes with him—"has previously in his mind"[27]—and on the kinds of encounters he has with its peoples.

Naipaul carries to India chiefly his exile and its opposite, idealized India as home, with its "great names," "great classical past," and "great civilization." This ideal, growing out of the context of an enclaved community in a faraway Caribbean colony, gave support and "racial identity" to the East Indian community of Naipaul's youth. A child's image of snow-capped mountains against a blue sky, this India expressed a fantasy of a mystical place of belonging. It is this that Naipaul recalls in his moods of alienation and withdrawal in London and it is what carries him to the subcontinent. But the ideal is qualified, upon his arrival in Bombay, by the litter, crowds, and poverty. India opens a wound in the self, brings back a sense of the stigma of the East Indian in the Caribbean colony, and feelings of entrapment and powerlessness to which his exile has been a response in part:

Most of us [East Indians] in Trinidad were still working on the colonial estates, and for most of us life was poor; many of us lived in thatched, mud-walled huts. Migration to the New World, shaking us out of the immemorial accepting ways of peasant India, had made us ambitious; but in colonial and agricultural Trinidad, during the Depression, there were few opportunities to rise. With this poverty around us, and with this sense of the world as a kind of prison . . . the India from which my ancestors had migrated to better themselves became in my imagination a most fearful place. This India was private and personal. . . . This India, or this anxiety about where we had come from, was like a neurosis. (*IMMN* 7)

The contexts of Naipaul's India are tangled—located in the colony, in his exile, in his ethnic heritage (the "Hindu sense of exile and loss is real," he writes ["LA" 68]). He sees and responds to India from within the frame of these contexts.

A mixture of anxiety and disillusionment shapes the encounters between Naipaul and his Indian others. Why, for example, in *An Area of Darkness*, does he so abruptly refuse the villager who asks for money concerning Naipaul's grandfather's land? One answer is that he does not want any connection with these villagers, although he does want a connection with the idea of India that he associates with his grandfather and that has brought him to the village. He must separate his idea of India from India itself, and himself from Indians—a task that becomes harder and harder. He feels that his very identity is threatened: "In Trinidad to be an Indian was to be distinctive. . . . To be an Indian in England was distinctive; in Egypt it was more so. Now in Bombay I entered a shop or a restaurant and awaited a special quality of response. And there was nothing. It was like being denied part of my reality. Again and again I was caught. I was faceless. I might sink without a trace into that Indian crowd" (*AD* 46).[28] Naipaul responds to this fear of a loss of his unique identity by differentiating himself from all those who may look like him but who, he is sure, do not see as he sees or think as he thinks. This is tragic, for he journeys to India in search of a sense of belonging, but once there, he feels that he must extract himself, be an "exile in the Motherland"—someone different from others like him ethnically. His account of India thus focuses on the difference between himself and Indian others, rather than on a connection between self and others, a difference yet a meeting on equal terms. It is important to note here, though, that *India: A Million Mutinies Now* does establish such a connection; in the author's conversations with Sugar and Kakusthan, for example, the reader finds a dialogue of difference yet equality. Some of the encounters are quite touching (and amusing), as when Kakusthan the Brahmin, with his rituals of cleanliness, offers food to the writer and wary traveler with his own Brahminic habits:

I had my own scruples, too, about eating far from home—far, at any rate, from the Taj Coromandel Hotel. But I felt ashamed of those scruples, and I accepted the food from Kakusthan's kitchen, and put my lips to the glass of coffee, though the breaking of bread (or a puri) in Kakusthan's back room did make my writing fingers oily. This became hard to ignore; it called for a more than ritual washing outside—Kakusthan pouring for me, not complaining, wasting precious water from the well, one of the six evening pots he was allowed. ( . . . When I next visited him at the colony, some days later, I told him straight that I was like him, too, and didn't eat away from home. He accepted that immediately. He laughed and said, 'All right, I'll be the untouchable this time.') (251–52)

The tone here is different, as is the kind of exchange, from those in earlier books on the country. Or perhaps in those books of the 1960s and 1970s Naipaul did not know how to treat the material from his more personal encounters with Indians and ended up focusing, instead, on a categorical, stereotyped "Indian" mentality.

India is a vast country with staggering socioeconomic problems; to read Naipaul's collection of essays and books is to get a real sense of that. By the year 2000, India will claim four of the twenty most populous cities in the world; in a twenty-year period, the population of Calcutta alone will likely grow from 4.6 million to 16 million.[29] Illiteracy—58 percent of Indians are illiterate—and inadequate education and educational development are linked to a poverty that forces parents to send their children into the work force rather than to school; of those children who do make it to the primary level, an estimated 80 percent go to school undernourished.[30] Nearly half of India's population exists below the poverty level, with an income "far too low to be able to afford the recommended nutritional requirement of 2400 calories per person per day in rural areas and 2100 calories in urban areas."[31] Poverty and social inequality go hand in hand: 75 percent of India's urban population have no private latrine, bathroom, water tap, or sewage facilities; while 3 percent of the urban households own 45 percent of the country's total urban wealth.[32] But to quote statistics and to consider the country's predicament from this perspective is to look at India in a way essentially different from Naipaul's. He writes of this vast country and its varied peoples from the perspective of a double-alienation: the alienation of Indians themselves, buffeted by collisions between the old and the new, and an alienation that grows out of his own exile. Although the two experiences are indeed different and distinct, they become tangled together in these essays and books.[33] All along Naipaul has looked at Indians through the lens of exile, sometimes consciously, sometimes unconsciously, mixing and juxtaposing his story with theirs.

# 6

# The Recursive Voyage

> I increasingly feel that my writing creates me. I am the invention of my own words.
> —Ledo Ivo, *Lives on the Line*

> I write. I write that I am writing. Mentally I see myself writing that I am writing and I can also see myself seeing that I am writing.
> —Salvador Elizondo, *The Graphographer*

> An oblong of stiff cloth lay before me, and I had the knowledge that if only out of this I could cut a smaller cloth, then the cloth would begin to unravel of itself, and the unravelling would spread from the cloth to the table to the house to all matter, *until the whole trick was undone.* Those were the words that were with me as I flattened the cloth and studied it for the clues which I knew existed, which I desired above everything else to find, but which I knew I never would.
> —V. S. Naipaul, *An Area of Darkness*

Recursion is a repetition of a special kind in which something is recognized or experienced or defined in terms of "simpler versions" of itself. "(Stories within stories, movies inside movies, paintings inside paintings, Russian dolls inside Russian dolls (even parenthetical comments inside parenthetical comments!)—these are just a few of the charms of recursion)," writes Douglas Hofstadter.[1] In Naipaul's dream of the oblong cloth, the author seeks obsessively the "clues" that will unleash a recursive unraveling of the world. In Elizondo's *The Graphographer*, the act of writing is a recursion of endless permutations, with reality itself captive in its dizzying sway.

For Naipaul, exile is a recursive voyage that leads back to the colony and his departure from it for other destinations. With each new voyage, he again experiences the liberation of exile and its potential for a new understanding of self and others; yet he also again experiences a sense of not-belonging and a malaise that can turn into a hypercritical attitude toward and rejection of those "others" who seem to him to resemble the people of the colony he has "left behind." Like the voyager in C. P. Cavafy's poem "The City," Naipaul the writer-in-exile always seems to end up in the same kind of place, to see the same kind of things, to have the same criticisms of colonial and postcolonial societies.[2] Critics such as Rana Kabbani have read his travel books and social commentaries in this vein, viewing his journeys as ones he emerges from largely unchanged: "his journey's progress [in *Among the Believers*] has been continuously impeded by fear—fear not only of the chaos that he saw surrounding him, but also of how that very chaos could return him to the pain of his own colonial past. Thus, his rejection of the world he has passed through is a very forceful one indeed, since he must at all costs avoid being sucked back into it having once escaped it."[3] Certainly this is an aspect of Naipaul's exile as a recursive voyage, and one that will be considered in this chapter.

There are, however, other aspects to the voyage. Inextricably tied to his exile as recursive voyage is the recursive activity of writing, the recurring need to reaffirm his identity as a writer and to construct and explain the world through words. Naipaul's exile and his writing thus feed upon one another symbiotically, such that to cease the journey of exile would almost be tantamount to cease being a writer—indeed to cease being a certain kind of writer. From the first departure from Trinidad for England, the voyage has become synonymous with the writer's challenge: to go forward, to return to self and words and to create one's world. Like trying to find the clues that will unravel the dreamer's oblong cloth, the challenge to wander and to write can seem for Naipaul an obsession.[4] The recursive voyage of exile, the recurring need to affirm an identity as a writer, and the recursive act of writing about the developing world create a sway, or a wake in which the writer is sometimes held captive. There is certainly a sense in which a writer's constructs can enclose even their maker, and this is perhaps what occurs in Naipaul's travel books and social commentaries. For him, the experience of exile is thus an experience of worlds *and* words. The recurrent voyage serves as a metaphor for the recursive act of writing: each new journey emerging from previous journeys; and words emerging from words, paragraphs from other paragraphs, essays from essays, books from other books. Because of a division between himself and others, the exile is constantly faced with the demand to create his world since it is not one that he shares with those others. In this sense exile becomes an aspect of the process of writing—it motivates it—and writing becomes an aspect of exile, a way of knowing self and world within a state of foreignness.

This chapter will examine a chronologically diverse group of nonfiction whose dates of publication span more than thirty years from the 1960s through 1990.[5] Journeys and subjects recur: the effects of culture and society on perception, the split identity of the exile and the concomitant divisions within colonial and postcolonial societies, the superimposition of ethnography and autobiography in the author's writings. Here my interest is in the recursive voyage and recursive creation of words and world: in voyages emerging from previous voyages, and essays and books emerging from previous essays and books. I am interested in the recurring experience of exile and the exile's manner of perception and construction of the world.

## *The Overcrowded Barracoon* (1972)

*The Overcrowded Barracoon* contains essays on colonialism and decolonization; the essays provide contexts for understanding fictional works such as *The Mimic Men, Guerrillas,* and *A Bend in the River.* A short but important essay in this collection, "Jacques Soustelle and the Decline of the West" (1968), treats the unconventional thought of the former governor-general of French Algeria. Naipaul is intrigued by Soustelle's concept of colonial "incorporation" within, in lieu of independence from, the metropolitan country, a design meant to foster a new socioeconomic order. Incorporation would have meant "equal rights and equal advance for all,"

Soustelle contends, but France rejected this because "'it was too difficult'" to achieve and thus it "'yielded to the "idol" of decolonization and the pressures of mercantile capitalism and converted the low cultures of black Africa into a *poussière* of petty dictatorships.'"[6] Soustelle's concept appeals to Naipaul—the idea of a new socioeconomic community uniting colony and metropolis as an alternative to, on the one hand, the old colonialism, and on the other, the pseudo-independence of colonies, most of whom are dependent on and indebted to former imperial powers. (A recent *Le Monde* article about postcolonial West Africa, "the most indebted region in the world," observes that a generation after decolonization, these states have come face to face with "the limits of their sovereignty"; with a debt of 134 billion dollars and under pressure from the International Monetary Fund to enact stringent reform, West African states have experienced a stagnant agricultural production, a cutback of industrial activity, and diminishing exports.)[7] Soustelle sees civilizations in decay, and this vision resembles Naipaul's own vision in essays and novels of the 1970s and 1980s: "'All civilizations have perished; even their ruins will go one day; there is no pattern and no goal'" (194). Although Naipaul detects a "romance" in Soustelle's predilection, whose sources lie in the dismantlement of the French empire and Soustelle's fascination with the vanished Mayan civilization, that sense of decay is also, ironically, Naipaul's—at least until his exorcism of it in "The Crocodiles of Yamoussoukro" in *Finding the Center* (1984) and *The Enigma of Arrival* (1987).

Romance is the theme of "Columbus and Crusoe" (1967), an essay that ponders the legend of Columbus and its connection with the story of Robinson Crusoe. The great explorer was "looking less for America or Asia than for gold," Naipaul explains.[8] Of Columbus's exploits (and of explorers' and *conquistadores*'), the author remarks illuminatingly: "In this adventure, as in today's adventures in space, the romance is something we have to supply" (205). A theme connects the Columbus legend, the quest for El Dorado, and the story of Robinson Crusoe, all variations on "an enduring human fantasy" and a "horror" concealed by it: "Crusoe makes good, in that very New World, but in the settled, beaten-down slave society of Brazil. The horror of the discovery, of being the first totally powerful man in the world: that happened a long time ago" (207). Naipaul treats these ironies—romance turning into horror, civilization into barbarity—in his major work of this period, *The Loss of El Dorado* (1969).

The subsequent essays in *The Overcrowded Barracoon* focus on ironies of independence in small former colonies, now island states, entities that appear to have little chance of any meaningful autonomy in a world of regional economic communities and global competition for markets. "St Kitts: Papa and the Power Set" (1969), "Anguilla: The Shipwrecked Six Thousand" (1969), and "Power?" (1970) grow out of the context of the fervor of West Indian independence and the Black Power movements that swept the region in the late 1960s and early 1970s. In the first of these essays Naipaul describes the struggle between the leaders of Saint Kitts's two political parties, which he calls "parties of protest, in the vacuum of independence."[9] He compares Saint Kitts's politics to comic-strip fisticuffs and points out that the Black Power slogan, which he sees stuck to a politician's car, derives from a petroleum ad: "Join the Power Set."[10] He concentrates on the hollowness of the rhetoric and the impotence of Saint Kitts's politics. He is right that the island's problems are not racial, as the slogan "Black Power" implies, but neither does the reader of this essay get a sense of what those problems are.[11]

"Anguilla: The Shipwrecked Six Thousand" (1969) considers what the author calls the "little black comedy" of one tiny Caribbean island seceding from two other tiny islands.[12] In a derogatory style that recalls *The Middle Passage* he quips that tiny, rocky, arid Anguilla "is like a mistake, a sport"; it is so minuscule and flat "that when Anguillans give you directions they don't tell you to turn right or left" but "say east or west" instead (232). The source of Anguillan disgruntlement stems from a British colonial policy that in 1966 declared Saint Kitts, Nevis, and Anguilla one associated state, a bureaucratic categorization that prevented Anguillans a voice in the government of their island; in response they seceded from the state in 1969.[13] This is the point at which Naipaul picks up the unfolding events, seeing in them an absurdist gesture ushering in a more acute dependence. "The Anguilla problem remains: the problem of a tiny colony set adrift, part of the jetsam of an empire, a near-primitive people suddenly returned to a free state, their renewed or continuing exploitation" (244).[14] The phrase "free state" anticipates Naipaul's collection of short stories and novella *In a Free State* (1971), which depicts the disintegration to which decolonization has often led.

"Power?" (1970) stands as a bellwether essay in Naipaul's oeuvre because it previews the inversions of his 1970s and early 1980s works; it constructs a worldview—the former colonial Caribbean as world turned upside down—that recurs in more complex forms in later essays on South America, Africa, and Asia. "Power?" connects the seemingly unrelated phenomena of carnival and the 1960s Black Power movement in Trinidad and the region; Naipaul inverts a common, Euro-American view of carnival as a pre-Lenten celebration and places its historical, sociopsychological roots elsewhere: "The bands, flags and costumes have little to do with Lent, and much to do with slavery" (246). But rather than consider Trinidad carnival for what it is—a "deeply meaningful anniversary of deliverance from the most hateful form of human bondage" and a multicultural celebration unique to the island[15]—Naipaul interprets it as a manifestation of a "secret world of fantasy" that symbolically transforms the "kingdoms of the night" to which slaves retreated as a defense against the despair of their daytime actualities. Fearing an imagined, pagan chaos, planters tried to break up the slaves' underworld with torture and executions, but "the fantasies remained," Naipaul contends, "because without that touch of lunacy the Negro would have utterly despaired," committing suicide by eating dirt, for example, as many in Trinidad did.[16]

Naipaul strips Trinidad carnival of its multicultural, syncretistic attributes and constructs a black "carnival" of inversions. "The Carnival the tourist goes to see is a version of the lunacy that kept the slave alive," he argues. "It is the original dream of black power, style and prettiness; and it always feeds on a private vision of the real world" (247). The kingdoms of the night create a double world, one of daytime illusion in which the Negro is enslaved and powerless, and the other of fantastic reality in which he becomes powerful and triumphant, a king. For Naipaul, carnival, Black Power, and Rastafarianism all express a vision of a "black millennium," "as much a vision of revenge as of a black world made whole again" (247).

Although "Power?" like other derogatory essays in this collection, is racist in its distorted view of Trinidad carnival, its focus is not on race, ultimately, but on the wounding legacy of empire. In Naipaul's analysis, the millenarian elements of carnival and Black Power derive from a malady of colonialism and marginality: "Something of the Carnival lunacy touches all these islands where people, first as slaves and then as neglected colonials, have seen themselves as futile, on the other side of the real world" (247). Trinidad and other neighboring islands lie "cut off" from the main currents of world affairs by their "geography, history, race"; thus, to be a colonial and West Indian is to live in an "unreal" place and to be oneself "unreal" (253). From their inclusion in European history, West Indian or Caribbean islands have been satellites of Europe, and today continue to be satellites of Europe, the United States, Canada, and Japan. The peoples of the Caribbean have been forcibly "dependent on empire for law, language, institutions, culture, even officials," argues Naipaul. "The island blacks will continue to be dependent on the books, films and goods of others; in this important way they will continue to be half-made societies of a dependent people, the Third World's third world" (250, 254).[17] But in critiquing this marginality, Naipaul falls victim to his own construct of Trinidad carnival as a solely black celebration. His failure to view it as a multicultural fete and art form (a theater in the streets) reveals a bias of his minority, East Indian background, as a member of an ethnic group that now participates in carnival but has been traditionally standoffish toward it. Naipaul's critique shows, ironically, a corresponding racism in its attack on racist Black Power in the Caribbean.

"The Overcrowded Barracoon" (1972), the collection's titular essay, depicts the plight of overpopulated, economically dependent Mauritius, a small Indian Ocean island seemingly trapped in a downward spiral of decay. The essay begins by citing a front-page story from a Mauritian newspaper that reports the departure of six Mauritian carpenters for jobs in Swaziland; Naipaul reads this news as an indicator of the island's desperation: "Six mouths less to feed; six families saved"[18] is page-one news in Mauritius, which is burdened by its overpopulation and high level of unemployment.[19] Of the crowding, limitations, and gap between the haves and have-nots, the author writes: "The sugar-cane, the cramped villages where the sugar workers and their families live, the little market towns: what the visitor sees is all that there is in Mauritius. There is little room for adventure, except at the top. . . . At the bottom, where life has been brutish, vision is more restricted, and there is only this communal sense of helplessness and self-disgust" (264). The essay poses a Soustellean question: to what end independence, given Mauritius's meager resources and possibilities for economic development? The island is less a nation than a jetsam, "an abandoned imperial barracoon" set adrift, "incapable of economic or cultural autonomy" (270).

Desperate as Mauritius's plight sounds, readers of the collection's essays should not forget that Naipaul is more a writer than a prophet. For although "The Overcrowded Barracoon" writes Mauritius's epitaph, in 1990, almost twenty years after the publication of this essay, the island has turned into a big success. An article in *Le Monde* calls Mauritius a "tiny dragon" and cites a number of favorable socioeconomic indicators, including a rate of unemployment less than 3 percent, a 7 percent rate of annual economic growth, a remarkably successful birth-control policy, and an attitude of tolerance among the island's ethnic groups.[20] When Naipaul wrote his essay, Mauritius had to export its people to employ them; today, it imports labor. Differences such as these between yesterday and today and between Naipaul's and others' evaluations of a country and people throw light on the literary quality of his essays, with their selectivity, repetition, and poetic sense of a world running down. His observations can be illuminating, yet they can also be imprisoning; by force of style, they can take on a definitive quality that belies the transitory, tentative nature of all observations on society.

*The Overcrowded Barracoon* considers the problems that decolonization and centuries-long colonial dependency and marginality have fostered. But even the overtly ethnological, sociological essays about Trinidad and Mauritius incorporate in their analyses a personal, autobiographical drama of choice and allegiances. Naipaul writes from the perspective of exile, his choice between the world of the colony and that of metropolis; as he explains during the Bryden interview in an anecdote about the Incan, Garcilasco, who chooses to leave Peru and to study and live instead in Spain: "I'm comforted because I think that Garcilasco made the correct decision—understanding that, the way the current was flowing, it was very silly for one man to try to pretend it wasn't flowing in that direction."[21] As former colonial and as exile Naipaul views developing countries from a privileged, double perspective; but from this perspective he constructs a certain kind of postcolonial world that grows out of his choice to belong nowhere. In this latter sense, exile limits rather than expands his vision, separating him from the other peoples he observes and projecting on them a choice that was his and not theirs. It seems as if Naipaul must reject the societies he visits in order to maintain his identity as an exile—in order to be secure in his not-belonging to these former colonial places that he must see in a state of their unmaking. But are not these places also in a state of remaking? And this is the other half of their destiny that—in the case of Mauritius, for example—Naipaul does not bring into the sinister postcolonial world that he constructs in these and other essays. This insight does not plainly appear in Naipaul's works until the breakthrough books, *The Enigma of Arrival* and *India: A Million Mutinies Now.*

### *The Return of Eva Perón* (1980)

The first of several essays in this collection, "Michael X and the Black Power Killings in Trinidad," rewrites the essay "Power?" of *The Overcrowded Barracoon*. In the events that lead to the killing of Joe Skerritt and Gale Ann Benson, Naipaul reads the signs of the "carnival lunacy" and "futility" that he believes are a heritage of colonialism and marginality in the Caribbean; the killings act out a fantasy of power whose source lies in the slave era's "kingdoms of the night." Michael X and colleagues are masqueraders: born Michael de Freitas, the former changes his name to Michael Abdul Malik; he is an "entertainer," a "Carnival" figure, "a dummy Judas to be beaten through the streets on Good Friday."[22] Steve Yeates, an ex-member of the British air force and Michael X's bodyguard, becomes the "Supreme Captain of the Fruit of Islam" and "Lieutenant Colonel of the Black Liberation Army." The Englishwoman Gale Ann Benson becomes the African "Hale Kimga." Naipaul reads this changing of identity or putting on of masks as an aspect of Black Power ideology in the Caribbean, with its "mystical sense of race" and "millenarian expectation of imminent redemption" (41). He calls Michael X's Black Power a "revolution without a program, without a head," and another instance of a West Indian mimicry of the world beyond the islands.

The essay responds to racist ideology in the West Indies, but more broadly, it responds to a pop concept of revolution as a universal, redemptive solution to the problems of the postcolonial world. Any social change depends on a matrix of particular conditions in a particular society, and that particularity is not transportable from one society to another: "Black Power—away from its United States source—is jargon . . . a sentimental hoax. It obscures the problems of a small independent country with a lopsided economy, the problems of a fully 'consumer' society that is yet technologically untrained and without the intellectual means to comprehend the deficiency. It perpetuates the negative, colonial politics of protest." The author adds: "While the dream of redemption lasts, Negroes will continue to exist only that someone might be their leader" (74). Whether the United States constitutes the source of the Black Power movement seems debatable; the Caribbean, with Marcus Garvey and others, can lay a strong claim of its own. But that is not Naipaul's interpretation.

Through ideology, through words, Michael X becomes the "false redeemer," remaking his past and giving a pattern to the future (15). Perhaps this essay's most interesting aspect concerns the latent relationship between Naipaul and Michael X, two exiles from Trinidad who construct their respective identities through the power of words. The author calls Benson's killing "a literary murder,"[23] but as if in a labyrinth, he then writes about this "murder" by writing about things literary: to explain the motivations and behavior of the personages he cites O'Neill's *Emperor Jones* and Conrad's "An Outpost of Progress." Not only this essay but others in the collection as well have about them a style and a circularity of images that make them wrought, artlike, even though they are about fact.

"The Return of Eva Perón," "Kamikaze in Montevideo," and "A New King for the Congo: Mobutu and the Nihilism of Africa" also critique myths and ideologies. In the first, Naipaul associates Peronism with a sociopolitical necrophilia, an obsession with the past symbolized by the Argentine veneration of Eva Perón and her apotheosis into national legend. Eva is loved and adored because she offered the people a "child's vision of power, justice and revenge" (113). Naipaul attacks the nebulousness of Peronism and its dependence on clichés, platitudinous slogans, and a rhetoric of "the enemy," observing: "where jargon ends by competing with jargon, people don't have causes. They only have enemies; only the enemies are real. It has been the South American nightmare since the breakup of the Spanish Empire" (119–20).

Above all, Naipaul views 1970s Argentina as a "colonial society, made deficient and bogus by its myths" (123). The myth of plenty distorts a history of "plunder": the theft of land, genocide, a victimization of the weak, and the waste of resources.[24] The myth of Europe as center of all civilization has produced an imitation and a reckless consumption, and thus the country has never become anything other than a "simple materialist . . . society," now "in the most rapacious and decadent phase of imperialism" (153, 162).[25] Political torture, which Naipaul calls an "Argentinian institution," persists because of a mentality that considers civilization as distant and the colony as a place where savagery is always a threat. Thus, ironically, the idea of civilization as an entity "far away, magically kept going by others," as "divorced from . . . intellectual life and equated with the goods and fashions of Europe," as "purchasable" and "always there, across the ocean," produces in Argentina its opposite, a barbarism (171). Is this a fair analysis? The 1970s in Argentina were a deplorable period, but readers of Naipaul's works have already heard the themes of this essay before in other contexts.

"Kamikaze in Montevideo" considers the effects of Eurocentric myths on Argentina's neighbor, Uruguay. Like Buenos Aires, Montevideo, Uruguay's capital, seems a city living in the past; its grand monuments deteriorating, it resembles a "fairy tale" city where a "hidden calamity" has taken place (141). The superficial cause of the calamity lies in the European-borrowed concept of the welfare state that, applied recklessly, has resulted in ineffectualness and bankruptcy in this once-rich South American country.[26] The deeper cause, however, stems from a distorting social myth: "Uruguayans say that they are a European nation, that they have always had their back to the rest of South America. It was their great error, and is part of their failure" (147). This mythic "European" identity led to success but also excess, rendering Uruguayans a dependent, imitative, colonial people: "educated but intellectually null, consumers, parasitic on the culture and technology of others" (147).[27] It has distorted Uruguayans' sense of their difference—their South American society, land, and selves.

"A New King for the Congo: Mobutu and the Nihilism of Africa" stands in the same relation to the novel *A Bend in the River* as "Michael X" does to *Guerrillas*. Both essay and novel treat the chaotic, postcolonial period of the Congo (Zaire) and reflect on history and development in 1970s sub-Saharan Africa; they depict Africa in a factual yet stylized, horrific manner that turns the bush and forest into a sinister, destructive force and symbol of the continent's repetitive cycles of making and unmaking. "A New King for the Congo" and *A Bend in the River* share such a vision and create a similar nihilistic world: Africa has no future; in an endless present, it dreams of its past. "To arrive at this sense of a country trapped and static, eternally vulnerable, is to begin to have something of the African sense of the void," the author writes. "It is to begin to fall, in the African way, into a dream of a past—the vacancy of river and forest, the hut in the brown yard, the dugout—when the dead ancestors watched and protected, and the enemies were only men" (219).

To Naipaul the African bush and forest signify both a presence and an absence—of words, of history, of men as makers of their world. They are holes in time that lie in the path of advancing "civilization." They resist it and engulf it, like the proliferating hyacinth lilies of the Congo River, which snag the propellers of boats, slowing down and stopping the advance of the modern world. The "great bush" seems always "close," as if waiting silently to strike; it seems to have "its own logical life" (191, 200). Naipaul associates the bush and forest with magic, irrationality, the "corruption" of men and corrosion of machines; bush and forest are a sempiternal monster, subduing, engulfing, overgrowing the "civilization" camped tenuously on its edges: "The bush grows fast over what were once great events or great disturbances" (203). Zaire remains a country still dominated by the timeless natural world: "So little has the vast country been touched: so complete, simple and repetitive still appears the African life through which the traveler swiftly passes"; along the river, people live the "immemorial ways of the bush," and even in the cities, "a more enduring kind of bush life" returns with the night (194–97, 215).

In the *Heart of Darkness* tradition in which Naipaul writes, the bush and jungle scrub, bury, and erase (203–5). They corrupt men's will and corrode their tools and machines, so it is only fitting that the African steamer on which Naipaul journeys has fallen into disrepair, with lights and light-bulb sockets, towel rails, and toilets out of order or missing altogether. Colonial monuments have worn down, been defaced and dismembered; of one such monument, and by extension of the European empire in sub-Saharan Africa, the author observes: "all that remains . . . are two tall brick pillars, like the pillars at the end of some abandoned Congolese Appian Way." Machines stand unused, or once used fall into disrepair: forklifts lie rusting, a lawn mower tilts on three wheels (201). Deteriorating colonial villas resemble "a tropical, overgrown Pompeii" (204). The bush swallows the things of time, whether "the towns the Arabs planted" or, more recently, the fashionable Belgian suburbs of Stanleyville (203).

Like the destructive action of the bush and forest, the Mobutu government has erased colonial history from school textbooks, with the effect that for a new generation of Zairians, the author writes, "the past is a blank"; for them, history does not extend beyond "their own memories" (204). The past becomes an enduring, undifferentiated time: "*le bon vieux temps de nos ancêtres*" (205). To Naipaul, Mobutu typifies the ambitions and the contradictions of leaders of postcolonial, 1970s sub-Saharan Africa, who seek to leap into the future based on a tribal past. On the one hand Mobutu presents himself as the builder of a modern state; on the other, he dresses and plays the role of the chief with "magical" powers that depend, ironically, not on the bush and forest but on Western military and economic support. In the essay's title, "A New King for the Congo," are intimations of a carnival world, whose core symbol is the crowning and dethroning of the king: *"the pathos of shifts and changes, of death and renewal. Carnival is the festival of all-annihilating and all-renewing time."*[28] Mobutu the carnival king-con man is like Michael X of "The Killings in Trinidad." Naipaul places Mobutu as modern African leader and Zaire as modern African state within a larger pattern or construct, including such diverse phenomena as slave revolts, Rastafarianism, and the Black Power movement in the Caribbean: "the dream of an ancestral past restored is allied to a dream of a future magical power. The confusion is not new, and is not peculiar to Zaire. Fantasies like this animated some slave revolts in the West Indies; and today, in Jamaica, at the university, there are people who feel that Negro redemption and Negro power can only come about through a return to African ways" (213). What Naipaul critiques here is the idea of a return to the source—whether purely "African" or innately "black"—that touches not only Zaire but also the 1970s Caribbean. In other places—in the essays on India, for example—he treats this idea as a myth of paradise lost and regained.

"Conrad's Darkness" reflects on Conrad and his work as they relate to Naipaul's subjects and development as a writer. Naipaul explains that as a youth he responded to the tropical element of Conrad's Eastern world and, later, as a writer from a West Indian colony, to his "colonial vision" (223). In Conrad's works Naipaul finds a recognizable, unstable world of colonies and margins, and a lens of perception through which he perceives the possibilities of his own identity and project as a postcolonial writer. Conrad wrote about collisions of cultures; he constructed a vision of the world's "half-made societies" continually making and unmaking themselves (233). In Conrad's manner of perception and evaluation Naipaul finds a model as writer in exile: a "satirical vision of the outsider" (243).

In reflecting on Conrad's work Naipaul reveals much about his own. "The world of illusions, men as prisoners of their cultures, belief and unbelief: these are truths one has to be ready for," he says of Conrad's story "Karain" (227). Are not these the "themes" of the essays in *The Return of Eva Perón*? Just as Conrad's works show "the moral degradation of the idea" by action(s), so too Naipaul's work concerns itself with ideas that control the lens of individual or group perception. The metaphor of vision—clarity and distortion—is thus important to both writers. In works about colonial and postcolonial societies Naipaul diagnoses "defect[s] of vision," but we should read these "diagnoses" not only as social commentary but also as artful constructs. The "peculiarity of art," Louis Althusser explains, "is to 'make us see,' 'make us perceive,' 'make us feel' something which *alludes* to reality. . . . What art makes us *see*, and therefore gives to us in the form of '*seeing*,' '*perceiving*' and '*feeling*' . . . is the *ideology* from which it is born, in which it bathes, from which it detaches itself as art, and to which it *alludes*."[29] In *The Return of Eva Perón*, the recurrence of observations and themes points to what Naipaul has said about himself as traveler and writer—that he looks at the world in a certain way. In these essays, the recursive voyage becomes more and more a voyage into words, rather than a voyage to worlds that surprise and carry the writer out of his usual constructs.

## *Among the Believers: An Islamic Journey* (1981)

Naipaul's 1970s essays reflect on "ideology" in the Third World.[30] In *The Middle Passage* (1962) and *The Loss of El Dorado* (1969), Naipaul critiqued such ideologically charged phenomena as the effects of American and British popular culture in Trinidad, French culture in Martinique, Rastafarianism in Jamaica, and the romance, legends, and myths that supported the pursuit of power and riches in the Caribbean and South America such as the romance of discovery, the quest for El Dorado, and the Arcadian-Christian myth of the slavery-plantation system. In *An Area of Darkness* (1964), "India" (1972), and *India: A Wounded Civilization* (1977), Naipaul critiqued the effects of religion and philosophy on Indian consciousness and society. *Among the Believers: An Islamic Journey* (1981) continues this critique of the effects of beliefs and culture on peoples in developing countries; it treats Islamic fundamentalism in the late 1970s, or more precisely, the confluence of Islamic fundamentalism and twentieth-century ideas about political and social revolution in four countries: Iran, Pakistan, Malaysia, and Indonesia.[31] As in earlier journeys, he not only comments on culture and society, but also constructs himself and his world through the journey and commentary. He travels among the believers—peoples who see the world through the lens of their Islamic beliefs and culture—and he critiques the effects of fundamentalist Islam on minds and nations.

It goes almost without saying that there are innumerable "Islamic journeys"; with the exception of Iran, the focus of Western media interest in the late 1970s and 1980s, and of Pakistan, the first modern state founded on Islamic principles, Naipaul's itinerary was not ready-made.[32] Muslims make up 90 to 100 percent of the population in more than twenty-five countries, more than 33 percent in another fourteen countries, and at least 5 percent in still another twenty-nine countries. In total, Islam claims the allegiance of 840 million people or one-fifth of humankind.[33] Naipaul's Islamic journey stops in only four countries; it does not include historically and politically important Egypt and Saudi Arabia, or the more moderate Maghreb (Tunisia, Morocco, Algeria). His Islamic journey is, therefore, a highly selective one. His book does not claim to comment on all Islamic societies, but rather on fundamentalist Islam, and more narrowly on the conjunction of Islamic religion and revolution in four nations. This limited scope, although not self-evident in the book's title, should make it clear that Naipaul travels and writes not exactly as a sociologist, but as a writer with a certain range of interests and a certain way of looking.

*Among the Believers* is divided into four sections, the first of which, "Iran: The Twin Revolutions," touches on the author's reason for embarking on this "Islamic journey." Naipaul notes that although he grew up in a society with a mixed Hindu, Moslem, Christian population, he took little interest in Islam because he considered it a religion with a glorious past but an impoverished present.[34] His interest is piqued by television coverage of the Iranian revolution; he is struck by contradictions in the attitudes of Iranians studying in the United States, like the student who proclaims "the beauty of Islamic law" while studying law at an American university. "What had attracted these Iranians to the United States and the civilization it represented?" he inquires. Not just the "need for education and skills," he responds, but an unadmitted attraction at whose center lies a "disturbance—expressed in dandyism, mimicry, boasting, and rejection" (13). His interest in Iran deepens through a reading of Nahid Rachlin's *The Foreigner,* which he interprets as a symbolic veiling of "hidden impulses" and an allegory of the collision between traditional culture and Western culture. His reading of the protagonist's (Feri's) story is doubly interesting because, like her, he is also "the foreigner." Both Feri and Naipaul are exiles; but whereas Feri chooses to return permanently to the motherland, Naipaul has rejected this possibility. Her story is the antithesis of his; her salvation under the veil is to him a retreat and an illusion. Naipaul draws on *The Foreigner* to focus the argument of his book: revolutionary Islam depends on a rigid demarcation between Islamic and Western civilization, but in actuality Islamic and Western civilization interpenetrate (e.g., Iranian hospitals depend on Western technology, while the West depends on Iranian oil), and thus a rigid demarcation belies their cultural and socioeconomic interrelationships. Revolutionary Islam withdraws from the world into the illusory purity and security of an ideological system that assigns to "others" the responsibility of running the world yet sets these others apart as alien and evil.

In "The Rule of Ali" Naipaul critiques the goals and program of

Iranian fundamentalist Islam, which seeks to establish a *jamé towhidi* or a society of believers "ruled purely by faith" (30–31). He critiques fundamentalism in terms of its demarcation of "what is" in the world by pointing out the difference between reality defined by revolutionary Islamic ideology and actualities in Iran.[35] He notes the contradiction between the anti-Western, antitechnological message proclaimed in a doctrinaire publication such as *The Message of Peace* and the country's open-armed, ready use of Western technology. "[T]echnology surrounded us in Tehran," he observes, "and some of it had been so Islamized or put to such good Islamic use that its foreign origin seemed of no account" (32–33).[36] What applies to foreign-produced cassettes, televisions, and telephones also applies to military hardware; Iranians speak of Phantoms (U.S.-built fighter planes) as if they were by nature Islamic or "as international as swords, part of the stock of the great world bazaar" (37–38). (Like Naipaul, other journalists and writers have been struck by the incongruity of fundamentalist Islam's use of high technology to spread its reactionary message. Robin Wright mentions a photo in *Jeune Afrique* showing bearded young men, with pictures of Ayatollah Khomeini pinned over their hearts, listening through headphones to lectures "extolling the virtues of death."[37] "The cassette," Bruno Etienne remarks, "is to Islamics what the printing press was to Calvinists."[38] Citing the effects of cassette tapes, television, and direct dialing on the revolution, Bernard Lewis calls the revolution in Iran "the first truly modern revolution of the electronic age": "Khomeini was the first charismatic orator who sent his oratory to millions of his compatriots at home on cassettes; he was the first revolutionary leader in exile who directed his followers at home by telephone, thanks to the direct dialing that the Shah had introduced in Iran and that was available to him in France.")[39]

Fundamentalist Islam has been called both the "ultimate ideology of the century" and the "new 'sleep of reason.'"[40] It is the latter that Naipaul perceives in fundamentalist scholarship and intellectual activities: the atmosphere of the holy city of Qom resembles medieval Europe, he writes, where faith prescribes the parameters of thought and where "there [is] no end to theological scholarship" (39, 46). The great teachers of Qom lecture, lead prayers, and produce tomes of religious exegesis, like the twenty-five-volume work on the Shia idea of the Imam: "Seven of those volumes had been published. A whole corps of scholars—no doubt collating their lecture notes: the medieval method of book transmission— were at work on the remaining eighteen" (17). Shia scholarship, like Qom, which is at its center, is frozen in the "Islamic Middle Ages"; its leaders are "figure[s] of high medieval learning" whose fields of study have "frozen . . . into a theological discipline" (70). In Naipaul's view, revolutionary fundamentalist Islam advocates, ironically, changelessness, not change; it is a return to the past, a death. He critiques the fundamentalist vision of the "theocentric society." Believers assert that Islam's strength is its totality, encompassing all aspects of private and public life, but Naipaul inverts this idea, regarding the purported totality of Islam as its weakness, a narrowing of thought and action into a prison of absurdity. Again citing an article from *The Message of Peace*, he describes a futuristic Islamic city, so carefully laid out that toilet fixtures in apartments, houses, and public buildings "'shall . . . make the user not to face the City of Mecca either from his front or back side'" (32–33). In this theography of water closets, Naipaul reads the defining tendency of revolutionary, fundamentalist Islam, its quest and zeal for a fantastic, ideological purity.

"Pakistan: The Salt Hills of a Dream" examines the gap between Islamic aspirations and actualities in a region of the Asian subcontinent to which the author first traveled in the early 1960s. Since 1947, Pakistan has linked religion and statehood by defining itself as a nation where "Muslims shall be enabled to order their lives . . . in accord with the teachings and requirements of Islam."[41] "Pakistan" stands for "the lands of the Paks," for peoples "spiritually pure and clean."[42] This idea of purity dominates the responses of the Pakistanis whom Naipaul meets, though the "purity" of which they speak is not an ethnic purity but a religious purity.

Naipaul's critique of Pakistan as Islamic republic focuses on the country's economic and political failures, the gap between its ideals and actualities, and the fundamentalist strategies that the Zia government used to conceal its failures. Above all, Pakistan is a failure economically. Though a country with more than twice the population of Iran (99.2 million inhabitants), Pakistan has a "dwarf economy" with an annual gross national product per inhabitant of $340, compared to $1,500 for

Iran and $14,090 for the United States. Its energy consumption per inhabitant—a rough measure of technological development—stands at a meager 20 percent of Iran's.[43] As Naipaul explains, the big difference between the two countries is that Pakistan has no oil: "here desert was desert. Iran . . . earned seventy million dollars a day . . . Pakistan . . . earned one hundred forty millions a month from its export of rice, leather, and cotton" (86). In the Karachi English-language newspapers he reads signs of Pakistan's feebleness and the narrowing economic horizons of its people, like an ad for $200-a-month jobs in Saudi Arabia: "It was on foreign earnings like this . . . that Pakistan lived" (86–87). The country's economy has become a "remittance economy" fueled by the earnings of overseas workers in the neighboring Gulf countries of Saudi Arabia and Kuwait and in Western Europe and North America. Pakistan is in such dire straits that its "manpower-export experts" scrutinize the "world's immigration laws and competitively gambl[e] with their emigrant battalions," determining how many and what kind of workers can be sent to each nation (101). A country that must export its own people in order to survive economically cannot be considered a success, he points out; about the difference between Pakistani vision and actuality, he concludes: "The dream of the Muslim homeland had had strange consequences. And strangest of all was this: the state that had appeared to some as God itself, a complete earthly reward for the faithful, lived not so much by its agricultural exports or by the proceeds of its minor, secondary industries, as by the export of its people. . . . The idea of the Muslim state as God had never converted . . . into political and economic organization" (100–101).

Pakistan's politics have rivaled the sad state of its economy, amounting to, in Naipaul's view, a thuggishness that has included two coups d'état, periods of martial law, capricious alterations of the country's constitution, and imprisonment and execution of public officials (99). Former president Zia-ul-Haq ruled tyrannically; in the name of Islamization, he proclaimed Islamic penal measures, appointed benches of judges with Islamic qualifications, introduced Islamic fiscal and economic measures, Islamic ideological and educational reforms, and promoted an Islamic life-style for public officials.[44] Referring to Zia's Islamization, Naipaul writes that Pakistan has, step by step, "undone the rule of law it had inherited from the British, and replaced it with nothing" (169). Its political failures stem broadly from a colonial legacy and a reliance on the faith to solve its problems; the country failed to develop political institutions because, at the time of its founding, the strongest Islamic political organizations resided in what is now India, and when politicians from these organizations moved to Pakistan, they lost their constituencies and were considered outsiders (89–90). In the political vacuum, the army flourished, but because the army recruited its personnel primarily from West Pakistan, a rift developed with the more populous East Pakistan. An unsuccessful war with India, a coup, and the secession of East Pakistan (Bangladesh) followed. President Zia came to power in the country's second coup, and later executed Ali Bhutto. "The state withered," Naipaul writes. "But faith didn't. Failure only led back to the faith" (90). Islam became the only bond in a country of diverse peoples and languages; instead of "sit[ting] down hard-headedly to work out institutions," Pakistanis trusted to "the saving faith" (91).

Naipaul argues that fundamentalism in Pakistan has created a myth of history that distorts or denies events that do not affirm Islam; fundamentalists withdraw into a millenarian fantasy of a pure Islamic epoch. Faith "nullif[ies] and overlay[s] the real world," he writes; it negates history by ignoring it or turning it into myth (143). History is "Islamized": "Before Mohammed there is blackness: slavery, exploitation. After Mohammed there is light: slavery and exploitation vanish" (142–43). This myth—of the golden age, an old, pure, sanctified epoch from which the decadent modern epoch has devolved and to which fundamentalists would seek to return—rejects science and technology and conceives of modern history as a story of decline.[45] Naipaul writes that fundamentalists want to "re-create something like a tribal or a city-state that—except in theological fantasy—never was"; that fantasy could be realized only if "the world outside could be shut out, and men could be made to forget what they know" (145, 167). For Naipaul, fundamentalism is, finally, a negation of thought, a turning out of the lights, for a weary, traumatized people: "In the days of Muslim glory Islam opened itself to the learning of the world. Now fundamentalism provides an intellectual thermostat, set low. It equalizes, comforts, shelters, and preserves" (167).

"Conversations in Malaysia: The Primitive Faith" looks at fundamentalism in a geographic region that Westerners may not automatically think of as Islamic.[46] Here Naipaul critiques myths of pastoralism and romantic innocence, both variations of the larger myth of a return to the source—to a golden age of purity—inherent in the appeals of Pakistani fundamentalism. Pastoralism privileges nature over technology, village over city, simplicity over complexity; it seeks a return to the earthly paradise that progress and development threaten or have already destroyed. Romantic innocence privileges the child over the adult and the primitive over the sophisticated; it reveres an earlier stage of human development and civilization.

"First Conversations with Shafi: The Journey Out of Paradise" offers an explanation for the author's choice of Malaysia as a stop on his itinerary: not just the fundamentalist revival there, but a fascination with Conrad's "Eastern world." His Malaysian stories depict the "remoter places of the Malay Archipelago a hundred years ago," with its mix of European, Arab, Chinese, and Malay (226). This mélange and its conflicts became Conrad's themes of East meeting West: "Separate, colliding worlds: the world of the Europeans, pushing on to the 'outer edge of darkness,' the closed tribal world of Malays" (226). Today, oil, tin, rubber, and palm oil have replaced rattan and coconut at the landing stations of Conrad's day. And Malaysia has become moderately rich, at least in the context of other developing countries; its gross national product per inhabitant, $1,870, stands significantly higher than Pakistan's ($390) and slightly higher than Iran's ($1,500).[47] Yet in becoming rich Malaysia has also become more dependent on the First World; in the rush for success, the country is exploiting its natural resources and overturning the old ways of its river and forest civilization.

The anger of the Malay villagers in the face of these changes is understandable in that they have not benefitted from the boom but have seen their way of life irrevocably changed. The "new men of the villages," Naipaul explains, "find their path blocked at every turn. Money, development, education have awakened them only to the knowledge that the world is not like their village. . . . Their rage—the rage of a pastoral people with limited skills, limited money, and a limited grasp of the world—is comprehensive" (227). Through forest exploitation, mineral extraction, a concentration on cash crops, and a stimulated consumerism, the country has gone forward, but in the bargain it has become more dependent on and open to transnational corporations and concerns of the world's economic powers: "Money magnified the limitations of places like Malaysia, small, uneducated, and coming late to everything. Money . . . changed old ways. But money only turned people into buyers of imported goods, fixed the country in a dependent relationship with the developed world, kept all men colonials" (266).

Fundamentalist Islam serves as an all-purpose response to the country's cultural and socioeconomic conflicts, themselves rooted in an "ethnic-economic split" among rural Malays, urban Chinese business owners, and Indian plantation workers. As sociologist David Drakakis-Smith explains, developments after the country's independence in 1957 have exacerbated this split and the concomitant racial and class tensions.[48] The Islamic revival which Naipaul dubs the Malay "way of getting even with the world," grows out of and exploits these tensions and inequalities. It "serves [Malay] grief, their feelings of inadequacy, their social rage and racial hate" (227). The author portrays this grief through the response of the young student, Shafi, who tells of a Chinese-run batik factory's contamination of a stream near his native Malay village. "[T]his disturbed our swimming activities," he says bitterly. "They spoilt our playground" (293). Shafi's metaphor aptly expresses a grief for a lost simplicity and the destruction of a village identity through industrialization. Naipaul also criticizes this destruction, such as the felling of forests to make tourist meccas in the Malay countryside (266), but he rejects, as he always does in Third World contexts, the backlash idea of a return to a former state of innocence or underdevelopment. The fantasy of a paradise regained will neither clean up the polluted stream nor save what is left of the Malay villages.

"Indonesia: Usurpations" considers fundamentalist Islam in neighboring Indonesia, the fifth most populous country in the world. Indonesians are different from Malaysians in their pre-Islamic history—Indonesia, or Java, knew a great Hindu-Buddhist civilization prior to the arrival of Islam in the fifteenth century—which has survived "half erased, slightly mysterious . . . still awesome," giving a "uniqueness" to Indonesians (298–99).[49] Like Malaysia, the country has known social turmoil in this century; it has experienced war and revolution, and in 1965 the twenty-year presidency of Sukarno ended with a military takeover, countrywide uprisings, and massacres of Chinese and purported communist supporters. One-half million to one million people were killed (299). In the 1980s, revivalist Islam taps the same ethnic, racial, and social energies, channeled by other beliefs and ideologies at other periods in Indonesia's history; it also taps a new "restlessness" that has come with money, education, and urban development. Fundamentalist Islam is a container for diverse ethnic and social passions and a fantasy of a return to a simpler time; it "makes people withdraw, the more violently to leap forward" (300).[50]

Although revivalist Islam has shown itself capable of channeling countercurrents of social passion and protest in Indonesia, it has produced, according to Naipaul, little constructive reform in either villages or cities. To look at Islam's impact on the villages he visits a traditional Islamic village school known as a *pesantren*, which purportedly integrates "community and school, village life and education" (317). The *pesantren*'s pedagogy and curriculum seem to have nothing to do with meeting the needs of contemporary Indonesia, however; students learn to withdraw from the world, not compete in it. Naipaul writes that the *pesantren* resembles a "sufi centre turned school" where the young learn "the discipline of monks and dervishes" instead of modern skills. He adds acerbically: "it wasn't traditional, and it wasn't education. . . . it was stupefaction, greater than any that could have come with a Western-style curriculum" (325). The practices of the *pesantren* amount to "the poor teaching the poor to be poor" (325). Why, Naipaul wonders, does the *pesantren*, which he likens to a "campus-turned-farmyard," expend such energies recreating the village life for students who are already villagers (341). It teaches backwardness.

Nor does Islam offer anything more than faith to those who, in moving from the village to the city, have lost their identity in Indonesia's rapid modernization. To the uprooted, Islam offers a sense of belonging, but it does not put forward institutionalized measures for coping with and managing the socioeconomic phenomena that produce the deracination. Islam thus surrenders to change, or reacts blindly against it: "This late twentieth-century Islam appeared to raise political issues. But it had the flaw of its origins . . . to the political issues it raised it offered no political or practical solution. It offered only faith. It offered only the Prophet, who would settle everything—but who had ceased to exist. This political Islam was rage, anarchy" (355).

Reflecting on the conversations and acquaintances of his journey in four Islamic countries, Naipaul perceives a pattern of response, which he calls "the interchangeable revolution." He thinks of Behzad, his Iranian guide, whose commitment to communism is filled with the "rage" of Shia Islam. He thinks of the Muslim businessman from Jakarta who wants a revolution in order to put "the Chinese . . . the multinationals, the successful, the ignorant men" who are running Indonesia in their place: "We will have to kill a lot of people," he declares (380). Naipaul thinks of the verse of celebrated Indonesian poet Sitor Situmorang, in which communist themes of "social life, solidarity and hope" interchange with nationalist and revivalist Islamic themes. For Naipaul, these three responses are all instances of the "interchangeable revolution," the comingling of ancient Islam and the spirit of modern revolution. "The Islam of protest," he concludes, "was religion that had been brushed by the ideas of the late twentieth century" (387). Fundamentalism is actually a hybrid—a mixture of old and new, of East and West—not a pure entity: this is the insight that makes *Among the Believers* a profound book, raising it above most other social commentary about contemporary Islam.

With ironic reversal, Naipaul contends that revivalist Islam is dependent on something external for its new identity; it has been energized by something outside of itself, that is, by the modern Western idea of revolution. This contention differs from those of other analysts of the Islamic revival, such as Robin Wright, who refers to the internal Islamic tradition of the holy war to explain the character of modern, militant Islam.[51] Naipaul views revivalist Islam in relationship to other ideologies—which can be understood by referring to Göran Therborn's concept of ideology: in the cluttered, cacophonous ideological universe all ideologies exist in dialogic relationship with one another, conflicting, reinforcing, reshaping one another's explanations of what is, what is good, and what is possible in the world.[52]

In "Reprise," the final part of *Among the Believers*, Naipaul sums up his main ideas by recounting the story of a second, unexpected stopover in Iran. In Tehran everyone is in a free state—"nervous," "waiting," pushed toward "hysteria" and "anarchy," living in a "battlefield, full of private wars" (425, 428). A society of believers has established itself, but from that society has come chaos, not law and institutions (428). Revolution has ushered in "Islamic Winter," a withering of the intellect and an indulgence in the illusion of power and wholeness. In answer to the question, What was the origin of the revolution? Naipaul gives the answer he always gives, whether the developing society he is "diagnosing" is West Indian, Indian, or Iranian: the origin lies in a collision of cultures, in that "division" in the "mind" of Iranians between faith and tradition on the one hand and the contemporary world on the other (429). Although the *Tehran Times* may call Islam a "comprehensive system" and vaunt the revolution as "unique and [the] most courageous . . . in the history of mankind," Iran and other Islamic countries will have to "make their peace with the world . . . beyond the faith," Naipaul concludes. Reiterating the book's thesis, he states:

The life that had come to Islam had not come from within. It had come from outside events and circumstances. . . . It was the late twentieth century that had made Islam revolutionary, given new meaning to old Islamic ideas of equality and union, shaken up static or retarded societies. It was the late twentieth century—and not the faith—that could supply the answers—in institutions, legislation, economic systems. And, paradoxically, out of the Islamic revival, Islamic fundamentalism, that appeared to look backward, there would remain in many Muslim countries, with all the emotional charge derived from the Prophet's faith, the idea of modern revolution. (429)

The thrust of this interpretation is twofold: first, revivalist Islam depends upon its "other," its purported enemy the West, as the ideological entity to which it responds and from which it takes its idea of revolution. Second, the religious fervor of Islam flows into the traditional society's new sense of revolutionary change, impacting on that society in unpredictable ways and even altering Islamic traditions—which in fact has already happened, if only temporarily, in Pakistan where, of all things, a woman was elected to head the first modern nation founded on Islamic ideology.[53] Naipaul deconstructs Islamic fundamentalism; he critiques its authoritarian ideology, inverting fundamentalism's cherished conception of itself: its wholeness, its antiquity, its purity, its independence of Western ideological frameworks.

*Among the Believers* has been read and attacked as a one-sided account of Islam; Rana Kabbani, for example, takes Naipaul to task for seeing "only negativity in Islam."[54] But his book is not about Islam per se but about fundamentalist Islam; more particularly, it is about the conjunction of fundamentalism and the idea of modern social revolution in four countries at a particular period, the late 1970s and early 1980s. Naipaul focuses on fundamentalism's intolerance and its hybrid identity; he views fundamentalism not as a solution to socioeconomic and political problems but as an expression of a cultural and social trauma. As we read this book, though, we the Western readers need a sense of the diversity of the Islamic diaspora that *Among the Believers: An Islamic Journey* does not provide and perhaps even conceals by the generality of its title. We need to be aware that people's responses to Islam do vary, and that there are, of course, moderate and progressive interpretations as well as reactionary ones.[55] For example, Jacques Berque, celebrated Islamologist and translator of the Koran, argues that the Koran expresses a "rationalist vision"; he explains that the word *reason* occurs forty-four times while the word *sacred* and its variants occur only seven times. Berque, a Muslim, inverts the idea that Islam is, by nature, irrationalist.[56] Throughout the Islamic diaspora people live according to differing interpretations of their religion determined, in their respective communities and societies, by factors such as ethnic history, geography, economic structures, gender, and occupational roles.

Very broadly, *Among the Believers* is not about Islam, but about cultural collisions, about Third World peoples' responses to change. It is about people becoming strangers to themselves and their responses to this new strangeness within. It is a book shaped by exile: during the author's journey among the believers he affirms his own identity through difference—through being a nonbeliever, through emphasizing his not-belonging. In his encounter with Islamic others, there can be no commonality, even though like the "believers" he feels a sense of estrangement. For the exile, it would seem that there can be no return to the past and a community of others, to a *society* of believers. Of Shafi's (his Malay interlocutor's) estrangement Naipaul writes: "I felt for him the wish to re-establish the rules was also a wish to re-create the security of his childhood, the Malay village life he had lost. . . . Some grief like that touches most of us. It is what, as individuals, responsible for ourselves, we constantly have to accommodate ourselves to" (242–43). Autobiographically, the author's "Islamic journey" is part of the recursive voyage of exile through which he analyzes his own "wound" by observing the estrangement of others, and it reaffirms his identity through not-belonging to their world. The rejection of a "return" is strong because the exile believes that he must not give in to what is at once a fear and an urge.

## *Finding the Center* (1984)

Any body of writing spanning decades, as does Naipaul's, will inevitably contain an array of positions and contradictions between some of those positions. Viewed in relation to *Among the Believers* or to his essays of the 1960s and 1970s about India and the Caribbean or West Indies, *Finding the Center* seems to embrace contradictions. After all, does Naipaul not critique Singh's centrist notions in *The Mimic Men* and, of course, those of fundamentalist Islam? Does he not say that Safi must accommodate himself to grief and not imagine that he can return to a mythic center located in the old Malay village of his childhood? And yet, "Prologue to an Autobiography," the first of two narratives in *Finding the Center*, adopts the idea of a return to one's origins. That, at least, is one interpretation of the book's title and object; a second, somewhat related but finally different interpretation, is that Naipaul seeks a balance between the urge to return to one's origins and the urge to go forward to new destinations. In the latter interpretation, the "center" of the book's title is not really a center, but an in-between, a sharing of and a balance between opposing forces.

The "Author's Foreword" and "Prologue to an Autobiography" consider Naipaul's "literary beginnings" and make interesting observations about his process of writing.[57] Alluding to early books such as *The Middle Passage* and *An Area of Darkness*, he explains that travel writing has been difficult for him: "My instinct was towards fiction; I found it constricting to have to deal with fact. I was glamoured by the idea of the long journey, but I had no idea how I might set about looking at a place in a way that would be of value to other people" (ix). He explains that he was "uncertain" how to treat "the traveler's 'I' " because of his identity as a colonial traveling in and writing about "a world still more or less ruled by colonial ideas" (ix). His early travel books show an author struggling to define a method of selection and emphasis of material—should he emphasize facts or impressions? should he be sociological or autobiographical?—and his position as a colonial and exile writing about a transitional, colonial and postcolonial world.

As traveler, Naipaul "carries his world with him" (x). His writing is thus a dialogue between a ready-made response and a new experience; the traveler-writer carries with him an already partially patterned interpretation of the world into which the experience of the new journey is set. Each journey is thus partly an old journey and a context for understanding future journeys. Each journey is recursive, and this, in part, is what the author means when he explains: "To become a writer . . . I had thought it necessary to leave [Trinidad]. Actually to write, it was necessary to go back. It was the beginning of self-knowledge" (34). Experience and the understanding of self and others are recursively tangled: to go forward, one must sometimes go back, yet one comprehends the need to go back sometimes only through going forward. This is part of the art and experience of exile.

"Prologue to an Autobiography" treats home and exile through the theme of "finding the center." By writing, Naipaul explains, the writer orders and gives "value" to his experiences; he finds his center, so to speak, though that "center" or "home" is a construct of his own making in the context of his culture and history (17–18). For Naipaul, the center is both a discovery and a construction. As Janet Varner Gunn explains in *Autobiography*, creation and understanding are not mutually exclusive but interrelated: "sense-making activity, basic to both narrative and life, involves what Schleirmacher identified as the 'hermeneutical circle,' that mutual shaping of parts and imagined whole which characterizes all of our efforts at understanding. It is simply a question of where we enter that circle and the degree of critical reflection we bring to our own interpretive performance."[58] The idea of a center can appeal to the exile, the outsider; in addition the idea shows a Hindu aspect of Naipaul's sensibility, for to find the center is to liberate oneself in the same sense that the sage seeks to liberate himself from the illusions of the world: "It is by 'knowledge' that man . . . 'awakens.' By knowledge . . . the effect of which will be to make him find his own center."[59] By understanding the self through others and through the reflection and constructs of writing, Naipaul seeks the center by balancing the forces of a double movement of going back and going forward.

Naipaul's exile has often been a tension between pulling and being pulled in opposite directions: "it was . . . fear, a panic about failing to be what I should be . . . that was with me when I . . . began trying to write in London. My father had died the previous year. Our family was in distress. I should have done something for them, gone back to them. But, without having become a writer, I couldn't go back" (72). His sense of duty struggles against his sense of mission: he should have gone back home but no, he says, "I couldn't go back." This personal dilemma—a collision of cultural values between his Hindu sense of familial duty and his Western individualist sense of his writer's calling—informs his exile. To go back home would be to raise doubts within his and other people's minds about his calling—maybe he was not cut out to be a writer after all; so Naipaul, with his anxiety and suppressed guilt, must be adamant about not returning and about going forward. He projects aspects of his dilemma onto peoples in developing countries, who in their own dilemma of cultural collisions are torn between a desire to go back (to return to the old ways) and an exigency to go forward (to modify their lives in the face of Western economic-technological hegemony). This personal dilemma runs like a hidden fault line through Naipaul's social commentaries, structuring them with a submerged autobiographical aspect and sometimes contradictory positions. Through exile, a traumatic change and a continual dilemma, the author constructs a new identity, and his usual position is to argue that so, too, must peoples from traditional societies whose world is in collision with the West. The solution is not a return to the past, but a construction of a syncretistic identity with aspects of both old and new. Conversely, in his position vis-à-vis peoples of *developed* countries, Naipaul seems to long for the way things used to be (like Singh's wish to bring back the "Old England") and views the latter half of the twentieth century as full of a decay—that sense of decay, in part, a displaced form of his remorse and anxiety.

A sense of decay dominates the second essay in *Finding the Center,* "The Crocodiles of Yamoussoukro," which can be read as another rewriting, more than a decade later, of "Power?" and "Michael X," essays in which the author traces the roots of Trinidad carnival and Black Power to the Caribbean slaves' "kingdoms of the night." The essay contrasts a dualistic world: the modern, sophisticated, economically successful Ivory Coast with the primitive, animistic world that, according to the author, still lives in the psyche of Ivorians and of which the palpitating bush and jungle are symbols:

In the slave plantations of the Caribbean Africans existed in two worlds. There was the world of the day; that was the white world. There was the world of the night; that was the African world, of spirits and magic and the true gods. And in that world ragged men, humiliated by day, were transformed—in their own eyes, and the eyes of their fellows—into kings, sorcerers, herbalists, men in touch with the true forces of the earth and possessed of complete power. A king of the night, a slave by day. . . . To the outsider, to the slave owner, the African night world might appear a mimic world, a child's world, a carnival. But to the African . . . it was the true world: it turned white men to phantoms and plantation life to an illusion. (149)

But the duality that Naipaul perceives in Ivorian society would seem to derive at least in part from his own conception of history: linear growth and progress in the First World versus repetitious cycles of half-making and unmaking in the Third World. The "'world is sand. Life is sand,'" Naipaul's Ivorian interlocutor tells him; the monuments of Yamoussoukro and the skyscrapers of Abidjan will vanish and be replaced by the bush and forest (173). Though this vision may be African, it repeats Naipaul's own view of a fragmenting, postcolonial world, as symbolized in his nightmare of a crumbling bridge: "I dreamed I was on a roof or bridge. The material of glass or transparent plastic, had begun to perish: seemingly melted at the edges. I asked whether the bridge would be mended. The answer was no. What had been built had been built; the roof or bridge I was on would crumble away" (155). In this dream the world is split, and the bridge that connects its two sides cannot hold: the traveler-exile fears he may perish in the in-between. The dream expresses a "fear of extinction" projected onto a landscape where Africa and the West seem to meet: for Naipaul, must the glass and plastic, products of the West, weaken and shatter in the bush and jungle? Can there be no bridge between different worlds?

In Yamoussoukro and Abidjan, Naipaul senses not a stability but an illusion of modernity and the fragility of the civilization flourishing there.[60] Listening to drummologist Niangoran-Bouah he ponders whether he himself has been bewitched: "I wondered—so far, after Yamoussoukro and the crocodiles, and the heads, and my own dream of the decaying bridge and general dissolution, had I been drawn into Mr. Niangoran-Bouah's spirit world" (161). But the author's sense of dualism and decay is a ready-made concept and perception, one expressed recursively in previous essays and novels. "I go to places which, however alien, connect in some way with what I already know," he writes (90). And what he already knows is articulated in the essay "A New King for the Congo" and "Conrad's Darkness," and before in *The Middle Passage* and *The Overcrowded Barracoon*, a vision of developing societies constantly unmaking themselves: "Africa can often seem to be in a state of becoming. It is always on the point of being made something else" (78). To arrive at this Africa in "The Crocodiles of Yamoussoukro," Naipaul does not travel directly to the Ivory Coast but takes a long, recursive journey that passes through the same vision of African and Caribbean or West Indian societies in "Power?" "In a Free State," *Guerrillas*, and *A Bend in the River*.

This vision of a double reality, of a circular African history always ending in erasure, derives from multiple sources: the colonial's split between margins and center, a Hindu heritage with its belief that the world is illusion, a response to Conrad's fiction about the faraway places of the world, travels in impoverished countries like India and Pakistan—above all, from exile. Through recursion the vision has become highly literary, a part of the author's way of looking at and constructing the world. "A writer . . . carries his world with him, his own burden of experience, human experience and literary experience (one deepening the other); and I do believe . . . that I would have found equivalent connections with my past and myself wherever I had gone," Naipaul explains (ix). Indeed, he has traveled to and written about many places and peoples in the Americas, Asia, and Africa, yet there is a sense in which, in all the particularity of impressions and observations of others, he is writing about the same place and about himself. He is always standing on the fault line of his split as exile; he is always going over a crumbling bridge that is also a world unmaking itself.

In *Pour une théorie de la production littéraire* (Toward a theory of literary production), Pierre Macherey remarks that Jules Verne's works are about the "straight line," about a belief in science and technology solving the problems of the world and carrying (Western) civilization forward.[61] Whether in novels or essays, Naipaul's works about developing societies are finally about the circle—the circle not as completion or perfection, but as repetition, a return to the zero degree. This vision of cycles of unmaking depends on actualities and observations, but it is equally a product of the recursive voyage of his exile: it derives, in part, from the experience of a life without a society, of a home left behind, of a need to reaffirm self and the self's relationship with others by finding what has already been found and writing what has been written before. *Finding the Center* is a work with a split identity, looking back to "Power?" and forward to *The Enigma of Arrival*, in which the author looks for a clue—in his past, in a West African country—to break out of that cycle.

# The Fourth World

> . . . style strives organically to assimilate material into language and language into material.
> —M. M. Bakhtin, "Discourse in the Novel"

> In the suburbs of Monrovia, near Paynesville, a dozen kilometers from the presidential palace, the combat continues. On the rebel side, the scenario is the same each morning: palaver for hours at crossroads, then the taking up of positions. The "freedom fighters" leave for the front dressed as if for carnival: in soccer shorts, an elegant hat with veil or a wig on the head, a multitude of necklaces or gris-gris on the wrist, face and arms smeared with clay ("to repel bullets")—or better still, dressed in a long black and purple gown, stolen from the closets of the University [of Liberia]. Anything is possible, and anything goes. Even militarily, it's the same fantasy and lack of strategy.
> —"Bloody Carnival in Monrovia," *Le Monde*

"Societies everywhere have been fractured by . . . change," Naipaul observes. "The whole world now requires another kind of imaginative interpretation."[1] Such a new interpretation the author attempts to put forward in his 1970s fiction: *In a Free State*, *Guerrillas*, and *A Bend in the River*. These works portray fractured postcolonial societies in which everyone is becoming an "exile," cut off from a community of others, at the mercy of the arbitrary laws of a dictator or the lawlessness of rivalries. The breakdown depicted in Naipaul's 1970s novels refers to a political and socioeconomic "free state" into which countries of sub-Saharan Africa and other regions of the developing world are falling or have already fallen. Lebanon—as captured in the French, coined term *libanisation*[2]— is an oft-cited, tragic example; for more than fifteen years it has been a country permanently at war with itself. Many African countries are little better off, and in some instances, worse off. Between their date of independence and 1983, fifteen sub-Saharan African countries experienced at least one coup d'état; thirteen had two or more. As of 1983, fifty African governments had been overthrown. In Benin (Dahomey) alone, there were five military coups, ten attempted coups, twelve governments, and six constitutions in the period between 1963 and 1972. Once known as the most stable country in sub-Saharan Africa, Liberia experienced six attempted coups since Master Sergeant Samuel Doe assassinated President William Tolbert, Jr. in 1980. In 1990, it was a country deeply in debt and engaged in civil war. Tribal or internecine wars have been waged in several African countries: in Sudan the war between the Islamic north and traditionalist African south has claimed 400,000 lives and created a million refugees; in Burundi, 200,000 Hutu were systematically slaughtered by Watusi in a three-month period in 1972, a slaughter repeated in 1988. Nigeria, Chad, Ethiopia, Angola, to mention but a few countries, have fought or are still fighting civil wars; several African countries have fought or are still fighting each other.[3] As of October 1990 there were thirteen wars in progress in Africa.[4]

This social breakdown can seem surreal. A case in point is the recent history of Comoros, islands off the east coast of Africa, which gained their independence from France in 1975. The country's first coup d'état took place twenty-eight days after the beginning of independence; three attempted coups followed during the next three years. Ex-president Ali Solih, who emerged in a coup six months after independence day, embarked on an ideological program that included the dismissal of 3,500 civil servants, destruction of records from the 134-year French administration of the islands, the lowering of the voting age to fourteen, and recruitment of a law-enforcement brigade composed of "teen-age dropouts" who roamed the streets robbing, raping, and killing. As president, Solih secluded himself in his palace, passing the time with young girls and slipping into a haze of whiskey, hashish, and all-night movies shown on his 16-mm projector. Disgruntled Comorian businessmen hired a group of mercenaries to assassinate Solih. Their leader, Frenchman Bob Denard—a veteran of the Congo and Biafra wanted in his own country in connection with a 1977 coup in Benin—was greeted by Comorians as a national hero. *Los Angeles Times* journalist David Lamb, who visited the islands before and after the Denard-led coup, was struck by Comorians' vacillations of loyalty and their acceptance of the surreal as the ordinary: "How could there be such a complete transition so quickly? People would shrug indifferently. 'We did what we were told to do,' explained a young man who had been a member of the youth brigade."[5] Incredibly, this drama replayed itself in 1989 when President Ahmed Abdallah was assassinated; Bob Denard and his mercenaries, who had recently returned to the island, were suspected, though Denard has claimed that the president was killed accidentally by stray gunfire from his own guards.[6]

Comoros is not such an exception in a postcolonial Africa that can appear, at least to Western eyes, to be the epitome of oppression and chaos—not a *Third World* (whatever that term might now mean), but a partly real, partly fantastic *Fourth World* toward which many countries are regressing. Naipaul's 1970s novels refer to this state of deterioration in which independence coincides, ironically, with increased economic dependence, political oppression, and *libanisation*. Naipaul writes about an actuality; he writes informed by his own background and his travels to Africa and other regions of the developing world.

Naipaul's Third World is fictional, though, as well as factual. "In a Free State" describes an East African country falling apart that is a mélange of Rwanda, Uganda, Kenya, and Trinidad. The Caribbean island of *Guerrillas* is a fictional Trinidad; the Central African country of *A Bend in the River* is a mixture of Zaire, Uganda, and again, Trinidad. From a literary perspective, there is a sense in which all of these places are images of a single, fictional state, a Fourth World of fear, the menace of violence, and horror. This vision of a Fourth World derives in part from European colonial discourse about sub-Saharan Africa, especially from Conrad's stories set in "half-made societies" forever making and unmaking themselves.[7] It derives from a particular ideological realm and literary-language consciousness, from a myth that exists before Naipaul, and that, in his novels, is reshaped by his colonial background, exile, and travels in the Third World, in conjunction with the historial contexts of the 1960s and 1970s. The Fourth World is at once an observation, a scenario of a regressing Third World, and a personal, mythic, literary landscape.

## In a Free State (1971)

*In a Free State* contains three pieces of fiction placed between two pieces of nonfiction, an arrangement that inserts the author into the collection as one of its characters, who are themselves exiles and expatriates; its theme, as the narrator of the semiautobiographical *Enigma of Arrival* suggests, is "freedom and loss."[8] The first piece, "Prologue, from a Journal: The Tramp at Piraeus," grows out of the instability of Naipaul's life as exile and travel writer and responds dialogically to glorification-of-the-road literature that Beats like Kerouac, Ginsberg, and others popularized in the 1950s and 1960s. In contrast to the romance of the down-and-out of *On the Road* and *The Dharma Bums*, "The Tramp at Piraeus" describes the plight of a traveler-tramp who has been knocking about the world for thirty-eight years. He presents himself as a geologist turned wanderer and a "world-citizen" who has cut himself loose from ties to society and the workaday world.[9] Naipaul considers him just a tramp, a man in an ironic bondage to the road: "He looked for company but needed solitude; he looked for attention, and at the same time wanted not to be noticed" (12). In his eyes Naipaul sees not the wisdom of a world citizen, but "fear."

The essay describes the tramp's odd behavior—such as randomly ripping pages out of a magazine—and his humiliation at the hands of other travelers who badger him. It poses a question: can the tramp's state, his belonging nowhere and being at the mercy of everyone, be called freedom? Only in the ironic sense of the book's title: the West has created a cult of the self-sufficient, societyless individual who exists, seemingly without ties, "in a free state." It has conceived of freedom as "freedom from," which leaves open the corollary question, "freedom to do what"? According to Erich Fromm, if freedom does not lead to involvement, "freedom from" leads to a new bondage.[10] In this essay—and in other works of this period such as "Michael X" and *Guerrillas*—Naipaul suggests that it is an illusion to suppose that individuals can shake themselves loose from their social context and exist as if unattached to any society, as world citizens who belong at once everywhere and nowhere. From his own exile Naipaul knows that the road takes its toll, and from this perspective the tramp can be viewed as a kind of secret sharer. The tramp has been swallowed by his freedom; as a destructive obsession this freedom is a displaced form of Naipaul's "fear of extinction," a loss of identity that can result either from being swallowed by society (e.g., the colony) or by societylessness (e.g., the alien metropolis).

"One Out of Many" and "Tell Me Who to Kill" treat the subject of culture shock and cultural collisions; they tell the stories of an Indian and a West Indian, respectively, who leave their traditional societies to begin new lives in the United States and England. Santosh, the story's narrator and protagonist, represents an Indian mentality controlled by caste and religion; his encounter with the alien West leads initially to conflict and withdrawal but eventually to a problematic acculturation in the society. He becomes a "free man," a citizen of the United States, but his new identity is fraught with irony: he lives as a "stranger" in a "dark house" in a ghetto, and feels that as a "free man" he has lost the peace and security of his former caste-controlled life on the sidewalks of Bombay (54–58).

Santosh begins his story with a flashback to his life as a domestic in Bombay, where he lived like millions of others as part of the ebb and flow of the streets (21). On the pavement he belongs to a caste-community, in which he has a daily program, an identity, an order of existence. "I was so happy," he muses (21). But all that changes when he departs for North America—and for misadventures that the author depicts in a darkly comic fashion. The allegory is clear: old India, shoeless and dressed in its domestic rags, is bewildered by the contemporary Western world, signified by airplanes, champagne, highrises, elevators. Confronted by the alien civilization, Santosh/India withdraws into the security of his employer's cupboard, which signifies his narrow caste identity and his retreat from the West. Santosh has left India, but he carries India with him, inside him culturally. He is its mental prisoner.

The story attributes to Santosh the preoccupation with self that Naipaul critiqued in caste-controlled, religion-minded India during his travels there in the 1960s and 1970s. Thus Santosh's account of his life in the

United States dwells on such self-centered topics as his misadventures on the airplane and in the apartment building, his discovery of his facial features, the first act of sex, the purchase of a new Western hat and suit. He experiences a tenuous awakening, a fissuring of his block caste identity; he notes, for example, his pleasure at regarding himself in the mirror and his astonishment at the experience of orgasm during his first act of sexual intercourse. But this awakening creates a division within him between Old World and New. He believes that his sexual encounter with a *hubshi* (a black woman) has left him impure, so he must, in ritualistic fashion, bathe and fast to cleanse himself. He believes that he must do penance, so he rubs his body with a lemon and rolls about naked on the floor and howls (39). He buys an American hat and suit as an expression of his new individuality, yet is unable to wear the suit because it is too big and because he feels guilty about the extravagant purchase: "When I considered all that cloth and all that tailoring I was proposing to adorn my simple body with . . . I felt I was asking to be destroyed" (36). After this minimalist shopping spree, Santosh feels so burdened that he has to lie down in his cupboard/bedroom. He never wears the suit—in fact, he never removes it from its box—as if to do so would be an offense against the Old India. Thus, although Santosh breaks out of his old caste identity little by little, he is constantly pulled back by its power over him.

It is not clear, finally, what he has achieved in leaving the sidewalks of Bombay for the ghetto of D.C. Through the fissuring of his caste identity, he has been awakened to a new sense of self but has lost the certitude of caste definition and the security of anonymity, of being "one of many" as he was among the sleepers on the Bombay pavement. Reflecting on his life he laments, "I was once part of the flow, never thinking of myself as a presence. Then I looked in the mirror and decided to be free. All that my freedom has brought me is the knowledge that I have a face and have a body, that I must feed this body and clothe this body for a certain number of years. Then it will be over" (57–58). In emerging from "the many," in breaking out of his block caste identity, Santosh enters a "shattered world," to use a key phrase from *India: A Wounded Civilization* (*IN* 31). He is left with a sense of his difference, with an awakened self that makes his new identity possible yet also fractures his former caste-ordered, religion-defined vision of the world. One of Naipaul's best stories, "One

Out of Many," recounts aspects of exile and its potential for fragmentation; in the lines of Santosh's narrative, the reader also hears overtones of the author's own story: "I am a simple man who decided to act and see for himself, and it is as though I have had several lives" (57).

"Tell Me Who to Kill" resembles "One Out of Many" in its treatment of cultural collisions and a shattered world: a West Indian's life in London ends in failure, loss, and a passion for revenge. The story is told by an unnamed, distraught, semiliterate narrator who mixes fact and fantasy; he travels to England to "look after" his younger brother Dayo who is supposedly studying aeronautical engineering and to whom he has transferred his aspirations for a better life. When Dayo does not meet him upon arrival in England, the narrator realizes that he is on his own and must survive in the alien world. He finds a day job at a cigarette factory and a night job at a restaurant; living like a "man in blinders," he manages to save fifteen hundred pounds and feels a sense of success and security. Eventually he is contacted by his brother, is reunited with him, and invites him to share a basement apartment. These "happy days" are short-lived though. The narrator learns that Dayo has abandoned his studies in engineering and in their place is taking short computer-programming courses, the kind the narrator sees advertised on buses; he also learns that Dayo is going to marry an English girl. Distressed, feeling abandoned, not knowing which way to turn, he quits his jobs out of the sense of security given to him by his savings account and then purchases a roti-and-curry shop that quickly exhausts the savings. He feels his life is now ruined: his brother has left him, he has lost his hard-earned money, and he is alone in an alien land. He dreams of returning to the West Indies: "life is over. . . . I come with nothing. I have nothing. I will leave with nothing. . . . I feel like a free man. I scorn everything I see" (96). Such is the "free state," a journey to the zero degree, of "Tell Me Who to Kill."

The story presents a collision between the marginalized, underdeveloped Third World (of the sensitive, hard-working, yet uneducated, unskilled narrator) and the modern, technological First World (here, England). In this confrontation the narrator has been programmed for defeat by his familial, cultural, and social circumstances. His parents do not educate him because his father fears being less educated and "throw down" by his son; the narrator's sensibility and class consciousness aggravate further his feelings of deprivation: "For the rich and the professional the world is not ordinary. . . . Where you build a hut, they build a mansion; where you have mud and a pará-grass field, they have a garden; when you kill time on a Sunday, they have parties" (70). The narrator inherits a circumscribed, patterned world of humiliation, diminishment, and dead ends; trying to break out of this world, he fails because of the disadvantages of his background and his collisions with an alien culture. "Tell Me Who to Kill" can be read as a story of exile and of the continuing effects of colonialism on peoples of developing societies. It is, perhaps, an allegory of the difficulty of the "slow" to survive in a global, socioeconomic order determined by the "fast."[11] At the story's conclusion the narrator, unable to ascertain the reason for his failure, can only vent his pain and bewilderment: "O God, show me the enemy. Once you find out who the enemy is, you can kill him. But these people here they confuse me. Who hurt me? Who spoil my life? Tell me who to beat back. . . . Tell me who to kill" (102).

"In a Free State," the novella from which the collection takes its title, conveys the first of Naipaul's visions of postcolonial Africa; its title alludes to the equivocal presence of European expatriates like Bobby and Linda in former African colonies and to the state of disorder and social breakdown in postindependent, sub-Saharan Africa. The novella explores three attitudes toward Africa: reactionaryism or old-style colonialism, cooperation, and separatism, all of which seem to be culs-de-sac.

"In a Free State" seems like a 1970s, postcolonial successor to Conrad's *Heart of Darkness*. The novella recounts a journey through bush and forest between outposts of European civilization in Africa. Bobby, an English administrative officer in a former British colony, drives by car from the nation's capital to a government compound up-country; Linda, an acquaintance and the wife of a British official who also lives at the compound, travels with him. Upon her urging, they stop along the way at a hunting lodge run by a crusty former British colonel with whom Linda apparently spends the night. The next day they continue their journey but encounter rain and bad roads and are unable to reach the Southern Collectorate before the four o'clock curfew that is in effect because a secessionist movement threatens the national government. Driving through the region of the rival, secessionist tribe, Bobby and Linda pass menacing army lorries, the abandoned vehicle of the tribe's king, who has been killed, and a line of his supporters now held as prisoners by government soldiers. Trusting to his illusory understanding of Africa, Bobby needlessly gets out of the car at a checkpoint and requests permission to continue the journey. As if in a 1930s Hollywood film about empire and the dark continent, Bobby says to the soldiers: "'Who your officer? Who your boss-man?'" But he loses this sense of authority when a soldier yells out "Boy!" and the white man hesitates (231). The soldiers perceive his loss of confidence and authority and respond by tearing his clothes and kicking him repeatedly until he loses consciousness. When he revives he is not prevented from returning to his car, where Linda waits in ignorance of what has happened; in spite of a broken wrist, he manages to drive away and reach the safety of the government compound in the Southern Collectorate. There he is further humiliated by his houseboy, who upon seeing Bobby's battered state, suspects that he has had a run-in with the soldiers, or perhaps he simply finds him laughable in this condition.

This plot, like that of Conrad's *Heart of Darkness*, moves from city and safety to bush and savagery. Also like *Heart of Darkness* and Naipaul's "Michael X" and *Guerrilla*, the novella creates a mood of fear and menace that intensifies as Bobby and Linda travel farther from the city and deep into the hinterland and culminates in a moment of horror: Bobby's symbolic loss of civilization and his beating at the hands of government soldiers. Within this journey the decaying hunting lodge stands as a beleaguered outpost between the capital at one end and the security of the compound at the other. A remnant of empire, the lodge signifies a bygone era of European penetration and influence on the continent; now it is slowly becoming a part of the jungle, of Africa, and the colonel waits in it, like a soldier in a fort under siege, for the final battle.

The colonel represents a racist and reactionary neocolonialism, an extremist judgment on the inability of Africa to maintain a "civilized" identity without a European authority to shape it—and punish it when it misbehaves. His deprecatory remark, "That's Africa," sums up his prejudice that the continent has always been a land of savagery that, at best, can only be controlled. Although the novella portrays the colonel as an unlikable racist, it supports his attitude toward Africa and Africans through the events of the plot, with references to tribal warfare, the killing of the secessionist tribe's king and torture of his supporters, and Bobby's brutal beating at the hands of government soldiers (185).

Bobby, the novella's main character, represents liberal-minded cooperation; he favors stronger ties between Europe and Africa and believes that, today, Europeans in Africa should listen and serve rather than criticize and command: "I'm not here to tell them how to run their country," he says. "What sort of government the Africans choose to have is none of my business. It doesn't alter the fact that they need food and schools and hospitals" (118). Bobby would seem to be making a persuasive point, but the novella undercuts his attitude of service if only by linking it with a political naïveté, a masking of differences between Europeans and Africans, and a combination of condescension toward and romanticization of Africa: "If I come into the world again I want to come with your colour," Bobby tells a Zulu man whom he tries to proposition (107). The Zulu spits in his face, and it is as if, symbolically, Bobby has sought to be humiliated in this way. His attitude of "service only" is flawed—at once a European guilt and a relinquishing of responsibility. There is no communication between Bobby and Africans; the exchange is always one-sided. The novella links his attitudes with postcolonial European equivocalness in regard to sub-Saharan Africa, a public expression of service yet a private sense of superiority expressed in Bobby's reactions to unexpected situations. After a service-station attendant unintentionally scratches the windshield of Bobby's car, Bobby erupts into a performance of the efficient, angry European confronting the inept African: "I'm going to have you sacked," he threatens, "sent back to your people" (147). Bobby's sense of superiority is expressed in his belief that he understands Africa, though events show the holes in his understanding and his miscalculation of Africans' responses to him: he is spat upon, rejected by Africans he propositions, kicked and beaten by soldiers, and laughed at by his houseboy. Through Bobby the novella critiques a liberalism that seemingly empathizes with the plight of Africa yet uses the continent as a setting for a personal adventure, thus perpetuating the colonial conception of Africa as exotic playground for Europeans.

Linda believes in the separateness of Europeans and Africans, and the events of the plot do not challenge the underlying racist component of that position. There is no interaction between her and black Africa, and therefore she does not risk a response or an examination of her attitudes. She gets along with the bullish colonel for a good reason: like his, her mind is a fortress largely blocked to the entry of any black African. Occasionally Linda's latent racist tendencies flare up—for example, in her response to Bobby's giving a lift to an African hitchhiker: she detests "the smell" of the African in the car (136). But through Linda the novella criticizes liberals like Bobby who in the name of African dignity and independence pretend not to notice the problems of underdeveloped societies and ignore brutalities, like the beatings of prisoners that take place in the Southern Collectorate compound at night. Linda reprimands Bobby for his superficial cooperation yet profound noninvolvement in the affairs of today's Africa (218). She tells him that Europeans should either "stay away" from Africans who support corruption and brutality, or "go among them with the whip." Linda says this offensively, but indeed what should be the European response, for example, to political torture in former African or other colonies, or to the slaughter of 200,000 members of one tribe by government soldiers from another tribe? "In a Free State" raises these questions and implies that no one has any workable answers; the novella is ahead of its time in exposing the contradictions of Western positions in relation to postcolonial Africa and the seeming inability of the West to play an effective part in its development.

The nature of the postcolonial, European presence in Africa is signified by the collectorate compound, which is at once home, fortress, and, ironically, prison. It keeps out the Africa of surrounding bush and forest, while it locks in Europeans like Bobby and Linda in their myths of Africa. Above all, it is the African landscape and its people that constitute the dominant presence in the novella; they become a point of reference, description, and conversation during Bobby's and Linda's drive from the capital to the collectorate compound. Villagers emerge from the bush and forest—as if from the earth—and then disappear back into them. Bobby and Linda are impressed by the seeming mystical expanse of land and sky, as if Africa is everything and nothing, infinity and hole in time: "This was the openness the sky had been promising. . . . The eye lost itself in the colourless distances of the wide valley, dissolving in every direction in cloud and haze" (116). The novella's images of Africa combine opposing meanings: ancient changelessness versus modern upheaval, Africa as sempiternal world versus Africa as shattered, postcolonial, human world. The narrator alludes to the "immemorial life of the forest" and its impact on European exploration and colonization. At the same time, though, he evokes a pathos for its displaced peoples: "They . . . lived, vulnerably now, in villages along their ancient straight roads: roads that had spread their power as forest conquerors, until the first explorers came. . . . But the road now was empty; and the villages [Bobby and Linda] passed were empty, dead, burnt-out" (234). The villagers, the people of the forest, have been swept up, dispossessed by political and social change in postcolonial Africa.

"In a Free State" anticipates violent events in East Africa, such as the breakdown of Uganda in the 1970s, and it taps into the old myth of the dark continent.[12] On the one hand, the novella refers to problems in postcolonial Africa such as tribal conflict and civil wars, the politics of oppression and torture, and the equivocal role of the First World in independent Africa's future development. Yet on the other hand, it superimposes its own mood of menace and horror on this actuality. The narrator of *The Enigma of Arrival* describes the landscape of a novella like "In a Free State" as a "made-up Africa." "Such violence in my Africa," he recalls. "So much had gone into that Africa of my fantasy" (*EA* 169–72). Here, the fantasy culminates in brutality—Bobby's beating—and a return to a simpler Africa of the hunter and the hunted.

The essay "The Circus at Luxor" closes the collection; it reflects on the rise and fall of civilizations and the ways of seeing that distinguish them. The tomb paintings that the author views at Karnak depict a stylized, "pure" time when the Nile was a "blue-green chevron," "a river in fairyland" (241). But surely no such time ever existed, Naipaul muses; the Nile is muddy, and the world of the living is filled with conflict and change. The Egyptian soldiers he sees near the ruins become his symbol for the decline of Egyptian civilization, from its grandeur at Karnak to contemporary poverty and humiliations: "Seventeen months later these [soldiers], or men like them, were to know total defeat in the desert; and news photographs taken from helicopters flying down low were to show them lost, trying to walk back home, casting long shadows on the sand" (246). Through this image, Naipaul inverts the vision of the Karnak paintings: the dark lines in the photographs replace the blue-green chevron of the ancient paintings. It would be reductive, though, to equate his description of the photographs with "reality" and the tomb painting with the "fabrication" of art. Naipaul describes the defeated soldiers poetically: they "[cast] long shadows on the sand," and this language conveys, once again, the vision of loss and unmaking of *In a Free State*. His comment on Jacques Soustelle's "romance" of defeat can serve as a gloss on his own reading of the wall paintings and the aerial photographs: "The pattern, too neat, belongs to art."[13] It is in this sense of reality shaped, refracted by a particular prism of the writer's attitudes, that history turns into story and sub-Saharan Africa in Naipaul's novels of the 1970s becomes a Fourth World.

### *Guerrillas* (1975)

*Guerrillas* contains some of the same elements as "In a Free State": a confrontation of attitudes about the postcolonial world, an unstable developing country, an uprising or rebellion, and a culminating moment of horror. Just as the plot of "In a Free State" progresses toward, and is about, Bobby's humiliation and beating, so too *Guerrillas* progresses toward, and is about, Jane's killing. Whether fairly or unfairly, convincingly or unconvincingly, the novel equates Black Power in the Caribbean not with a profound empowerment of the people, but with racism and regression, with a return to a kind of mentality of the tribe. The novel attempts to invert the 1960s romanticized concept of guerrillas and revolution, just as Naipaul's earlier novels about West Indian politics ironically inverted concepts like universal adult suffrage and island independence. The author has written three novels about politics in the Caribbean—*The Suffrage of Elvira*, *The Mimic Men*, and *Guerrillas*—and it is worth noting that each of these depicts a breakdown or an emerging breakdown of society. In *The Suffrage of Elvira*, an election campaign divides a rural community and ends with the populist burning of the winning candidate's new, expensive British automobile; in *The Mimic Men*, independence eventually brings the overthrow of Singh's nationalist party, Singh's exile, and the worsening socioeconomic plight of Isabella; in *Guerrillas*, a popular uprising fizzles into vandalism against Chinese merchants, the humiliation of a government official ("They strip him naked. Joseph say somebody even put a knife to the man's balls"), and the hacking to death of a white Englishwoman.[14] Behind each of these books is a distrust and fear of the "people"—a fear overpowering the author's countersense of the Trinidad-like island's beauty and vitality.

Very little happens in *Guerrillas*, and perhaps because of this what does happen stands out more starkly. Much of the novel consists of reflections and dialogues in which, as at Harry de Tunja's Sunday beach parties, individuals mark off their positions vis-à-vis one another and their unstable island world. Three of the main characters are exiles of one sort or another. Jane, an Englishwoman, and her husband Peter Roche, a white South African, have recently emigrated to this Trinidad-like island where class and racial tensions are mounting. Jane has no occupation other than that of an intellectual vaguely sympathetic with revolutionary causes. Author and former guerrilla in South Africa, where he was imprisoned for his opposition to the racist white government, Roche has settled into a comfortable public relations position at Sablich's, an island firm that became a success through the slave trade (76–77). Hiring Roche the celebrated activist-author is the company's way of trying to improve its image on the island. The company also seeks to change that image by supporting Jimmy Leung's (alias Jimmy Ahmed's) commune, a back-to-the-earth project run by Jimmy and poor blacks as a cover for a guerrilla base. Roche supports Jimmy's efforts, though he does not perceive that the commune, named Thrushcross Grange, is a cover. Jane recognizes this immediately and pursues Jimmy for the adventure and out of disappointment with her marriage to Roche, a now middle-aged man worn out by his South African experience and finally passive with her and others. After a fellow guerrilla, Stephens, is shot on a city street by police, Jimmy and others carry the body through the neighborhood and set off a looting of shops and calls for revolution by the Arrow of Peace; the government declares a state of emergency and hints at an American intervention to restore order. Believing that her life has run into another dead end, Jane decides to leave Roche and the island and to return to England. She pays a final visit to Jimmy, who uses her to get his revenge on an empire that has given him a fractured identity as a partly Chinese, partly African, partly Anglicized West Indian. Jimmy and his lover Bryant hack Jane to death and bury her body on the commune. Visiting Thrushcross Grange the same day, Roche senses a "slaughterground"; he realizes that Jane has been killed and that he must run for his life. Back at his comfortable house on the Ridge, a fashionable suburb of the city, he destroys Jane's ticket and passport, which has no record of her entry on the island, and when Jimmy calls, Roche lets him know tacitly that he will remain silent and do nothing about her murder.

*Guerrillas* grows out of events in Trinidad in the late 1960s and early 1970s and out of the author's identity as an East Indian, a significant minority group on the predominantly black island. In spite of Trinidad's gap between rich and poor—the top 10 percent of the households receive a third of the income and the bottom 40 percent, only about 10 percent[15]—the island has been fairly stable politically since its independence in 1962. However, two notorious exceptions were the Black Power riots in 1970 and the attempted coup d'état of a radical Islamic group, Jamaat Al Muslimeen, in 1990.[16] Referring to the former, as well as to East Indians' status in Trinidad society, the narrator of the semiautobiographical *Enigma of Arrival* sheds light on the background of *Guerrillas:* "Twenty years [after I left for England] the Negroes of Trinidad, following those of the United States, were asserting their separateness. They simplified and sentimentalized the past" (*EA* 159–60). The narrator recalls seeing young blacks "marching in the streets" and "threatening another false revolution," and he interprets their motives as "a wish to destroy a world judged corrupt and too full of pain, to turn one's back on it, rather than to improve it" (*EA* 161). He interprets Black Power less from a socioeconomic perspective than from that of his own ethnic community— "the people mainly threatened, not black, not white" (*EA* 161). "Part of the fear of extinction which I had developed as a child had to do with this," he confesses, "the fear of being swallowed up or extinguished by the simplicity of one side or the other, my side or the side that wasn't mine" (*EA* 152–53). This personal sense of ethnic tensions informs *Guerrillas'* portrait of a schizophrenic Jimmy Ahmed, Bryant, and Stephens and explains something of the acerbity of the novel's attack on Black Power, which the author interprets as an intimidation of non-"blacks" in a multiracial society. The novel attacks what he perceives as the inapplicability, programlessness, and millenaristic fantasy of the 1960s and 1970s Black Power movement in the region. As a West Indian, as one who understands the gradations of "color" in these islands, Naipaul considers Black Power a myth of ethnic purity used as a weapon.

The vivid descriptions of landscape and the multivoiced, lyric Caribbean dialogue aside, *Guerrillas* is Naipaul's most narrowly focused, overtly ideological novel, with the characters representing different positions and points of view about the postcolonial world. Of these characters, four stand out: Jane, Roche, Meredith Herbert, and Jimmy Ahmed. Jane represents a middle-class liberalism of the times that Naipaul attacks here and elsewhere for its hollowness: Jane can do little more than wish that the world were different. As a middle-class English expatriate, she has the privilege to act out a revolutionary identity while at the same time remaining attached to her distanced, safe identity as an Englishwoman in a former British colony. This is symbolized by her "return ticket," her ability to change back from one identity to another and to fly away when trouble arises. She enjoys the privilege of her white, English identity as well as the sense of her rejection of that identity that her relationship with Jimmy Ahmed and her life on the West Indian island afford. Jane carries within her, the narrator says, "scattered, unrelated ideas," "the debris of a dozen [ideological] systems" (56). Her macabre murder analogizes a split within her self.

Peter Roche and Meredith Herbert form contrasting portraits of activists whose commitments have carried them in opposite directions. Roche has spoken out against "white aggression" in his country and been jailed and tortured for the blowing up of bridges and other guerrilla acts; now a political exile—Jane calls him a "refugee"—he works as a public relations officer, a "doer of good works, with results that never showed, someone who went among the poor on behalf of his firm and tried to organize boys' clubs and sporting events, gave this cup here and offered a gift of cricket equipment there" (54). The biggest thing about Roche is that he's burnt out; no cause can really move him anymore: "he knew that to many people he appeared as a man given over to a cause. It was understandable, but it was strange; because he had no political dogma and no longer had a vision of a world made good, and perhaps had never had such a vision" (99–100).

Along with Harry de Tunja, a character to be discussed momentarily, Meredith Herbert is one of the novel's best realized portraits. Solicitor, political star, then political dropout, a radio show interviewer, a family man, Meredith has grown up on the island and has a stake in its future. He can be domineering, a performer, less than straightforward with friends about unfolding events; yet his words carry with them the weight of someone who truly belongs to his society. These differences between Meredith and Roche are highlighted during the radio interview in which Meredith questions him on his South African past and his present life on the island. Meredith tells Roche that his credentials as a South African guerrilla are irrelevant in the West Indies: "You've endured terrible things. . . . But it's a dead end. It doesn't do anything for the rest of us" (243). Meredith exposes as simplistic any analogy between issues in South Africa and those in the West Indies; he portrays Roche as ineffectual and manipulated by the very elements that he is supposedly struggling against. When, at the end of the radio interview, Roche blunders into an equation of "guerrillas" with "gangs," Meredith's victory is complete (245–46).

Through Jimmy Ahmed as character and caricature, the novel attacks the idea of the portable revolution and peripatetic revolutionaries, that is, the notion that revolution can be transported from one social context to another and that men like Jimmy are its vehicles. Jimmy views himself as carrier of "the burden" of Fanon's damned of the earth: "all the suffering people in the world . . . the people who live in shacks and grow up in dirty little back rooms" (39). But the novel undercuts this position by setting up an incongruity between his life and his fantasized identity. Meredith notes that Jimmy's class origins are less proletarian than they may appear; he points out that a shopowner's son, unlike many others on the island, would not go hungry. He also points out that if a revolution ever begins, Jimmy (Leung), who imagines himself a "Black Stallion," will be viewed by the people as just another Chinaman. As Mrs. Stephens says to Roche: "What is the sweetness with that Chinee man . . . ? Who give him all that big fame in England? What he doing with those boys? Knolly was a good, good boy" (120–21). The novel portrays Jimmy as a man made half-foreign by his exile in England and as a revolutionary manqué out of touch with the underlying currents of ethnic attitudes in his own society. Returning to the theme of mimicry that is so much a part of earlier works, the author portrays Jimmy as a mimic of others' ideas and actions, which are especially European.

In one sense, *Guerrillas* is a kind of Afro-Gothic horror story. It portrays Jimmy as the "programmed" monster, a Frankenstein or creation of bits and parts of 1960s revolutionary ideology; Harry de Tunja calls him a "succubus." Thrushcross Grange, the decaying agricultural commune, and the slums of the city beyond it represent the Gothic castle and dangerous environs (27). Jane is the unsuspecting victim—humiliated, sodomized, pierced by machetes and hacked to death—whose brutal murder is a premonition of a Trinidadian and West Indian breakdown that the author feared might come to be and that he thought of as a "return to the bush," a postcolonial dead end.[17]

In trenchantly attacking Black Power in the Caribbean, does Naipaul write a racist novel? *Guerrillas* has a racist element, but its target is not an ethnic group per se but the idea of a pure, ethnic group and the idea of "guerrillas." Naipaul seeks to appropriate the word *guerrillas*, to remove it from leftist, 1960s and 1970s discourse about revolution, strip it of its progressive connotations, and "populate" it with meanings that grow out of his understanding as Trinidad Indian and as exile.[18] In the novel's authorial evaluation, guerrillas do not create a new, better society, but rather push society backward. By appropriating the word *guerrillas*, Naipaul seeks to call into the question the idea of revolution—especially a revolution based on a concept of racial purity—as a viable mode of social change in the Caribbean.[19] A major problem in the novel, though, is that Jimmy's portrait and those of the other guerrillas seem to be caricatures, and thus the novel's attempted revision of the concept of "guerrillas" falters because that attempt partakes of the exaggeration or distortion.

Asked by interviewers Boyers and Mukherjee about other controversial aspects of the novel such as Jane's sodomy and murder, Naipaul replied: "I was appalled." *Guerrillas* "is the only book I know," he added, "which is really about an act of murder. That is why it's shocking—and the fact that it shocks you is part of its success."[20] But is the novel, a fictionalization of the material of "Michael X and the Black Power Killings in Trinidad," a success? Called a masterpiece by some, attacked by others, *Guerrillas* is difficult to read with an unbiased mind. Three points are worth noting here: first, the novel's constructed vision of Caribbean society brings together elements of other works from other periods about Trinidad politics and democracy, particularly *The Suffrage of Elvira* and *The*

*Mimic Men,* and to consider these three novels together might offer an illuminating analysis. Second, although *Guerrillas'* denouement has given it a notoriety, for me the novel's most interesting aspect is not the shock of what happens, but the portraits of three characters—Roche, Meredith, and especially Harry de Tunja—and the dialogues in which they engage. In this otherwise grim book, the portrait of Harry de Tunja and the banter between Harry and Merry-boy (Meredith) show the author's affection for the people and land about which he has written. There is a vitality there that outlasts the novel's shock appeal. Third, more than two decades after his exile from the colony, Naipaul seems still to need to construct a vision of an island flawed by carnival and calypso. "This is a country that has been destroyed by music," Harry remarks half-jokingly. "If I had my way I would ban music. And dancing. Make it a crime. Six months for every record you play. And hard labor for the reggae. . . . You just have to think what is going on right now on that beach. And think how lovely and quiet it would be, eh. None of that reggae-reggae the whole blasted day" (144–45). Was it Borges who wrote that Argentina will never progress until it bans the tango? Harry's diatribe can be read in the same vein, although there is something else here. Harry, an East Indian who immigrated to the island from South America, is hypersensitive because he believes that his own identity gets swallowed by this culture not quite his own; he does not want to be known as "Calypso Harry," as he was in Toronto, Canada, just because he had lived on the Trinidad-like island. At one of his Sunday beach parties he explains playfully: "How the hell can you respect a guy who starts tapping his feet to music and jigging up in his chair? Apart from everything else, I find it looks so damn common. Especially if the guy is a little old. You feel the feller has no control at all, and that at any moment he is going to tear his clothes off and start prancing about the room." Harry's diatribe reveals something of the author's attitude toward the island from which he lives in exile—an island that, in his construct, limits abilities, swallows identity, and renders everyone finally "so damn common." Harry seems to have all the answers—or at least he thinks he does. During the uprising, when looting breaks out in the city, radio reports from the BBC blame the troubles on unemployment and foreign domination of the economy, but Harry, not unlike the author, sees things a bit differently; what is happening, he says, is a craziness (220). Although

*Guerrillas* contains passages that show the author's inverted affection for the island he left behind, and although the novel is based on events in the region, what dominates is the resonance of an exile's not-belonging and a sense that, as in a myth or fairy tale, some malady, some irrationality, lingers over a land and its people.

## *A Bend in the River* (1979)

*A Bend in the River* refers to the sociopolitical turmoil of postcolonial Zaire: ethnic conflicts, secessionist movements and governmental retaliation, periods of boom and bust tied to the price of copper, a dictator's ideological program, the nationalization of businesses, corruption, and bribery. Salim, the novel's narrator and main character, a shopowner of Indian Muslim origin, tries to remain outside of the country's turmoil but is inevitably drawn into it. He recounts, in retrospect, his journey from an East African coastal community ("an Arab-Indian-Persian-Portuguese place") to a town at the "bend in the river" of a central African country where he reopens the shop of a friend and counsel, Nazruddin.[21] He accepts Nazruddin's offer to take up shopkeeping because he has come to a dead end in his life; he believes that he must leave his effete Indian Muslim community or be washed away by change along with it. In time Salim the shopkeeper prospers as the river town undergoes a boom tied to the rise in copper prices. His relative prosperity and contentment are short-lived, though, for the country and his situation in it as an Indian Muslim businessman are permanently unstable. Through a visit from a childhood friend, Indar, he begins to see his life from a new perspective and recognizes his unfulfilled ambitions. University educated in England, the son of a banking family, Indar has come to the river town as a consultant to the Domain, a newly established university city and research institute whose objective is to produce the modern African. When tribal and political turmoil erupt again, Indar leaves, but not before introducing Salim to a group of European intellectuals at the Domain, particularly Raymond, a historian and adviser to the country's president, and Yvette, Raymond's wife, with whom Salim is immediately fascinated. Salim and Yvette begin a relationship based on their mutual disappointments in life and their need for a sense of self-worth, realized through each other.

Copper prices fall, another rebellion breaks out, and the Domain is abandoned, the expensive project falling into disrepair and dereliction. Yvette and Salim eventually recognize the differences in their situations, and their relationship ends in his battering of her. Salim goes to England to visit Nazruddin; comprehending that he no longer has a future in Africa, he decides to marry Nazruddin's daughter and stay in England. But first he must return to the town at the bend in the river to sell his shop and collect the valuables he has cached in its backyard. On his arrival he finds that the shop and other European businesses have been nationalized by the "Big Man," the country's messianic president. Salim turns to black-marketing, is reported by his houseboy, and is jailed. Fortuitously, he is released by a former acquaintance, Ferdinand, the son of his first client at the shop, who is also the newly appointed commissioner of the region. Ferdinand tells Salim to leave the country for good or risk being arrested again, beaten, and perhaps killed. Taking only a suitcase, Salim barely manages to escape on the next river steamer.

Like the characters of "In a Free State" and *Guerrillas*, those of *A Bend in the River* present various ideological attitudes and positions in the postcolonial world. Salim looks at the town at the bend in the river through the eyes of an exile; he seeks to prosper in that community, but he remains an observer and outsider. He belongs nowhere—neither in central Africa nor in the effete Indian Muslim community of the East African coast: "We couldn't protect ourselves; we could only in various forms hide from the truth. To stay with my community . . . was to be taken with them to destruction. I could be master of my fate only if I stood alone" (20). Salim conceives of history as a "tide" that is sweeping him and other Indians in Africa away: "One tide of history . . . had brought us here. . . . Now . . . another tide of history was coming to wash us away" (20). He rebels against the "old ways," with their authoritarianism, fatal acceptances, and self-contained vision (19). His restlessness and rebellion serve him well, enabling him to break away from his dying, enclaved community and to prosper in the midst of social instability and breakdown. But they carry with them a price, a sense of homelessness and a lack of a social sensibility.

Salim is a hybrid of "voices" and attitudes, a mixture of insight yet self-deception, practicality yet adventure, skepticism yet naïveté. He is a shrewd shopkeeper who knows how to make a profit, yet he has a hunger for experience and can be reckless, as in his relationship with Yvette (the wife of a presidential adviser) and in his black-marketing in ivory and gold. At times he seems not quite an adult, only partially developed intellectually and socially: he looks up the meaning of *uranium* in a children's encyclopedia, and is oddly attracted by the photos of Yvette as a girl (94, 184). Yet he sees clearly the cracks in the facade of the expatriate Europeans at the Domain and the fallacies of the "new," postcolonial African society. He can critique himself, as in the following passage where he describes his reading as an expression of both curiosity and self-deception: "[I was reading] a magazine of popular science, the kind of reading I had become addicted to. I liked receiving little bits of knowledge; and I often thought . . . that the particular science or field I was reading about was the thing to which I should have given my days and nights, adding knowledge to knowledge, making discoveries, making something of myself, using all my faculties. It was a good feeling; from my point of view, it was as good as the life of knowledge itself" (43). As "narrating self" Salim can critique the illusions of Salim as "experiencing self"; the former perceives the difference between illusion and actuality. His story, in fact, constitutes an autocritique in which the narrator evaluates the attitudes and actions of the character in the narrative.

Salim then exists as two entities in the novel; he exists dialogically: his present self (i.e., Salim as a raconteur) describes, reflects on, and evaluates his former self (i.e., Salim as a personage in the events of the story). Moreover, within Salim as raconteur there exists a division, an unsynthesized dialectic whose poles are the conflicting worldviews expressed at the beginning and end of the novel. The novel's first sentence—"The world is what it is; men who are nothing, who allow themselves to become nothing, have no place in it"—asserts a belief in individualism and will (3). Yet images and views at other points in the novel, particularly at the end, present a determinism that stands in opposition to this ideology of will. For example, Salim, echoing Indar's words, alludes to the "tides" of history that overwhelm peoples and civilizations; he compares the community of the town at the bend in the river to ants marching, as if programmed, in regimented columns; he describes the chthonic power of the bush and jungle to erase the "civilization" built on its margins. At the end of the novel, Salim escapes town not through his own willpower but through Ferdinand's fortuitous intervention in his behalf. The final sentences focus on the bush and jungle, which envelop the steamer and Salim its passenger, making men seem small amid nature's profusion and giantism: "The steamer started up again and moved without lights down the river, away from the area of battle. The air would have been full of moths and flying insects. The searchlight, while it was on, had shown thousands, white in the white light" (278).

Indar, Salim's alter-ego, presents an extremist response to the condition of the postcolonial Third World, to the cultural collision between traditional and Western values. For Indar, the only liberating response for someone in the developing world to this collision of cultures is to reject the past; the past exists only in the mind, and through an effort of will the individual can master it and go forward, he believes: "You trample on the past, you crush it. . . . That is the way we have to learn to live now" (112–13). Indar's is less a philosophy of will, though, than the rebound of the Third World refugee-exile, who has rebelled against tradition, authority, fate. "We make ourselves according to the ideas we have of ourselves," he tells Salim (152). Yet to "trample" is not to make anew syncretistically; it is, in part, to repress and mask. Thus for Indar one bound (from the values of his coastal Indian Muslim community) will eventually lead to a rebound; he becomes a prisoner of his own dialectic, first trampling on the past and then instilling it with all value. He returns to India to look for "some dream village in his head" (244).

Father Huismans represents a neocolonialism whose contradictory mission is to implant European culture while collecting and preserving African culture. Like other equivocal, liberal-minded Westerners in Naipaul's 1970s novels who seek a bond with African or Afro-American peoples, Huismans comes to a brutal end—he is beheaded, his connection with Africa literally and symbolically sundered. The values of his European identity constitute his strength and his weakness, causing him to misunderstand Africa: "The idea [he] had of his civilization had made him live his particular kind of dedicated life. It had sent him looking, inquiring; it had made him find human richness where the rest of us saw bush or had stopped seeing anything at all. But his idea of civilization was also like his vanity. It had made him read too much in that mingling of peoples by our river; and he had paid for it" (82). Huismans represents a certain Western viewpoint that looks at Africa as a museum (or wildlife reserve) rather than as a changing, human world of cultures in conflict and collision. He is killed by his idea of the "True Africa," into which he is, finally, absorbed: "His body was put in a dugout, and the dugout drifted down the main river until it caught against the bank in a tangle of water hyacinths" (64, 82).

Raymond, historian and the "Big Man's white man," represents still another facet of the First World's relationship with the Third World: he is the mediocrity that it sometimes exported there. Raymond occupies an ideological niche adjacent to Father Huismans: both are bearers of European culture; both are more attuned to the past than the present, Huismans with his collection of African masks and Raymond with his history of African development. The diligent, inspired Huismans is portrayed sympathetically, however, whereas Raymond is not. Salim considers Raymond's historical work sterile, uninformed by African people and places. He remarks disparagingly of his writings, methods, and sensibility as an ethnologist: "He gave no reasons and looked for none; he just quoted from the missionary reports. He didn't seem to have gone to any of the places he wrote about; he hadn't tried to talk to anybody. . . . he had less true knowledge of Africa, less feel for it, than Indar or Nazruddin or even Mahesh; he had nothing like Father Huismans' instinct for the strangeness and wonder of the place" (182). Both Raymond and Huismans reflect a receding European presence in the central African country, just as the names of its towns have been Africanized and the statues of King Leopold and his colonial explorers defaced or removed. Raymond is symbolically beheaded, removed from his purported position of influence as adviser to the president; he becomes, Salim hears, the Big Man's catcher of evil spirits, the "white man" who draws on himself all "the bad things" directed at the president (260).

Yvette, Raymond's wife, is another of Naipaul's superficial, Western females. (Other than the domineering Mrs. Tulsi, there is no strong female character in his novels.) Salim associates Yvette with the glamour of the Domain; although she half wants to flee its stifling environment, its tendrils of privilege pull her back and divide her identity. In characters like Yvette the author, as someone who has grown up in a developing country, seems to invest a mixture of attraction and repulsion for certain aspects of Western culture, its seductiveness and shallowness. Other female characters who evolve out of this tendency are Laraine of *An Area of Darkness*, Linda of "In a Free State," and Jane of *Guerillas*.

The Big Man, the president of the central African country of the novel, symbolizes an ideological distortion paralleled by the country's defaced monuments and deteriorating buildings and machinery. The epithet "Big Man" (one is reminded of Orwell's "Big Brother") links the president with totalitarianism; it also links him with the pretentious inscription on the steamer-service monument ("he approves of the mingling of peoples and their bonds of union") and with the Domain, the gigantic development project that was the president's brainchild. The president has fostered a personality cult, exemplified by images and photos that depict him as larger and taller than other men. He is a grotesque just as the bush and jungle, in the novel, are grotesque or monstrous.[22]

Son of a sorceress, Domain educated, and rising to the post of regional commissioner, Ferdinand embodies the conflict between the old and the new Africa. Salim talks of him demeaningly: "He could never be simple. The more he tried, the more confused he became. His mind wasn't empty, as I had begun to think. It was a jumble, full of all kinds of junk" (54). In Ferdinand's attitudes and responses Salim imagines a savage "history of the land" where "men ha[ve] always been prey" (55). " 'This is the rage that flattened the town,' " he says of the young Ferdinand's response to a humiliating remark (59). But Salim's judgment turns out to be one-sided. For it is Ferdinand who releases Salim from jail and, in a sense, saves his life. Ferdinand comprehends better than Salim the trauma of contemporary Africa and the plight of so many people caught in the cross fire: "You mustn't think it's bad just for you. It's bad for everybody. . . . We're all going to hell, and every man knows this in his bones. . . . Everyone wants to . . . run away. But where? That is what is driving people mad. They feel they're losing the place they can run back to" (272). Salim escapes, Ferdinand and his people do not.

Through dichotomies between history and timelessness, Western progress and African unmaking, "rational" Europe and "irrational" Africa, *A Bend in the River* overlays its references to postcolonial Congo (Zaire) with a myth of Africa the dark continent. The African bush and jungle are infused with a primitive, chthonic, sempiternal power. Salim muses: "In daylight . . . you could believe in . . . the future. . . . But at night. . . . You felt the land taking you back to what was there a hundred years ago, to what had been there always" (9). In his vision of the "True Africa," no matter the continent's efforts to develop, it always returns, in cycles of half-making and unmaking, to a primitive stage identified with the bush and forest: "People lived as they had always done; there was no break between past and present. All that happened in the past was washed away; there was always only the present. It was as though, as a result of some disturbance in the heavens, the early morning light was always receding into the darkness, and men lived in a perpetual dawn" (10, 12). In this vision of Africa, time runs backward, and people and land blend mystically into one prehistoric being.

Salim mystifies the African landscape, investing it with special powers; this, coupled with a mood of breakdown and a menace of violence, define the Afro-Gothic quality of *A Bend in the River* and of Naipaul's 1970s novels. Salim has a special eye for decay; he points out the irony of the Latin inscription on the monument commemorating steamer service on the river: "two-thousand-year-old words [from the *Aeneid*] to celebrate sixty years of the steamer service from the capital! . . . And almost as soon as it had been put up the monument had been destroyed, leaving only bits of bronze and the mocking words" (63). Like the monument, the grandiose Domain, a university city and research institute set in bush and jungle, begins to fall into disrepair even before its completion: the waterless swimming pool is capped with wire mesh; the tractors for the envisioned, yet never completed, farm stand idle and rusting. The Domain loses its Western aura and becomes Africanized, overrun by bush and appropriated by townspeople; it devolves from university city to "housing settlement": "Maize . . . grew in many places; and the purple-green leaves of the cassava . . . created the effect of garden shrubs. This piece of earth—how many changes had come to it! Forest at a bend in the river, a meeting place, an Arab settlement, a European outpost, a European suburb, a ruin like the ruin of a dead civilization, the glittering Domain of Africa, and now this" (260). Like the colonial monuments, the Domain becomes an ironic testament to unmaking.

*A Bend in the River*'s vision of Africa can be viewed from three intersecting planes: history, myth, and autobiography. In Salim's vision, Africa is flawed by the very nature of its Africanness; the continent is "going back to its old ways with modern tools," as if its turmoil and underdevelopment were endemic (201). It is as though "some disturbance in the heavens" has made Africa what it is, fixing it forever in state of primitiveness (12). The continent's identity takes on a mythic element: the "light . . . always receding into darkness" is like Sisyphus' stone, always rolling back down the hill after he has laboriously pushed it to the top. Though also limited, Indar's analysis of Africa is closer to the truth: "'Everything had conspired to push black Africa into every kind of tyranny,'" he remarks (154). We need to separate the myth from the reality: historically, the plight of Africa originates not in a debilitating Africanness, but in colonialism; today that plight has worsened because of a postcolonial, economic order that virtually assures that the continent will remain indebted and underdeveloped. Similarly, tribal warfare—a bane's of the town at the bend of the river—may be ancient, but today's wars in Africa, although they often have an ethnic dimension,[23] are rooted in today's political and socioeconomic problems, not in an endemic Africanness.

Sub-Saharan Africa is not innately flawed, but it is still recouping from centuries of colonialism, which left it with a scarcity of doctors, teachers, administrators, scientists, and technicians. When Belgium, the final colonizing power in the Congo (Zaire), departed in 1960, it left an artificially demarcated, regionally divided country with an uneducated and untrained people. At its independence, the Congo had a bewildering 120 political parties, the majority with an ethnic connection. Only 16 Congolese had graduated from a university and only 136 had completed secondary school. Of 1,400 civil service posts, only 2 were held by Congolese. In other professions, there were no Congolese doctors, secondary school teachers, or army officers.[24] Similarly in Angola, at the time of its independence in 1975, after five centuries of Portuguese rule, 98 percent of the country's native population were illiterate, and only a few people had any technical skills or an education beyond high school.[25] Their peoples uneducated and unskilled, by Western standards, economically dependent on and caught in an uneven exchange with the former colonial powers, the countries of sub-Saharan Africa were never prepared to compete in a postcolonial, global economy, though they were incorporated into it—to the First World's advantage.[26]

Naipaul's 1970s novels at once look back to Western discourse about the "dark continent"[27] and forward to a contemporary Western evaluation of the illusion of development in the Third World. They put forward a scenario of the Africa of tomorrow in which development is, ironically, a movement backward, a dissolution. In the 1970s Naipaul observed what Africa became in the 1980s—the "dead-end decade"[28]—and what some social and economic analysts fear that Africa will become more acutely in the 1990s and twenty-first century: a region of accelerating breakdown. Salim's Africa as a perpetual dawn fading into darkness is a myth, but Africa's and the Third World's backward movement is very much a reality. According to the Agency for International Development, "most developing countries are actually regressing"; "citizens of the world's poorest countries were better off 10, 20, or even 30 years ago."[29] Nineteen of the twenty-five poorest nations are African.[30]

On this actuality, Naipaul's 1970s novels superimpose myth and autobiography. The myth—their "dark vision" of a continent running down—has helped shape the style of Western journalists who write about the continent. Is it not something of Naipaul that we hear in this passage that describes breakdown in postcolonial Angola?

Walking through Luanda . . . I was struck by the eerie notion that I had entered a living ghost town, that here was the African city of the twenty-first century. It had people but no sense of life or purpose. Block after block of stores were closed, their windows broken and boarded up. Neon signs flashed mysteriously about IBM, Sony and Singer shoprooms that had been empty for years. Hotel employees snoozed at the reception counters, and government workers slouched behind desks that were barren of telephones, typewriters, pencils or paper. Elevators were stuck where they had jammed two or three years earlier, and air conditioners coughed and sputtered and threw out blasts of hot air.[31]

Writing about postcolonial Africa in this way has become a discourse that dialogically links it with earlier colonial discourse about the "dark continent": today the signs say IBM, Sony, and Singer, whereas a century ago it was another technology abandoned in the jungle. Actuality and myth are tangled together such that to write about dissolution in contemporary Africa from a Western perspective is sooner or later to write about or within the myth.[32] (A related instance of this entanglement of discourses and of art and actuality concerns the controversy in India over the film, *La*

*Cité de la joie*, and the book that the film is based on. Some Indian intellectuals accuse the filmmaker and the author of portraying India in neocolonial stereotypes—the India of beggars, lepers, *tuberculeux*, criminals, and prostitutes—but the filmmaker, Roland Joffé, and author, Dominique Lapierre, have defended their portrayals as ones based on actualities. The title of a *Le Monde* article states the problem well, "Peut-on filmer la pauvreté?" [Can you film poverty?].) Even so, we need to realize that there are other visions of Africa and the developing world. Naipaul finds a different, less dismal vision of India in *India: A Million Mutinies Now*. Others—but not many—have as well: former United Nations ambassador Andrew Young has pointed out that Africa can have a promising future; it has immense natural resources and a youthful population.[33] The very breakdown that is taking place in Africa may be a sign of a difficult postcolonial democratization of the continent.[34]

Finally, there is an informative autobiographical element in Naipaul's 1970s novels. *A Bend in the River*, as well as "In a Free State" and *Guerrillas*, is pervaded by an exile's sensibility; to the novel's construction of a Third World regressing into a "Fourth World" of people without places, Naipaul brings his sense of homelessness and his colony-induced "fear of extinction." Although the novel's controversial opening would seem to speak unfeelingly of those people in Africa and other regions of the developing world who are, indeed, being squeezed into nothing, in that sentence we can also hear an exile's anxiety and his understanding of recent history's pitiless course.

# 8

# Exile and Enigma of Arrival

> . . . everyday life can become literature, and literature can become life.
> —M. M. Bakhtin and P. N. Medvedev, *The Formal Method in Literary Scholarship*
>
> . . . man is the novelist of himself.
> —José Ortega y Gasset, "History as a System"

In "The Mourners" (1950), Naipaul's earliest piece of published writing, the narrator Romesh observes the grief of a mother and father at the death of their young son. " 'It makes you think, doesn't it? . . . Here today. Gone tomorrow. It makes you think about life and death, doesn't it?' " the father laments.[1] "The Mourners" suggests Romesh's awakening to a sense of loss and his turning to art (the story that he is telling) as a response to his own grief and that of the mother and father, who cannot stop thinking about their son and want to show a photograph album of him to Romesh. He does not have the heart to tell them that he has already seen the photographs.

Readers familiar with Naipaul's works may recall "The Mourners" while reading "The Ceremony of Farewell," the final section of *The Enigma of Arrival*, in which the narrator spreads photographs of his deceased sister, Sati, on a coffee table and thinks of her on the day she is to be cremated in faraway Trinidad: "I felt purged," he explains. "I had

had no rules to follow; but I felt I had done the right thing. I had concentrated on that person, that life, that unique character; I had honored the person who had lived."[2] Through this recollection and its transformation into art (by the narrator's writing about it), the deceased sister is honored and grief is dispelled. The world needs words, and life needs art to understand it, commemorate it, and safeguard it, if only briefly, from the extinction of forgetfulness and thoughtlessness. Without words the world remains full of incomprehensible spirits, or as the narrator wonders of a simple family he meets in Waldenshaw: "What terrors must there have been in the town for them! How could people like these, without words to put to their emotions and passions, manage? They could, at best, only suffer dumbly. Their pains and humiliations would work themselves out in their characters alone: like evil spirits possessing a body" (34). Through words the narrator commemorates Sati, Jack the gardener, and others at Waldenshaw, and through them he understands himself as a maker of "his own world" (93). Through words he creates a sense of beginnings and endings, and enacts a concord between self and world. "Men, like poets," Frank Kermode writes, "need fictive concords with origins and ends, such as give meaning to lives and poems."[3]

From the first, Naipaul has responded to loss and exile through art: "The Mourners" commemorates a boy; *A House for Mr Biswas*, a father; *The Mimic Men*, an East Indian-West Indian exile in England; *The Enigma of Arrival*, a sister (Sati) and a brother (Shiva).[4] The novel is dedicated to the memory of the latter, an international novelist and journalist who died of a heart attack at the age of forty in 1985; a semi-autobiographical novel, it honors a brother and fellow author by writing about the subject of the writer and the act of writing. It reflects on death, and change generally, from autobiographical and historical perspectives, and synthesizes recurring themes in the narrator's and author's life and art. The novel attempts to heal a division between "man" and "writer" that the narrator-author has experienced since his departure as a youth from Trinidad for England. The writer and the man unite in acts of creation and commemoration; as in a ritual, the narrator-author heals a wound, banishes "evil spirits," and constructs a new self and world. He affirms life— people must be doers "every day of their lives," the narrator-author declares—and he affirms words in their therapeutic power to serve life by releasing its energies and by creating a sense of belonging in the world (343).[5]

Written as a first-person narrative, *The Enigma of Arrival* (1987) comprises five chapters: "Jack's Garden," "The Journey," "Ivy," "Rooks," and "The Ceremony of Farewell." The first chapter describes the rhythms and personages in the life of the novel's unnamed narrator at Waldenshaw, a manor and village near Salisbury, England, where he has rented a cottage for ten years. A Trinidad Indian in his forties, he has come to this corner of the Wiltshire countryside to escape the city and to overcome the exhaustion of his peripatetic life as an international writer. At Waldenshaw he feels as if he has reentered his childhood "romance of [a] Constable reproduction"; he inhabits a place where "time had stood still" and where people live "in a version of a book of hours" (7, 13, 15). Like Thoreau, the narrator finds and creates at Waldenshaw (the roots of whose name, "walden" and "shaw," both mean "wood") a "safe house in the woods"; he experiences a sense of a "second childhood," seeing in the landscape and its inhabitants an actuality commensurate with his schoolboy fantasy of the England of Shakespeare, Gray, Wordsworth, Hardy, and other literary masters (88).[6] The narrator enters the mythology of Englishness from which Naipaul, as a youth in Trinidad, felt separated.[7]

At Waldenshaw and in the surrounding Wiltshire countryside he perceives a quaintness and perfection of nature that match the literary England of his imagination. He describes the pleasures of his walks and encounters with the personages of Waldenshaw, employees of the manor such as Mr. and Mrs. Phillips, the caretakers, Pitton the gardener, Bray the driver, the dairyman and farm workers, Jack the gardener and his father-in-law. The latter two in particular seem remnants of another, "better" age: "Of literature and antiquity and the landscape Jack and his garden and his geese and cottage and his father-in-law seemed emanations" (21). The narrator admires Jack's heartiness and dedication to the land; his robust manner and carefully tended garden seem innately English—as if part of the soil and environs—and together Jack and the Wiltshire countryside become the central images of the narrator's romance of Old England. Initially the narrator thinks of Jack as an embodiment of tradition, as part of the same essentially English world as Chaucer and Shakespeare, but later he realizes that, on the contrary, Jack might well be a foreigner of sorts, that he lived "in the middle of junk, among the ruins . . . that the past around his cottage might not have been his past; that he might at some stage have been a newcomer to the valley; that his style of life might have been a matter of choice . . . that out of the little piece of earth which had come to him with his farm worker's cottage . . . he had created a special land for himself, a garden, where . . . he was more than content to live out his life" (15). The narrator realizes that Jack is perhaps no more rooted, except through a choice and conscious act of belonging to this little plot of land, than he. As much as possible, given his circumstances, Jack's has created his home, of which his garden, like the narrator's writings, is the central symbol.

With Jack's death—the garden and greenhouse soon falling into disrepair and the cottage eventually burning down—the narrator looks at Waldenshaw differently, less as a remnant of Old England than as part of a fragile, constantly changing world. He comprehends that what seemed Waldenshaw's perfection is a construct of his own eye, that this "perfection" would certainly be viewed as decay by previous generations, and that his very presence there is an instance of that decay, a consequence of the decline of empire and the movement of former colonial peoples, like himself, to the metropolitan country.

"The Journey," the second chapter of the novel, consists of a fascinating, thinly veiled autobiographical account of Naipaul's career between his departure from Trinidad as a scholarship student bound for England in the early 1950s and the publication of *Among the Believers* in the early 1980s. The chapter continues, in fictional form, the narrative entitled "Prologue to an Autobiography" in *Finding the Center* (1984). Where fact and fiction diverge, here, the reader cannot say; only the author can know for sure. As Serge Dubrovsky has remarked of his own semiautobiographical novel, *Le Livre brisé* (1989), in a world without beliefs where there are only individuals, the writer, perhaps like all of us, stands face-to-face with himself.[8]

The titular motif of the "journey" forms the theme of this chapter and of the novel: the narrator's journey as a young scholarship student from Trinidad to England; return journeys to the West Indies and the Caribbean; journeys as part of his work as a journalist and novelist to Central and South America, Asia, and Africa; the writer's journey of words about those worlds; and life itself as a journey. The narrator recalls his disillusionment upon arrival in England where, drawn by a romance of faraway places, expecting to encounter a city like the literary London in the novels and short stories he has read, he finds instead a "strange and unknown" city (133–34). In his boardinghouse he meets not colorful English personages waiting to be characters in a story, but strangers from other countries, the "flotsam of Europe" after World War II (141). He describes his initial attempts to write "metropolitan" stories according to his preconception of England and English writers, and his chagrin at not finding suitable material in this fractured, immigrant world. He explains his realization that his writer's subject matter was not "sensibility"—"the ideas of the aesthetic movement of the end of the nineteenth century and the ideas of Bloomsbury, ideas bred essentially out of empire, wealth and imperial security"—but the collision of incongruous "worlds" and his own life as a "version" of the "great movement of peoples" taking place "in the second half of the twentieth century" (141, 146–47). Thus, in turning to his own life as a colonial and exile as his subject matter, he realizes that by trying to be an English writer, as he imagined English writers to be, he had been falsifying his experience, hiding from his identity, and widening the fissure between writer and man that had opened when he first left Trinidad for England.

The narrator reflects on his "writer's journey," with numerous allusions to places traveled to and the books written about them. He reflects on an idea inspired by the photograph of a Giorgio de Chirico painting, *The Enigma of Arrival*, which he sees while flipping through an art booklet left behind by the former tenants of the Waldenshaw cottage. The painting depicts a wharf, a mast, a voyager, and "muffled" figures in a deserted street of an ancient Mediterranean city. It conveys "desolation" and "mystery of arrival," the narrator surmises, and he imagines a Borges-like tale of a traveler who arrives at an ancient port: on the quai the traveler passes a mysterious figure and walks through a walled gate; within he is swept up by the activities of a crowded city and blends into its human flow. After "encounters and adventures" he feels a weariness and sense of being lost; he tries to return to his ship but cannot find the way. He opens a door and sees the port, "the world" almost as it was on his arrival, except for one thing—his ship has departed, time has passed, the traveler has lived his life (98–99). The narrator writes that the traveler will finish his days as a wanderer, "a man on the run . . . passionate to get away to a clearer air" (172). Only later does the narrator comprehend that this tale tells the story of his own exile and enigma of arrival.

"Ivy," the third chapter, returns to the countryside and the personages of Waldenshaw manor, particularly its landlord, whom the narrator never meets. He catches glimpses of him and forms an impression of his personality based on what he is told by others and what he surmises about him through the landlord's writings and drawings. The landlord sends him poems, written decades before, that tell an "Indian romance" of Krishna and Shiva and "the days of imperial glory" (212). He also sends a mischievous 1920s novel, illustrated with drawings reminiscent of Beardsley, about a ready-to-serve missionary in Africa who, ironically, gets eaten by cannibals (282). Arriving in Waldenshaw "at a time of disappointment and wounding" in his life, the narrator empathizes with the landlord who out of a malady of the spirit—an acedia—has ceased to be a doer and wishes to "hide" from the world (192). The narrator and landlord are inversely related, at "opposite ends of wealth, privilege, and in the hearts of different cultures" (191). The decline of the British empire, which on one plane the landlord's acedia symbolizes, has led to the rise of the narrator's fortunes—carried him to England, provided him a university education and an opportunity to become a writer, and set him up in a cottage of Waldenshaw. The narrator's presence there exemplifies the "great movement" of colonial peoples after World War II and is linked to the decline and fall of European empires.

The landlord's acedia, the deteriorating manor, and, in this chapter, the ivy signify that decline. The landlord is very fond of ivy, Mrs. Phillips the caretaker tells the narrator, and has ordered that it not be cut even though it is smothering the trees. The narrator notes the coincidence between the landlord's withdrawal and order not to cut the ivy and his own journey from Trinidad to England and the beginning of his exile. The landlord's acedia coincides with the beginning of the split within the narrator between writer and man; it is as if the landlord and the narrator are secret sharers of a historical pattern and a vision of decay. Initially the narrator sees Waldenshaw as a safe island, an almost perfect world, yet with time he begins to see it differently. On the one hand he begins to perceive Waldenshaw's fragility, a paradise that could be destroyed in one "morning's work with a chain saw." On the other hand, in the landlord's decision not to trim the ivy smothering the manor's trees, the narrator sees a corruption within the pastoral ideal of perfection and changelessness, a deleterious effort to maintain (and maim) the world according to one's old, fond image of it (263). The landlord prefers to let himself and his manor go to ruin rather than, like Jack and his garden, tend it and remake self and world.

"Rooks" reflects on change in the lives of the servants of the manor and other persons connected with the landlord: the suicide of Alan, a literary friend; the death of Mr. Phillips, the caretaker; the religious conversion of Bray, the landlord's driver; the change of jobs of Pitton, a gardener; the respiratory illness of the narrator. In Alan the narrator recognizes an earlier version, years past, of his own divided self (288). A talented critic but a writer manqué and flatterer of other, accomplished writers, Alan is divided between a wit and gaiety, broadcast to the English literary world in his radio programs, and an insecurity and feeling of failure. Alan suffers "a moral attack," the narrator writes, a malady that erupts in ravaging bouts of drinking and a debilitating, imitative aestheticism (291). Alan kills himself because, like the landlord, he prefers to live in the past. The circumstances of his suicide are coincidental—he mistakenly takes an overdose of pills after a night of heavy drinking—but his unbearable solitude, the narrator concludes, would have "brought him there again" sooner or later (295).

"Rooks" takes its title from an "old wise tale"[9] that the birds' nesting announces the arrival of death or money (297). With the death of Mr. Phillips—not only the caretaker but also the human force behind the landlord's stable condition—the narrator senses the approaching end of his own ten-year sojourn at Waldenshaw (36, 331). He falls seriously ill—partly, it would seem, from melancholy for Waldenshaw's disappearing pastoral world, for like Alan and the landlord, he lives in his idea of Old England as a better, more beautiful world: "The beauty of the place, the great love I had grown to feel for it . . . had kept me there too long. My health had suffered. . . . the cold of the cottage, and the damp and mist of the glorious riverbank" (88–89). His respiratory illness is roughly the equivalent of the acedia and the suicide; the three symbolize a decay overcoming the living through their respective fantasies of the past. Alan and the landlord prefer the dead, and their circumstances and choices—the landlord's acedia and Alan's suicide—fulfill their latent wishes. Similarly, the narrator's respiratory illness ages him, symbolically making him like the decaying manor and the ruins that dot the Wiltshire countryside (88). The narrator judges that there is always "some kind of exchange" in one's life; he has to pay for his ten years in a quaint but damp Wiltshire cottage with his respiratory illness and a too early middle age (88).

"The Ceremony of Farewell" explores the paradox of death as lifegiver and of art and ritual as means of responding to loss and of safeguarding life from oblivion. The narrator reflects on change in his own life and recalls his "Mediterranean fantasy" of the "traveler, the strange city, the spent life," which he now perceives as an allegory of his own exile, of his lifelong "writer's journey" (343–44). Like the allegorical traveler he has "always" been "a stranger, a foreigner, a man who . . . left his island and community before maturity, before adult social experience" (244). In the traveler, the narrator recognizes his own exile, sense of loss, and fear of extinction.

The death of his sister, Sati, takes the narrator back to Trinidad. There he observes the many changes that have occurred during his and Sati's lifetime: the "sacred world" of the Indian villages of their childhood has vanished, and the island has been transformed, remade in a late twentieth-century, industrial image. In confronting these changes, the narrator feels grief, but he is also revitalized by Sati's death, put back in touch with the living, the changes in his family, and the transformation of the island of his childhood and youth. Although only briefly, the exile rejoins his community. His violent dreams cease, and his melancholy ends. With these changes and his new dedication—to "life and man as the mystery"—he becomes, again, a doer; he loses his writer's block and begins to write the book that is in fact the book he is writing and we are reading: "faced with a real death, and with this new wonder about men, I laid aside my drafts and hesitations and began to write very fast about Jack and his garden" (354).

But what is the meaning of the narrator's "new wonder," and why does the narrator write both "very fast" and specifically "about Jack and his garden"? His wonder is existential: confronted with our inevitable death, we choose to do, create, each day, even though what we do and create is always inevitably undone; we choose to "remake our world." We are like Camus's Sisyphus, who pushes the stone up the hill while knowing that it will roll back down and that he will have to take up its burden still another time. "I leave Sisyphus at the bottom of the mountain!" Camus writes: "We always return to take up our burden. But Sisyphus teaches the superior fidelity that denies the gods and raises the rocks. He too judges that all is well. This universe, henceforth without master, appears to him neither sterile nor futile. Each of the grains of this stone, each sparkling mineral of this mountain full of night, forms a world to him alone. The struggle itself toward the summits is sufficient to fill the hearts of men. We must imagine that Sisyphus is happy."[10] In a world without gods, Sisyphus takes up his absurd burden—he takes it up with Jack's courage and dedication. Like Jack in his garden, Sisyphus creates his own world of stone, mountain, and night.

The narrator writes "very fast" because he has been brushed by "real death"—Jack's, Alan's, Mr. Phillips's, Sati's—and he feels his own middle age and mortality. He writes specifically about Jack and his garden because they symbolize a new understanding of a response to death, and change, and homelessness. The narrator is a writer in exile, and Jack too, who lives in a rented cottage and tends a rented plot of land, is an exile of sorts, owning little and coming to Waldenshaw perhaps only to work. The narrator admires Jack for his courage and dedication, but even more important, because he creates his home, his world.

## Recursion and Synthesis

The novel's narrator remarks that with each new book he writes, he seeks a "synthesis" of the "material," the "worlds," and the "way of seeing" of his previous books (173).[11] *The Enigma of Arrival* is perhaps Naipaul's most recursive and synthetic work in terms of three interlocking motifs: change, voyages, and art and life. Like a fugue, these motifs are variations on a theme, on what Bakhtin and Medvedev call the overall thematic unity of a work or works. For Naipaul that overall theme is exile and its opposite, home.[12]

Change is a complex motif throughout Naipaul's works carrying two different, sometimes contradictory representations and evaluations. In the early 1950s novels like *Miguel Street* (1959), change means escape from a limiting milieu and a chance for success, and it is thus often charged with a positive value; the boy of the story, through his maturation, perceives the traps of the slum and steps out of its patterns of failure and desperation for a chance at success in a faraway country. *A House for Mr Biswas* (1961) also views change as positive; it is through change that Biswas breaks out of his inherited identity as the son of a laborer and the stifling hierarchy of the traditionalist Tulsi family. Socioeconomic change creates opportunity: because his West Indian society is changing, industrializing, Biswas is able to leave his traditionalist Indian village for the city and, rather amazingly, find a job as a reporter without any training or specialized education. Change also creates opportunity for Anand, Biswas's son, who excels at school and wins a scholarship to study in England. A change of jobs makes it possible for Biswas to own a car and later to put down a deposit on the house on Sikkim Street. In short, through socioeconomic change Biswas steps out of his caste identity as the son of a laborer and tenuously joins the middle class. In this context, change equals social progress; it fractures the authoritarian caste order signified by the Tulsi family and pushes the largely agricultural East Indian community into the center of Trinidad society and the urban, industrial age.

In *The Middle Passage* (1962), Naipaul's first travel book and social commentary, and in essays and books on India (*An Area of Darkness* [1964], "India" [1972], and *India: A Wounded Civilization* [1977]), the author diagnoses the "maladies" of Caribbean or West Indian and Indian societies, one of which is stagnancy or an absence of change. The former peoples persist in a colonial mentality; the latter, in a caste- and religion-dominated mentality. In essays and books about Third World societies, absence of change equates with a "wounded" society. The author often critiques a distorting myth of the past that expresses a society's longing for a simple or pure epoch that in reality never existed. Rastafarianism, Black Power, Africanism, Gandhianism, Peronism, Islamic fundamentalism: for Naipaul, each is based on a myth of a return to simplicity and a looking backward to an imagined paradise. Throughout his works he critiques false revolutions that go backward rather than forward and that advocate, finally, changelessness and not change.

Although early works, such as *The Suffrage of Elvira* (1958) and *The Mystic Masseur* (1957), also critique social change—that is, the novels' respective narrators look satirically on Elvirans' equation of democracy with buying and selling and Ganesh's social climb by hook or by crook— it is not until *Mr Stone and the Knights Companion* (1963) and *The Mimic Men* (1967) that Naipaul writes works whose protagonists embrace retreat from change and construct fantasies of the past. It is in these two novels that the theme of change turns into the theme of mutability, a view of the world in decay, regressing from a former, better time thought of as a paradise lost. In *Mr Stone* change is equated with degradation and human destructiveness, an attitude that reflects the protagonist's alienation in the metropolis, where he feels little sense of community and where privacy becomes an imprisonment, a state of "each man returning to his own cell" (*MSK* 18–19). Stone believes that the principle of destruction rules the human world: "it [is] not by creation that man demonstrate[s] his power and defie[s] this hostile order, but by destruction" (*MSK* 125–26). In *The Mimic Men*, nostalgia becomes the protagonist's dominant response to change; in the context of the mechanical, impersonal metropolis, Singh the colonial creates a fantasy of the communal, pastoral aspects of the Caribbean island world from which he has been exiled.

Set in part or entirely in England, *Mr Stone* and *The Mimic Men* convey a sense of First World decay; interestingly, Naipaul does not write another novel about England until almost twenty years after the publication of *The Mimic Men*, although he continued to live there when not traveling for his work as a novelist-journalist. The reason for England's absence in Naipaul's 1970s works is intimated by the narrator of *The Enigma of Arrival*, who confesses that on his arrival there he loses his "dream of the future" (134).[13] The exile experiences a *déchirement*, a splitting of self and world; for the colonial who has finally arrived in the metropolis, the land of his ambition, and is immediately estranged from it, memories replace dreams. For the divided self of the exile, the past becomes more real than the present or the future, and the author thus writes books about that past, the past of the land of his ancestors and the past of colonies and empire: about Trinidad, the Caribbean and West Indies, India, and other regions of the developing world. The contradiction that develops in these works concerns the author's criticism of traditionalist, "static" societies in the Third World, yet his own sense of change as a destroyer; the position of the author who critiques a lack of change in Third World societies is inconsistent with the position of the narrator of *The Enigma of Arrival*, for example, who retreats from change to the safe island of Waldenshaw.

That novel conveys a nostalgia, and in its myth of Englishness shows the imprint of the narrator's-author's colonial British education and his off-and-on thirty-year residence in the "kingdom by the sea." *The Enigma of Arrival* picks up the themes of Naipaul's two previous novels set in England: in response to exile and alienation, the protagonists of *Mr Stone* and *The Mimic Men* perceive change as destruction and withdraw into fantasy. *Mr Stone* depicts an urban world where work is devoid of meaning and where men and women are alienated from each other and from nature; though a vehicle of reductive parody, the idea of the Knights Companion looks nostalgically to "Old England" as reflected in chivalric romance, its value system embodied in the quest, gallantry, and knightly camaraderie of the Round Table. *The Mimic Men* presents a related romance through Singh's daydream of sheep grazing in Soho Square, which expresses his alienation and his desire for retreat to a pastoral world. In *The Enigma of Arrival* the narrator's situation relates inversely to Singh's: he writes from and inhabits the pastoral to which Singh in his standard, characterless London hotel room can escape only imaginatively; he lives within Singh's fantasy. Twenty years after the publication of *The Mimic Men*, *The Enigma of Arrival* reenters Singh's daydream and awakens from it by understanding it as a debilitating myth.

The England of the novel refers to an actuality, but this actuality is overlaid by a kind of fairyland. At Waldenshaw the narrator takes pleasure in the sight of sheep and shepherds, cows grazing in verdant pastures, and solitary, rustic figures that seem to step out of English poesy. The landscape is imbued with and hallowed by literature or the mythology of Englishness that the narrator, as boy in Trinidad, has constructed from the literature he has read. He finds the beauty of the Wiltshire landscape greater than any he has known because it matches his childhood image of beauty exemplified, for instance, in paintings of the English countryside; he experiences a reawakened "knowledge of natural things" and "the fulfillment of the child's dream of the safe house in the wood" (88). (As noted in chapter 2, it is this dream that the son as exile writes about through the father's dream of a house of his own, especially in "The Shorthills Episode" of *A House for Mr Biswas*.)

*The Enigma of Arrival* is about perceptions of and responses to changes of various sorts. The narrator describes changes in the landscape, both seasonal change and profound changes that have come individual by individual, generation by generation, through the epochs. He explains that, since his childhood, he has seen the world with decay "in his eye," and in a passage that recalls the short story "The Mourners," he laments: "I lived with the idea of decay. ( . . . It was like my curse: the idea, which I had had even as a child in Trinidad, that I had come into a world past its peak.) Already I lived with the idea . . . that one's time on earth . . . was a short thing" (15, 23). His dual perception of cows in a field illustrates his nostalgic idealization of the Wiltshire landscape in contrast with his sense of a decaying world: at first sight the cows and countryside seem a perfect match with his childhood memory of a tranquil, pastoral scene on a milk-can label, yet as he looks closely he notices that some of the cows are malformed, with "additional lumps of flesh," "extra cattle material hanging down their middles . . . like heavy curtains" (11). From a distance the pastoral can be dreamed, but close up it dissipates. As Ralph Singh says, the gold of the imagination inevitably turns to the lead of reality (*MM* 10). The narrator sees the Wiltshire world through this split lens of perception, which expresses the *déchirement* within the exile, still not yet completely healed after thirty years. He perceives a generalized, late twentieth-century decline of England in the decaying Waldenshaw manor. Constructed "at the zenith of imperial power," the manor has become obsolete and monumentally difficult to repair; like the deteriorating Roman villa at nearby Chedworth, it is a colossus "exaggerat[ing] human needs," its own grandeur ironically assuring its decline and fall (260–61, 269). Changes in the manor grounds and Wiltshire countryside deeply distress the narrator because they make it harder to maintain his fantasy of an Old England somehow surviving amid the turmoil of this fin de siècle.

He overcomes this sense of decay and loss through acts of commemoration; he constructs an understanding of change and death by writing the book that he is writing. He reflects on the landlord's acedia, on Alan's suicide, on Mrs. Phillips's response to her husband's death, and on Jack's and Sati's deaths. Sati's death has the most profound effect on the narrator because she is not only a beloved family member, but also a link with and symbol of the narrator's Trinidadian past. Sati signifies family, home, and Trinidad, with which the narrator as exile has still not been reconciled since his departure from the island thirty years before. Returning there for Sati's cremation, he notices the many changes that have occurred: where forest once stood, huts and shacks of illegal immigrants cling to the hills at the edge of Port of Spain; a swamp has been drained and turned into "a landscape of Holland" with vegetation and canals; the East Indian villages of his childhood are now only barely recognizable: "No narrow roads; no dark, overhanging trees; no huts; no earth yards with hibiscus hedges; no ceremonial lighting of lamps, no play of shadows on the wall; no cooking of food in half-walled verandas, no leaping firelight; no flowers along gutters or ditches where frogs croaked the night away. But highways and clover-shaped exits and direction boards: a wooden land laid bare, its secrets opened up" (352). Grief infuses this litany of a "sacred world" vanished, but by reflecting on these and other changes and, above all, by finding the words to fit his feelings, the narrator constructs an understanding of loss, comprehending that each generation necessarily remakes the world in its own image. Ritualistically he is purged and revitalized; he banishes the "evil spirits" that have tormented him with nightmares and writer's block. He reenters the world and becomes again a "doer," affirming "life and man as the mystery," and in this energy he composes *The Enigma of Arrival*—about Jack and the old and the new England, Sati and the old and the new Trinidad, the writer and the man becoming one through the celebration of words and worlds.

The final paragraph of the novel sweeps up the reader in its affirmation, but does it say something that Naipaul has not said before? Recursively, its final sentence recalls the final sentence of *Miguel Street*, written almost thirty years previously: "I left them all and walked briskly towards the aeroplane, not looking back, looking only at my shadow before me, a dancing dwarf on the tarmac" (172). In these passages, the narrators of

*Miguel Street* and *The Enigma of Arrival* embrace their respective destinies; in the face of their past and the unknown—a "shadow" for one narrator, "real death" for the other—they go forward with their lives. The young man walks "briskly," the middle-aged man writes "fast"—as if emphasizing both their determination and the extinction that may overtake them at any moment. Nor is the affirmation at the end of *The Enigma of Arrival* totally different from the affirmation of *A House for Mr Biswas:* "life has to be lived," the narrator writes simply of Biswas's definitive understanding. But one important difference between these affirmations as opposed to that of *The Enigma of Arrival* lies in the phrase the "religion of men." This should not necessarily be read as a statement of faith that Naipaul puts forward, but as an affirmation of community that his narrator and protagonist, a man for a long time in exile from other men, has put forward. Out of context, the phrase rings arrogant and passé. In context, however, it is more than a banality because it is the *narrator as exile's* affirmation of self and others. It is freedom as "escape to" rather than "escape from," to use Fromm's distinction.[14] The boy of *Miguel Street* separates himself from others, whereas the narrator of *the Enigma of Arrival* joins others, a community.[15]

The novel's second motif, the journey or voyage, also combines opposing attitudes and evaluations in Naipaul's works. The journey or voyage can signify openness, discovery, growth, potentialities in general; conversely, it can mean a futile wandering, homelessness, the individual cut off from his community, a wasted life. Images of the voyage occur throughout Naipaul's work. In *Miguel Street*, for example, the boy's voyage signifies new possibilities, an escape from the patterns of failure of the Port of Spain slum and the beginning of a new life. In *A House for Mr Biswas* Mohun's bus ride from the village of Arwacas to Port of Spain signifies much the same thing, a challenge accepted and a new life begun. In essays of the late 1950s and early 1960s Naipaul writes of his need to travel, to leave London and England, in order to recharge his energies and reawaken his wonder; the voyage signifies an openness to the stranger within and without, and the "adventure" of writing itself. The voyage becomes a metaphor for the author's delving into his ancestral past; essays and books about India develop from this theme of the journey of discovery. Naipaul's fascination with voyages permeates his histories and social commentaries on the Caribbean and West Indies, but the journeys he writes about are also problematic: *The Middle Passage* takes its title from the nightmarish voyage of slaves from Old World to New; similarly, *The Loss of El Dorado* tells the story of the quest for a city of gold in the South American jungle and the failures of Old World conquest and colonization in the New World.

In these accounts of Trinidad and Caribbean history, the voyage loses its positive connotations and equates negatively with enslavement, delusion, oppression of peoples, and the rape of the land. The negative image of voyage dominates in these works, as it does in Ralph Singh's account of his exile in *The Mimic Men*, in which life in England constitutes the "greater shipwreck," a fragmentation of self and world. In *An Area of Darkness*, Naipaul's first of three travel books and social commentaries on India, the description of landfall in Bombay—"the margin of the sea unremarkably littered"—symbolizes the disillusionment that that voyage will bring (45). The negative image of the voyage culminates in the sequence of stories of *In a Free State* that recounts journeys of loss, waste, absurdity, humiliation, brutality: the geologist "tramp" at Piraeus wastes his life wandering the world; Santosh ironically rises from the pavement of Bombay to the slum of Washington, D.C.; the narrator of "Tell Me Who to Kill" leaves his West Indian island for London, loses his familial, cultural connections and finds instead a rage against an enemy that he cannot identify; the journey of "In a Free State," a car trip from an East African capital into the bush, ends in Bobby's humiliation and brutal beating; the author's trip to the temple of Karnak in "The Circus at Luxor" culminates in his irate response to the whipping of beggars and a dark reflection on the rise and fall of empires. The motif of the voyage also structures Naipaul's subsequent 1970s novels. In *Guerrillas* Jane's journey to a West Indian island ends in her horrific slaying. In *A Bend in the River* Salim seems to lose everything but his life. In the novel's final paragraph he is wrapped in the enigma of the voyage; carrying but a suitcase, escaping to an unspecified destination, he is within the voyage, poised aboard the steamer between departure and arrival, between old and new identities.

*The Enigma of Arrival* treats the voyage motif within the double experience of the exile's *déchirement* yet construction of a new identity. Journeys constitute a splitting, a fracturing of the narrator's self and world. Of his initial departure from Trinidad for England he recalls his "magical vision" from the airplane of the island and ocean far below; yet it is also at this time that he begins to feel the pain of the "two sides" of his personality "separating one from the other, the man from the writer" (120). Many voyages follow and exacerbate this sense of division and decentering signified by the flight of the airplane carrying him above and away from the familiar landscape and the connection with his community. Voyages divide the self, but at the same time they serve as recursive vehicles for its unification in a greater complexity or a syncretistic synthesis: only through the fracturing of the narrator's identity can a synthesis or new construction of identity become possible. The voyage from Trinidad to England leads to a university education and a career as an international writer. Subsequent voyages, writing itself as a voyage, take the narrator to new places and a new understanding about other peoples and himself. The journey takes him to Waldenshaw, where after a ten years' residence he heals the split between writer and man by reconciling his past and present and by recognizing that, like Jack, we create our selves and worlds. Voyages sweep him up in the movement of former colonial peoples in the second half of the twentieth century; he shares the experience of exile with many others and comprehends that now more than ever before people must create their own sense of being at home in the world (141–42, 147). The voyage of exile eventually leads back to Trinidad and to a new understanding of solidarity in the community of others: "the true religion of men."

The novel's third motif is the relationship between art and life, literature and actuality. As a young writer the narrator tries to mask his cultural identity as a Trinidad Indian and thus in his stories, art and life are unrelated: in his juvenile attempts to be an "English" writer—like Ackerley, Maugham, Huxley, or Waugh—he produces stories such as "Gala Nights," whose very title suggests a glasses-clinking, dancers-twirling, social world distant from his immigrant actuality (120, 135). Only by focusing on his identity as a Trinidad Indian and colonial exile in England does he find his true subject matter and begin to write stories full of the voices of his world. In order to be a writer he must bring his life into his art.

Art and life exchange and interpenetrate, Bakhtin and Medvedev state: "everyday life can become literature, and literature can become life."[16] A syncretistic synthesis of earlier literary works and of aspects of the self would seem to be the project of the narrator of *The Enigma of Arrival*, at once Naipaul's most literarily allusive and autobiographical novel. The key to this project is the novel's titular image, *The Enigma of Arrival*. An art-book photograph of de Chirico's painting inspires the narrator's "fantasy" of a traveler whose arrival in an ancient, Mediterranean city is in reality an ending. The narrator recounts:

> My story was to be set in classical times, in the Mediterranean. . . . [A traveler] would arrive . . . at a classical port with the walls and gateways like cutouts. He would walk past that muffled figure on the quayside. He would move from that silence and desolation . . . to a gateway or door. He would enter there and be swallowed by the life and noise of a crowded city. . . . The mission he had come on—family business, study, religious initiation—would give him encounters and adventures. . . . Gradually there would come to him a feeling that he was getting nowhere; he would lose his sense of mission; he would begin to know only that he was lost. His feeling of adventure would give way to panic. He would want to escape. . . . But he wouldn't know how. . . . At the moment of crisis he would come upon a door, open it, and find himself back on the quayside of arrival. He has been saved; the world is as he remembered it. Only one thing is missing. . . . The antique ship has gone. The traveler has lived out his life. (98–99)

The narrator's fantasy springs from an exchange between art and life: his encounter with the art-book photograph of de Chirico's painting as it evokes images of or connections with his own life. His fantasy contains in symbolic form his life as exile: his travels, estrangement, sense of loss of past and home. The story also contains the larger, historical subject of his writings, that is, the movement of peoples of the world, especially refugees and exiles of the Third World, in the second half of the twentieth century.

In its self-referencing, tangled hierarchies the novel resembles the art of M. C. Escher, such as *Self-Portrait* and *Drawing Hands*.[17] The former shows a hand holding a reflecting globe in which the viewer sees the image of Escher holding up the reflecting globe; the latter shows a drawing of a drawing in which two hands, a right and a left, have just drawn each other. Has the right hand drawn the left hand, or vice versa? One cannot be certain, because the hierarchy is braided or intertwined.

Similarly, although one can point out the recursion in *The Enigma of Arrival*, one cannot establish a hierarchy of self-referencing that is not tangled, capable of being meaningfully rearranged in another way. At the novel's "base" of superimposed images lies a photograph of de Chirico's *The Enigma of Arrival*, the painting itself perhaps inspired by literary reflections—Nietzsche's sketches of northern Italian cities[18]—and evocatively entitled by French poet Guillaume Apollinaire, who may have seen something of his own life in de Chirico's metaphysical painting. Superimposed on this already complex interaction between art and life lie several interlinked levels of images: the narrator's tale or "Mediterranean fantasy"; his perception of his own life as it is reflected symbolically in that tale; his autobiography, *The Enigma of Arrival*, that grows in part out of the tale; the novel, *The Enigma of Arrival*, about a writer who writes an autobiographical book that grows out of a "Mediterranean fantasy" inspired by an art-book photograph of the painting by de Chirico inspired by Nietzsche's Italian sketches and entitled *The Enigma of Arrival* by Guillaume Apollinaire, who was perhaps thinking about the enigma of his own life when he gave the painting its title; and in all of the above, Naipaul's life informing his art and Naipaul's art informing his life. Just as in Escher's *Drawing Hands* this hierarchy is tangled or intertwined postmodernistically: for it is Naipaul's sense of the *étrangeté* of his life that creates the enigma perceived in the art-book photograph, and thus the image listed last could also be listed first.

The point of this is not that Naipaul is playing a game but that this semiautobiographical novel is highly self-referential: it is about itself, but in being about itself it is about what is "extrinsic" as well, the author's life. This extrinsic reality is reflected in the novel, and thus the extrinsic is in a sense the intrinsic as well, and vice versa. The novel illustrates an intertwining exchange that Bakhtin and Medvedev explain in this way:

every literary phenomenon . . . is simultaneously determined from without (extrinsically) and within (intrinsically). From within it is determined by literature itself, and from without by other spheres of social life. But, in being determined from within, the literary work is thereby determined externally also, for the literature which determines it is itself determined from without. And being determined from without, it thereby is determined from within, for internal factors determine it precisely as a literary work in its specificity and in connection with the whole literary situation, and not outside that situation. Thus intrinsic turns out to be extrinsic, and the reverse.[19]

On the one hand, elements of Naipaul's life are there in the novel; yet on the other, the novel is about itself, about writing, about constructing one's self and world. In a tangled hierarchy, life and literature are woven through each other, refer to each other.

In the commemorative, therapeutic, celebrative ritual of writing, writer and man overcome a sense of *déchirement*. And that is the project of this novel. Like the protagonist of Borges's "The Circular Ruins,"[20] whose ambition is to dream a man and insert him in reality, Naipaul writes a novel about a writer who lives in the daydream of a character of one of his earlier novels (i.e., Ralph Singh of *The Mimic Men*); through this dream the narrator creates a new man who ceases to be divided, who becomes whole again and goes forward with his life and art. The exchange is beautifully tangled, for through his creation, the narrator-writer creates a new man within the author. And that is one meaning of the enigma of arrival, this double sense of creating and having been created by one's creations.

But to say that the narrator lives in a dream is, in another sense, not to do justice to his or Naipaul's experience. The enigma of arrival is the process of "presencing," of becoming real: through autobiography the narrator (and Naipaul) not only understand aspects of their pasts, but also place themselves firmly in the world and take up the burden of going forward into the future. In *Autobiography: Toward a Poetics of Experience*, Janet Varner Gunn explains: "Autobiography is a presencing, in Augustine's words, of 'man in his deep.' What is made present is not merely a past that is past. What is presenced is a reality, always new, to which the past has contributed but which stands, as it were, in front of the autobiographer. To lay claim to one's life, and thereby to become 'fierce with reality,' is to understand that reality as something to which one is continually trying to catch up but which one can never outstrip."[21] In *The Enigma of Arrival* the narrator-author lays claim to his life; through words, through literature, he becomes "fierce" with life, with reality. The writer and man become one, yet oneness is fleeting for it is an idea that the narrator-author brings into presence briefly and will inevitably be exiled from. To catch that reality he must *write* as well as live, for by writing he has sometimes learned to understand himself and others and to construct a home.

# 9

# Toward a New Pluralism

> So, with Al's help, my eye changed. And where at first I had seen only Harlem and gloom, I began on the high balcony to see the comparative order of the area where Al lived. And the splendor of the original Harlem design.
> —*A Turn in the South*

> When you travel for a book like this, you often don't know what you are looking for until you have found it. You need a lot of help on the way. On this journey many people helped.
> —*India: A Million Mutinies Now*

In writing about himself, Vidiadhar Surajprasad Naipaul has written about others; through an art at least partly autobiographical, he has tapped experiences and constructed fictions that define aspects of the colonial and postcolonial world.[1] The key to this link between self and others is the experience of exile, which has enabled him to treat his own alienation and dislocations as an instance and analogue of the changes and search for identity of colonial and postcolonial peoples. Like societies in transition and development, the exile lives in an in-between that must be constructed syncretistically into an identity.[2] It is through this in-between, this sharing of both origins and ends that he "finds his center"; it is through dislocations that he locates who he has been and is becoming.

The experience of the author's exile relates then not only to the experiences of other exiles from the developing world, but also to society's experiences of change, cultural collisions, and trauma of development, and to the future shocks of our already post-postmodern world.

In *Etrangers à nous-mêmes*, Julia Kristeva writes that a "secret wound" pushes the stranger into his wanderings.[3] Naipaul's exile begins within the circumstances of his family, Indian community, and colonial society. In one sense, his exile is forecasted by a grandfather's voyage of exile from India to Trinidad. In *India: A Million Mutinies Now* the author reflects on this inheritance: "my ancestors had left as indentured servants for the sugar estates of Guyana and Trinidad. I had carried in my bones that idea of abjectness and defeat and shame" (517). That Naipaul recognized the importance of those ancestral voyages to his identity shows in his fascination with and travels on the Asian subcontinent. He has written the better part of five books about India and Pakistan, more than on any other subject or geographic region except Trinidad and the Caribbean. The enclaved status of East Indians in the West Indies also prepares for the author's exile and his position or persona as an outsider; it has helped form his sense of difference and his attitudes toward ethnic groups and racial issues. Finally, the colony as a margin and a metahistory, a not quite "real" version of England, has prepared him for his exile. In the essay "Jasmine" Naipaul expresses his sense of divided reality deriving from a linguistic, cultural, and economic inheritance as a colonial. This division pushes him toward England; alienation in the metropolis and a division within between traditional and Western culture lead to recurring voyages of exile to the far ends of former empires. Although the "wound" that pushes Naipaul into exile may have been a need to exorcise a "shame," through that dislocation he has located an identity. Exile has been full of pain, but it has also been a key to the treasure. As another Trinidadian, C. L. R. James, writes of his own exile and its key to his self-understanding: "If the ideas [of *Beyond a Boundary*] originated in the West Indies it was only in England and in English life and history that I was able to track them down and test them. To establish his own identity, Caliban, after three centuries, must himself pioneer into regions Caesar never knew."[4]

Exile shapes Naipaul's works, impacting on their narration, characterization, subjects and themes, readings of other societies, and modes of intercultural encounter between author and those others. The divided self of the exile is manifest in the narrative point of view of the 1950s fiction, which through double-voicedness seeks to mediate that division. A split exists between the narrator as experiencing and knowing self, or between the third-person narrator and the authorial narrator. The use of irony and satire allows the author to say one thing yet mean another, thus creating a duality that depicts a two-sided colonial world and engages differing aspects of the author's colonial and metropolitan selves.

Naipaul's characters show the mark of exile in their sense of fragmentation, their not-belonging or their sense of being strangers to themselves and others and being observers from the margins, their fantasies that "real" life lies somewhere else or is better "anywhere but here," and their appetite for others' experiences in other worlds. Biswas, Singh, Salim, and the narrator of *The Enigma of Arrival*, for example, embody some or all of these qualities. None of these characters truly belongs in his community or society; each tends to observe rather than act, and through those observations of others, experiences new territories of seeing and feeling. One thinks of Camus's remark, in *Le Mythe de Sisyphe*, that Don Juan chooses "to be nothing" because for him it is "a question of seeing clearly."[5] Whether Naipaul's characters do see clearly is moot, but a character like Salim does seem to choose to be nothing, to live without a fixed social identity, in order to be a watcher and an evaluator of others and thus to know them (or have the illusion of knowing them). We find some of these same qualities in the author as "character" in autobiographic social commentaries such as *The Middle Passage*, *An Area of Darkness*, and *Among the Believers*, where he emphasizes his difference from the people he observes and his not-belonging to their world—yet partly through these others he sees himself and knows more about his world.

Cultural collisions and culture shock have become the subject matter of Naipaul's works, particularly the trauma of colonial and postcolonial peoples seen through the lens of an exile from the developing world. Exile generates motifs such as change, the voyage, the divided self and social breakdown, the seduction yet illusion of a definitive return to one's origins. The author is divided between fits of masked nostalgia and assertions of "trampling on the past," between an old identity in a traditional community and a new identity in a postindustrial society. This division translates into contradictory attitudes toward social change, viewed as progress on the one hand and decay on the other; as an exile caught in the cultural collisions of his epoch, Naipaul does not escape unscathed their fragmenting effects. His sense of decay presupposes that there existed a better time from which the present has devolved, and such a sense of decay or decline renders the present "empty and fragmented—since everything affirmative, ideal, obligatory, desired has been shifted, via the [historical] inversion, into the past . . . en route, [the past] has become weightier, more authentic and persuasive."[6] Naipaul is of two minds: in works set in Third World contexts, he rejects historical inversion (e.g., he deconstructs the myth of the past and purity implicit in Islamic fundamentalism), yet in works set in First World contexts he laments decay and fragmentation (e.g., Stone and Singh long for "Old England"). For the exile, someone between two worlds, the appeals of motion and rest play themselves out in contradictory positions such as these.

Exile shapes Naipaul's evaluations of traditional societies. He views them from the perspective of one who has chosen to leave his traditionalist community for a fast-paced society in which the individual must actively construct his meaning and self-identity. That choice leads to critiques of cultures and societies that privilege tradition and teach the fixity of origins and the unalterability of fate; for the exile chooses flux over fixity and authority, insecurity over security, constructed identity over inherited caste identity. Similarly, exile shapes Naipaul's attitudes toward individual and social development; he has had to believe not in karma, but in will, work, and ambition. In the interview with Charles Michener he explains: "Coming from a place like Trinidad which I always felt existed on the edge of the world, far away from everything else, not only physically but also in terms of culture, I felt I had to try very hard to rejoin the Old World. So I had this great drive to achievement."[7] But there is a price to pay for this drive and the severing of ties with one's community and past. The exile is troubled by insecurity, a threat of failure, a "neurosis" and a projection of the demands of his road to success onto peoples of the developing world. "When I was in the fourth form I wrote a vow . . . to leave [Trinidad] within five years," he has pointed out proudly. "I left after six; and for many years afterwards in England, falling asleep in bedsitters with the electric fire on, I had been awakened by the nightmare that I was back in tropical Trinidad."[8] But is the nightmare the past, or a shame or fear in the present? For almost four decades Naipaul has moved forward by turning to the past; as the narrator-author of *The Enigma of Arrival* explains:

> To be what I wanted to be, I had to cease to be or to grow out of what I was. . . .
>
> So the past for me—as colonial and writer—was full of shame and mortifications. Yet as a writer I could train myself to face them. Indeed, they became my subjects. (244–45)

Naipaul's critique of developing societies cuts in two directions: it is an attack on ideologies advocating a return to the past; at the same time it is a commentary on the author's attitudes toward his own past and his sense of the future. In short, exile for Naipaul has been an ambiguous two-way journey: a break with the past, yet a constant recollection of it in other places—Asia, Africa, North and South America. In leaving the past behind, the exile, like the boy-adult narrator of *Miguel Street*, must redefine it in order to move forward.

Exile has shaped Naipaul's readings of other societies and his modes of encounter with their peoples; it has perhaps reinforced a tendency, in part growing out of his enclaved, Trinidad Indian community, to observe strangers rather than interact with them. In certain of his writings about developing societies, Naipaul has dealt in stereotyped categorizations and created a closed, egocentric persona, neurotic at times, at times paranoiac. But it would be reductive to judge Naipaul's travel books and social studies solely on the basis of how well the author's persona does or does not interact with those people he portrays. Naipaul has gained insights from his insider's-outsider's perspective, even though that insight can sometimes seem only an unilluminating attack on others' beliefs and values, more of a darkness, a gazing into the nightsky.[9] Naipaul's works are valuable not because they consistently show communication (between the author and peoples of other cultures and societies), but because they powerfully record cultural shocks and collisions. The recent books, *A Turn in the South* (1989) and *India: A Million Mutinies Now* (1990), do show a shift, however, in the mode of encounter between authorial self and others toward a dialogue in which the differences between that self and the people the author portrays are acknowledged but those differences do not prevent a sharing, a certain commonality.[10] Both books seem composed from the words and voices of people rather than according to a ready-made idea recursively expanded; through interviews and collaboration, the author enters into a relationship of difference yet equality with the people about whom he has written and does not judge them in a categorical way as he did, particularly in the books on India and the colonial Caribbean and West Indies.

Exile shapes the relationship between Naipaul and his readers[11] during the three phases of his works, which can be characterized, respectively, by mediation, alienation, and syncretism. In the initial phase (the 1950s and early 1960s works), the author mediates between the differing aspects of his identity, between Trinidad and England; these works, which look back to the colony, use irony and satire to bridge the different ideological and social evaluations of the author and his intended English readers. By writing about the colony, he acknowledges it as the source of his identity and material, but in writing about it ironically and satirically, he can view it, as do the metropolitan readers who will buy his books, from a judgmental distance. In the second phase, which includes 1960s and 1970s works such as the essays and travel books on India, *Mr Stone and the Knights Companion*, *The Mimic Men*, *A Free State*, *Guerrillas*, and *A Bend in the River*, he expresses an alienation from English society, whose impersonality and decay he describes, and from colonial and postcolonial societies, whose problems he continues to analyze. These works often express disgust and repulsion; his social studies and travel writings about developing societies sometimes offend readers from those societies, while works like "In a Free State," "The Killings in Trinidad," and *Guerrillas* turn off certain other readers with their portraits of uncomprehending, impotent Westerners, moods of menace and aggression, and moments of violence. In the third phase, Naipaul reconciles his New World and Old World identities and comprehends the world as a changing one of diverse realities and irrationalities. This period bridges the differences between the author and his English readers through a nostalgia and a sharing of humanistic values, as in *The Enigma of Arrival*; it bridges the difference between the author and his readers from developing countries through a sympathetic dialogue, as in *India: A Million Mutinies Now*. The titular metaphor of the mutiny on ship combines an old way of seeing the world with a new: that is, the author still sees a decay in the world about him, but this change, he points out in the course of the book, may be a necessary stage in Indians' coming to grips with their postcolonial identity. In this third phase of Naipaul's works, two extreme attitudes toward the writer and writing, both of which have tended to isolate Naipaul from the people he writes about, are syncretized. The first conceives of the writer as "the last free man": "As prophet, as journal-keeper, as traveller and observer, deviser of tales or magician with words, [the writer] has always been felt to be above society. . . ." Conversely, the second conceives of the writer as an underground man of sorts. In an interview with Israel Shenker, Naipaul has lamented: the "thought of writing for the rest of one's life is a nightmare. . . . The romantic vision is gone. I'd be delighted to stop—now."[12] In his works of the 1980s and 1990 Naipaul passes beyond these extreme attitudes or positions and conceives of the writer not as divorced from society, either as the "last free man" or the "underground man," but as implicated in the lives of the people he writes about.

An author whose publications span decades, Naipaul has overcome more than a few crises in his long career. These crises, I have argued, have grown out of the experience of exile, with the most recent having come to a head in the 1970s novels *Guerrillas* and *A Bend in the River*;[13] it is worth considering the symbolic representation of this crisis in those novels. In the former novel, Meredith Herbert plays an antagonistic game with the guests at Harry de Tunja's Sunday beach party; he asks them to image what they will be doing in the future and shows each of them that they are really not prepared to change: "*The life being described is the life the speaker lives or a life he has already lived. The setting may change, but no one will make a fresh start or do anything new*" (169). As if to affirm this dead-end vision, the novel concludes with the macabre murder of a confused Englishwoman. A related vision occurs in *A Bend in the River*; the world is what it is, Salim says, and those who allow themselves to become nothing have no place in it. Jane of *Guerrillas* and Salim and Indar of *A Bend in the River* are divided between a need to go forward and a need to return; in various forms they play out that same division in the author. Jane's slaying, Father Huismans's beheading, Indar's vacillation between "trampling on the past" and searching for the village world of Old India, Salim's battering of Yvette (a European) followed by his decision to marry Nazruddin's daughter (an Indian Muslim)—all show various rejections or attempts at resolution of a division between cultures and between past and future.

These novels erupt with violence as their characters are confronted by strangers without and the stranger within. The crucial change for Naipaul during this period of his works begins with the autobiographical shift of *Finding the Center* with the author's return to Trinidad, his meeting with Bogart (on whom the character Bogart of *Miguel Street* was based), and his reflections on his father, Seepersad Naipaul. The key phrase distinguishing this shift is "the need to return," a phrase used in *India: A Million Mutinies Now* and one signaling a direction of Naipaul's recent books. In *Finding the Center* (1984) and *The Enigma of Arrival* (1987) the return is very personal; in *A Turn in the South* (1989) and *India: A Million Mutinies Now* (1990), the return is personal but also infused by a sense of other peoples' destinies. The insight that informs these four works, from *Finding the Center* through *India: A Million Mutinies Now*, is that exile, an in-between state, is not one-directional but two-directional; as an "in-between," exile partakes of its origins (the past) as well as its destination (the future). Exile is not a choosing between the past *or* the future—the predicament in which characters in Naipaul's 1970s novels are trapped—but rather, a two-directional movement. It is not a fixed state in either origins or ends.

It is tempting to sum up the phases or periods of Naipaul's works with words such as *outside, in-between,* and *among,* but such shorthand inevitably oversimplifies. For Naipaul exile has been both an outsideness and a state in-between different cultures and worlds. His recent works place him among the peoples he has written about, in dialogue with them and sympathetic to the problems of their lives. Exile has been a paradoxical movement; by leaving Trinidad, Naipaul comes to understand himself better as Trinidadian. By breaking ties with his community, he begins the long process of making new ties, though that does not extinguish the need to return and understand anew his Trinidad community. Exile is marked by a sharing of opposites, and the four works from *Finding the Center* through *India: A Million Mutinies Now* show a Naipaul both returning to familial and social aspects of his colonial past—to his father's life, to African Americans and their struggles in the shadow of a heritage of enslavement, to the India of previous sojourns—and moving beyond that colonial past through revisions and rewriting of earlier journeys and ways of seeing. These works show a new pluralism in the exile's vision, a sense of a million realities interacting in a rapidly changing world. It is a *new* pluralism in that the author, as Trinidadian, has always appreciated the values of a cosmopolitan, multicultural, and multiracial society—he specifically cites them in the chapter on Trinidad in *The Middle Passage*—but these values do not emerge in his works of the 1960s and 1970s.

In *A Turn in the South* and *India: A Million Mutinies Now* the interaction between Naipaul and those people he meets on his journeys comes through unmistakably; though the writing is his, in a sense he collaborates with others in the books' making. Both books compile perspective on perspective and open up heretofore closed texts by rereading earlier journeys that they record. In the following passage, for example, Naipaul contrasts his 1962 and late 1980s response to a Shia procession: "It had been hard for me [in 1962] . . . to believe what I had so suddenly come upon: bloodied bodies, blood-soaked clothes, chains, whips tipped with knives and razor blades, the exalted, deficient faces of the celebrants, and their almost arrogant demeanour. . . . I was ready to believe, what I was told then, that much of the blood on display was really animal blood. I hadn't understood the religious-historical charge of the occasion, the undying grief it sought to express. I had only been alarmed by it, and glad to get away from it, glad to return to myself and what I knew" (*IMMN* 507). The single-minded laser-beamlike interpretations of the earlier essays and books on India shift to the scattered light of pluralistic interpretations and ways of looking—by Naipaul then, Naipaul now, by Aziz his guide, by Aziz's son Nazir, and by those Shias in the religious procession. Others' perspectives inform the self's perspective, and Naipaul the traveler embraces a profound sense of reality's multitudinousness.

The reader can find similar passages, though fewer of them, in *A Turn in the South*, a work that from one perspective concerns the author's attempt to understand the history of Africans in the New World through his Trinidad background and his travels and dialogues with blacks in the American South. Recalling lines of James Baldwin that he had read thirty years before—"the most difficult (and most rewarding) thing in my life has been the fact that I was born a Negro and was forced, therefore, to effect some kind of truce with reality"—Naipaul reflects: " 'Reality'—it was what I remembered and what I accepted; but now, in the South, in the middle of my own journey, I began to wonder whether the truce that every black man looked for hadn't in fact been with the irrationality of the world around him. And the achievement of certain people began to appear grander" (*TS* 120). In this passage Naipaul rereads his experience— going backward to his old assumptions and forward to a new understanding—making connections with the experiences of other people and becoming through those connections changed, capable of seeing and comprehending more than before.

It is dangerous to critique the works of a living author, and more dangerous still to write a conclusion about one as consistently productive and of such significance as V. S. Naipaul, with decades of books behind him and perhaps decades more to be written. It seems most worth saying at the end of this study that Naipaul's best works face in two directions; at once commemorative and current, they honor those who have lived and describe the losses and dislocations that the living must respond to as best they can. In his best works, Naipaul writes with lucidity and poignancy— about worlds changing, about colonial and postcolonial peoples confronted with change that at once destroys and, perhaps, will liberate and create. One particular passage toward the end of *India: A Million Mutinies Now* eloquently reflects his deep understanding of that domain, commemorating one generation of Indians and forecasting the exile of the next generation from an older world of certitudes. Contrasting the two, Naipaul writes of his acquaintances, Aziz and Nazir:

[Aziz] had never been out of Kashmir. At the moment the valley (and the mountains around it) was all the world he knew. He was still part of it. Twenty-seven years after I had got to know him, Aziz had remained more or less the same. It wouldn't be like that with Nazir. Already he had intimations of a world outside.

Already, through the monthly exchange of letters with a foreign girl, there had come to him the idea of the possibility—always in Allah's hands—of a foreign marriage. In 27 years—hard for me now, in late middle age, to imagine that stretch of time, that boundary in the shades—Nazir wouldn't be the same. New ways of seeing and feeling were going to come to him, and he wasn't going to be part of the valley in the way he was now. (516)

We read Naipaul, and our ways of "seeing and feeling" are enriched by the exchange. Cultural shocks and collisions, the world's need for words to commemorate and comprehend itself, the knowing of self by knowing others: Naipaul's art of exile, of the margins and the space between origins and destinations, is about all of us in a world radically changing and in our awakening to the stranger without and within.

# Notes

All translations are my own, unless otherwise indicated.

### Introduction

Naipaul conveys the idea expressed in the epigraph quotation from "Jasmine" in other works as well. In *The Middle Passage*, for example, he quotes Stephen Dedalus's laments in James Joyce's *A Portrait of the Artist as a Young Man:* "The language in which we are speaking is his before it is mine. How different are the words home, Christ, ale, master, on his lips and mine! . . . My voice holds them at bay. My soul frets in the shadow of his language." See *The Middle Passage: Impressions of Five Societies—British, French and Dutch—in the West Indies and South America* (London: Andre Deutsch, 1962; New York: Vintage Books, 1981), p. 163.

1. V. S. Naipaul, "Jasmine," *The Overcrowded Barracoon* (New York: Vintage Books, 1984), pp. 29, 25.

2. Language is part of the conquest and transformation of others. There is an interesting passage in Cheikh Hamidou Kane's *L'Aventure ambiguë* (The ambiguous adventure) in which the protagonist explains that it was through language in part that the French conquered his African people. He explains his own fascination with the signs, structure, and musicality of French; through it he comprehends his world anew. Yet this language also transforms him and sets him at a distance from his native world. He becomes a divided man, an "exile," through the language of the conquering culture and society. See *L'Aventure ambiguë* (Paris: Union Generale d'Editions, 1961), pp. 172–73.

3. For a discussion of colonial alienation, see Bill Ashcroft, Gareth Griffiths, and Helen Tiffin, *The Empire Writes Back: Theory and Practice in Post-Colonial Literature* (London and New York: Routledge, 1989), pp. 9–10. For a discussion of "map" and "territory," see S. I. and Alan R. Hayakawa, *Language and Thought*, 5th ed. (San Diego: Harcourt Brace Jovanovich, 1990), pp. 20–21, or

Alfred Korzybski, *Science and Sanity: An Introduction to Non-Aristotelian Systems and General Semantics* (Lancaster, Penn.: Science Press Printing Company, 1933).

4. "The English language was mine; the tradition was not," Naipaul writes in "Jasmine," p. 26.

5. Maurice Merleau-Ponty, *Phénomenologie de la perception* (Paris: Gallimard, 1945), p. viii.

6. Tzvetan Todorov, *Nous et les autres: La Réflexion française sur la diversité humaine* (Paris: Editions du Seuil, 1989), pp. 382–83. The majority of this paragraph paraphrases Todorov's commentary on the concept of exile.

7. For an elaboration of the concept of in-between, see Daniel Sibony, *L'Entre-deux ou l'origine en partage* (Paris: Editions du Seuil, 1991).

8. See "Without a Place," *Savacou* 9–10 (1974); reprinted as "Without a Place: Interview, Ian Hamilton," in *Critical Perspectives on V. S. Naipaul*, ed. R. D. Hamner (Washington, D.C.: Three Continents Press, 1977), p. 45.

9. Paul Bowles, *Their Heads Are Green and Their Hands Are Blue* (New York: Random House, 1957), p. vii.

10. Todorov, *La Conquête de l'Amérique: La Question de l'autre* (Paris: Editions du Seuil, 1982), p. 245.

11. Julia Kristeva, *Etrangers à nous-mêmes* (Paris: Fayard, 1988), p. 13.

12. Edward W. Said, "The Mind of Winter: Reflections on Life in Exile," *Harper's Magazine*, 269 (September 1984): 50.

13. On the topic of Naipaul and exile, see, for example, Andrew Gurr, *Writers in Exile: The Identity of Home in Modern Literature* (Sussex: The Harvester Press, 1981); Ling-Mei Lim, *V. S. Naipaul's Later Fiction: The Creative Constraints of Exile* (Ph.D. diss., Indiana University, 1984); and Gareth Griffiths, *A Double Exile: African and West Indian Writing Between Two Cultures* (London: Marion Boyars, 1978).

14. Kenneth Ramchand, *The West Indian Novel and Its Background*, 2d ed. (London: Heinemann, 1983), p. 12.

15. Wilson Harris, *The Womb of Space: The Cross-Cultural Imagination* (Westport, Conn.: Greenwood Press, 1983), pp. 120–22.

16. In Todorov, *Nous et les autres*, pp. 382–83.

17. Todorov, *Nous et les autres*, pp. 382–83.

18. Todorov, *La Conquête de l'Amérique*, pp. 253, 133.

19. Mircea Eliade, *Yoga: Immortality and Freedom*, trans. Willard R. Trask, Bollingen Series 56 (New York: Pantheon Books, 1958), p. xiii.

20. See Todorov, *La Conquête de l'Amérique*, p. 34.

21. Kristeva, *Etrangers*, pp. 13, 219, 282, 152, 250, 283.

22. Camara Laye, *L'Enfant noir* (Paris: Plon, 1953), pp. 169–70.

23. Cheik Hamidou Kane, *L'Aventure ambiguë*, p. 163.

24. V. S. Naipaul, "One Out of Many," *In a Free State* (London: Andre Deutsch, 1971; New York: Vintage Books, 1984), p. 29.

## Notes to Introduction

25. Naipaul, "Prologue, from a Journal: The Tramp at Piraeus," *In A Free State*, p. 9.
26. C. P. Cavafy, *The Complete Poems of Cavafy*, expanded ed., trans. Rae Dalven, intro. W. H. Auden (New York: Harcourt Brace Jovanovich, 1976), p. 27.
27. Naipaul, "East Indian," *The Overcrowded Barracoon*, p. 37.
28. See, for example, V. S. Naipaul, "Prologue to an Autobiography," *Finding the Center: Two Narratives* (New York: Alfred A. Knopf, 1984; New York: Vintage Books, 1986).
29. See V. S. Naipaul, Foreword, *The Adventures of Gurudeva* (London: Andre Deutsch, 1976), p. 18. See also "The Novelist V. S. Naipaul Talks to Nigel Bingham about His Childhood in Trinidad," *The Listener* 88 (7 September 1972): 306.
30. Todorov, *Nous et les autres*, p. 390.
31. M. M. Bakhtin, "A Response to a Question from the *Novy Mir* Editorial Staff," *Speech Genres & Other Late Essays*, trans. Vern W. McGee, ed. Caryl Emerson and Michael Holquist (Austin: University of Texas Press, 1986), p. 7. The word *exotopy* is Tzvetan Todorov's coinage to match M. M. Bakhtin's coinage of a term that signifies "outsideness." Todorov explains: the "second aspect of creative activity is named by Bakhtin with a new Russian coinage: *vnenakhodimost*, literally 'finding oneself outside,' which I shall translate, again literally, but with a Greek root, as *exotopy*." See Tzvetan Todorov, *Mikhail Bakhtin: The Dialogic Principle*, trans. Wlad Godzich (Minneapolis: University of Minnesota Press, 1984), p. 99. Throughout this study I will use *exotopic* as the adjectival form of the noun *exotopy*.
32. In Todorov, *Nous et les autres*, pp. 391, 392.
33. Ashcroft, Griffiths, and Tiffin, *The Empire Writes Back*, p. 12.
34. Lim, *V. S. Naipaul's Later Fiction*, p. 269.
35. In Todorov, *La Conquête de l'Amérique*, p. 253.
36. Bowles, *Their Heads Are Green*, p. vii. The word *jumblies* comes from an Edward Lear poem. Paul Bowles quotes from the poem as the epigraph to *Their Heads Are Green:*

> Far and few, far and few,
>  Are the lands where the Jumblies live;
>  Their heads are green, and their hands are blue,
>  And they went to sea in a Sieve.

37. Muneo Jay Yoshikawa, "The Double-Swing Model of Intercultural Communication between the East and the West," in *Communication Theory: Eastern and Western Perspectives*, ed. D. Lawrence Kincaid (San Diego: Academic Press, 1987), pp. 320–23.
38. Carmel Camilleri, "La Communication dans la perspective interculturelle,"

*Chocs de cultures: Concepts et enjeux pratiques de l'interculturel*, ed. Carmel Camilleri and Margalit Cohen-Emerique (Paris: Editions L'Harmattan, 1989), 363.

39. Charles Michener, "The Dark Visions of V. S. Naipaul," *Newsweek*, 16 November 1981, 105, 109.

40. E. H. Gombrich, *Art and Illusion: A Study in the Psychology of Pictorial Representation*, Bollingen Series 35, 5 (Princeton: Princeton University Press, 1972), p. 172.

41. Naipaul notes that between his birth and the age of seven he lived in seven or eight different houses: "I think it is because one has lived this disordered life that I haven't been able to settle down, even as an adult." See the Bingham interview, p. 306.

42. In an interview with Ian Hamilton, Naipaul remarks: "London is my metropolitan centre; it is my commercial centre; and yet I know that it is a kind of limbo and that I am a refugee in the sense that I am always peripheral." See "Without a Place: Interview, Ian Hamilton," p. 41.

43. Foreword, *The Adventures of Gurudeva*, p. 22.

44. In *V. S. Naipaul: A Materialist Reading*, Selwyn R. Cudjoe insightfully observes that "the subtheme of home (what or where is home?) and displacement (trying to find a center) arose with enormous force, persistence, and urgency in [Naipaul's] early texts. Adaptation and change carried a price; the resulting psychic pain subtends his work." See *V. S. Naipaul: A Materialist Reading* (Amherst: University of Massachusetts Press, 1988), p. 29. There are similarities between Cudjoe's analysis of exile in Naipaul's works and the analysis in this study; on the whole, I believe that this study views exile as more of a transformative movement toward creative understanding of self and others than does Cudjoe's, but to voice that major difference is not to disagree with his "materialist reading" of Naipaul. I have reflected on his reading while revising drafts of this study and have reformulated certain concepts (like "carnival" in chapter 1) and sharpened the focus in part through that reflective dialogue.

## 1. Carnival

1. V. S. Naipaul, "London," *The Overcrowded Barracoon* (New York: Vintage Books, 1984), p. 11. In the Foreword to *The Adventures of Gurudeva* Naipaul notes the mixed romantic-satiric mood and East Indian-West Indian ethnic perspective of his father's short stories as an influence on his own writings: "my father's early stories created my background for me." These stories constitute "a unique record of the life of the Indian or Hindu community in Trinidad in the first fifty years of the century. They move from a comprehension of the old India in which the community is at first embedded to an understanding of the colonial Trinidad which defines itself as their background, into which they then merge."

See Foreword, *The Adventures of Gurudeva* by Seepersad Naipaul (London: Andre Deutsch, 1976), pp. 15, 19.

2. Mikhail Bakhtin, *Problems of Dostoevsky's Poetics*, ed. and trans. Caryl Emerson (Minneapolis: University of Minnesota Press, 1984), p. 107.

3. "Something of the Carnival lunacy touches all these islands where people, first as slaves and then as neglected colonials, have seen themselves as futile, on the other side of the real world." Naipaul, "Power?" *The Overcrowded Barracoon*, p. 247.

4. Ernest Mirville, *Considérations ethno-psychanalytiques sur le carnaval Haïtien* (Port-au-Prince: Collection Coucouille, 1978), p. 76.

5. The modern Trinidad carnival, Erroll Hill explains, originates in the ritualistic canboulay (*canne brûlé*) procession, a celebration of the slaves' emancipation; its origins evolve out of the African culture of the island, one with which the East Indians who came to Trinidad as indentured workers in the nineteenth century did not identify. Especially those East Indians who clung to caste traditions remained aloof from carnival, a "leveler of social distinctions." Naipaul's "carnival culture" derives from this history of difference between Afro-Caribbean and Asian Indian cultures; it echoes an earlier, nineteenth-century discourse that was "antipathetic and frequently hostile" toward carnival. For a discussion of the history of Trinidad carnival, see Erroll Hill, *The Trinidad Carnival: Mandate for a National Theatre* (Austin: University of Texas Press, 1972), pp. 10, 16.

6. M. M. Bakhtin, "Discourse in the Novel," *The Dialogic Imagination: Four Essays*, ed. Michael Holquist, trans. Caryl Emerson and Michael Holquist (Austin: University of Texas Press, 1981). In double-voiced works, "the author manifests himself . . . not only in his effect on the narrator, but also in his effect on the subject of the story—as a point of view that differs from the point of view of the narrator. Behind the narrator's story we read a second story." See pp. 429, 313–15.

7. Naipaul, "London," p. 11.

8. Postcolonial theory and criticism use the words *syncretism* and *hybridity* to define this phenomenon. The former designates "the process by which previously distinct linguistic categories, and, by extension, cultural formations, merge into a single new form"; the latter emphasizes the plurality of the self and the dialogic nature of the literary work. Bill Ashcroft, Gareth Griffiths, and Helen Tiffin, *The Empire Writes Back: Theory and Practice in Post-Colonial Literatures* (London and New York: Routledge, 1989), p. 15.

9. Kenneth Ramchand cites George Lamming's *In the Castle of My Skin* (1953) and Michael Anthony's *The Year in San Fernando* (1965) as Trinidadian works on the same subject. Kenneth Ramchand, *The West Indian Novel and Its Background*, 2d ed. (London: Heinemann, 1983), p. 205.

10. V. S. Naipaul, *Miguel Street* (New York: Penguin, 1971), p. 72. All further quotations are taken from this edition, which henceforth will be abbreviated as *MS* in parenthetical citations.

11. For a discussion of these concepts, see F. K. Stanzel, *A Theory of Narrative*, trans. Charlotte Goedsche, preface Paul Hernadi (Cambridge: Cambridge University Press, 1984), pp. 112–14, 146–47. Stanzel also makes a distinction between "teller-characters" (e.g., the adult of *Miguel Street* as narrating self) and "reflector characters" (e.g., the boy of *Miguel Street* as experiencing self): "A teller-character always functions as a 'transmitter,' that is, he narrates as if he were transmitting a piece of news or a message to a 'receiver,' the reader. Communication proceeds differently with a reflector-character. Since he does not narrate, he cannot function as a transmitter in the above sense. In this case the mediacy of presentation is characteristically obscured by the reader's illusion that he is witnessing the action directly—he feels he is perceiving it through the eyes and mind of the reflector-character. These differences between the two processes of communication have consequences for the interpretation of a narrative text, in that the narrative assumes varying degrees of credibility or validity depending on whether it is conveyed by a teller-character or by a reflector-character."

12. The casual acceptance of violence, particularly violence against women, children, and the powerless, is a disturbing aspect of the ghetto and what Naipaul calls the "picaroon" world of the colony; directly and indirectly, both he and his father (in *The Adventures of Gurudeva*) critique this acceptance of violence as part of husband-wife and parent-child relationships. In the latter Seepersad Naipaul describes the brutal beating of Ratni by her husband Gurudeva: "And he pounced on her . . . and bundled her out into the yard. Artfully he entwined her long hair around his fists and dragged her in a circle over the rough ground as though she were a sack of potatoes. And when she neither wailed nor wept, he disengaged his hands from her hair and cuffed her and kicked her frantically" (31). For his part, V. S. Naipaul writes that nowhere are children beaten as harshly as they are in the West Indies. See *The Middle Passage: Impression of Five Societies—British, French and Dutch—in the West Indies and South America* (London: Andre Deutsch, 1962; New York: Vintage Books, 1981), pp. 183, 190. Henceforth abbreviated as *MP* in parenthetical citations.

13. Bakhtin, *Problems of Dostoevsky's Poetics*, p. 126.

14. Of the sources of the characters and stories of *Miguel Street*, Landeg White notes: "It is significant that much of the material is based on anecdotes which are still widely current in Trinidad. See *V. S. Naipaul, A Critical Introduction* (New York: Barnes & Noble, 1975), p. 50.

15. See V. S. Naipaul, "The Mourners," *A Flag on the Island* (London: Andre Deutsch, 1967), pp. 55–62.

16. In 1949 Naipaul won a government scholarship to study in England; in 1950, at the age of eighteen, he left Trinidad. For a lively account of the scholarship process in Trinidad, see C. L. R. James, *Beyond a Boundary* (London, 1963; New York: Pantheon Books, 1983).

17. V. S. Naipaul, *The Suffrage of Elvira* (London, 1958; New York: Penguin, 1969), p. 9. All further quotations are taken from the 1969 edition.
18. Bakhtin, *Problems of Dostoevsky's Poetics*, p. 127.
19. Naipaul, *The Middle Passage*, p. 72.
20. Bridget Brereton, *A History of Modern Trinidad: 1783–1962* (Kingston: Heinemann, 1981), p. 227.
21. V. S. Naipaul, *The Mystic Masseur* (New York: Vintage Books, 1984), p. 11. All further quotations are taken from this edition.
22. Erich Fromm describes the interrelationship between economic, psychological, and ideological forces in this way:

man reacts to changing external situations by changes in himself, and . . . psychological factors in their turn help in molding the economic and social processes. Economic forces are effective, but they must be understood not as psychological motivations but as objective conditions: psychological forces are effective, but they must be understood as historically conditioned themselves; ideas are effective, but they must be understood as being rooted in the whole of the character structure of members of a social group. In spite of this interdependence of economic, psychological, and ideological forces, however, each of them has also a certain independence. This is particularly true of the economic development which, being dependent on objective factors, such as the natural productive forces, technique, geographical factors, takes place according to its own laws. As to the psychological forces . . . the same holds true; they are molded by the external conditions of life, but they also have a dynamics of their own; that is, they are the expression of human needs which, although they can be molded, cannot be uprooted. In the ideological sphere we find a similar autonomy rooted in logical laws and in the tradition of the body of knowledge acquired in the course of history.

See *Escape from Freedom* (New York: Rinehart & Company, 1941), pp. 297–98.
23. Foreword, *The Adventures of Gurudeva*, p. 7. Also see "Prologue to an Autobiography" in *Finding the Center* and "The Voyage" in *The Enigma of Arrival*.
24. Ganesh is a con man not unlike Valmond "Fatman" Jones, the "impresario" of the scam Sam Cooke concert that Naipaul writes about in *The Middle Passage*. The Fatman promotes two concerts that never take place, pockets the money, and flies "unexpectedly" to Martinique thirty-six hours before Cooke's purported arrival. Valmond Jones fleeces the gullible, but people admire him just the same for pulling it all off, Naipaul writes (*MP* 75–76).
25. There are, of course, other interpretations of Ganesh. In his excellent *V. S. Naipaul: A Materialist Reading*, Selwyn R. Cudjoe writes: "Ganesh's life parallels that of Gandhi in many essential details. Most important, his participation as a mystic in social and political life becomes the point of departure for understanding his life in the Wilderness." See *V. S. Naipaul: A Materialist Reading* (Amherst: University of Massachusetts Press, 1988), p. 45. See also Paul Theroux, *V. S. Naipaul: An Introduction to His Work* (New York: Africana Publishing Corporation, 1972).

## 2. A House for Mr Biswas

1. Kenneth Ramchand, *The West Indian Novel and Its Background*, 2d. ed. (London: Heinemann, 1983), p. 204.
2. For a discussion of Seepersad Naipaul and his East Indian community, see Bruce King, *The New English Literatures—Cultural Nationalism in a Changing World* (New York: St. Martin's Press, 1980), pp. 100–102. For a discussion of the impact of Seepersad Naipaul's stories on his son's early writings, see Anthony Boxill, "V. S. Naipaul's Starting Point," *The Journal of Commonwealth Literature* 10 (1975): 1–9. Also see Ramchand, *The West Indian Novel and Its Background*.
3. V. S. Naipaul, "Prologue to an Autobiography," *Finding the Center: Two Narratives* (New York: Alfred A. Knopf, 1984; Vintage Books, 1986), p. 60.
4. V. S. Naipaul, *A House for Mr Biswas* (London: Andre Deutsch, 1961; New York: Penguin, 1981), pp. 17–18. All further quotations are taken from the 1981 edition, which henceforth will be abbreviated as *HB* in text citations.
5. Eric Williams, *From Columbus to Castro: The History of the Caribbean 1492–1969* (New York: Vintage Books, 1984), p. 348. See, in general, the chapter entitled "Asian Immigration" for a discussion of this topic. About the status of the Asian laborer and the nature of the contract, Williams writes: "The Asian labourer was not a slave. He was a freeman, and he came to the Caribbean on contract, generally for five years. . . . The contract specified that the Asian labourer was to have a free passage to the West Indies before 1898, a free return passage at the end of his contract; those who arrived after 1898 were entitled to half the return passage in the case of males, two-thirds in the case of females. . . . The contract further provided for medical attention during his employment, and housing accommodation at the expense of the employer" (351–52).
6. The exact figure is 143,939. See Bridget Brereton, *A History of Modern Trinidad: 1783–1962* (Kingston: Heinemann, 1981), pp. 101–3.
7. Naipaul's grandfather "was brought to Trinidad as a baby from eastern Uttar Pradesh"; as a Brahmin he received a Hindu education and was trained as a pundit. See the Foreword to *The Adventures of Gurudeva* (London: Andre Deutsch, 1976), pp. 11–12. In the Foreword Naipaul also writes: "My father's elder brother, still only a child, was sent out to work in the fields at fourpence a day; but it was decided that my father, as the youngest of the children, should be educated and perhaps made pundit, like his father" (12).
8. The word *tulsi* means *basil* in Hindi. See V. S. Naipaul, *India: A Wounded Civilization* (New York: Alfred A. Knopf, 1977; New York: Vintage Books, 1978), p. 79.
9. In the Foreword of *The Adventures of Gurudeva* Naipaul writes that after the attempt to make his father a pundit failed, he began to do "odd jobs, attached to the household of a relative" (12–13). For Seepersad Naipaul's portrait of Trinidad village life, see "In the Village," pp. 172–75.

10. The barracks described in the novel seem to be related to but different from the typical housing of indentured laborers in Trinidad. Eric Williams describes them in this way: "One of the worst features of the [indenture] system was the housing provided the workers. In Trinidad the separate cottages of slavery gave way to 'barracks'—long-rooms partitioned off, without washing or sanitary facilities. Each family had a single room in the 'barracks'—there was no privacy, morality was impossible." Williams, *From Columbus to Castro*, p. 357.

11. In the Foreword of *The Adventures of Gurudeva* Naipaul writes: "I do not know how . . . the wish to be a writer came to my father. But I feel now, reading the stories after a long time and seeing so clearly (what was once hidden from me) the brahmin standpoint from which they are written, that it might have been the caste-sense, the Hindu reverence for learning and the word, awakened by the beginnings of an English education and a Hindu religious training" (12–13). Naipaul states that his father began writing for the *Trinidadian Guardian* in 1929 and that he was very much influenced by its new editor, Gault MacGowan, who "had come from *The Times* [of London] and in Trinidad was like a man unleashed." He looked at the island with a newcomer's eye and created a sensation with stories on voodoo, obeah, "prisoners escaping from Devil's Island," and vampire bats. "He saw stories everywhere; he could make stories out of nothing; his paper was like a daily celebration of the varied life of the island" (14).

12. Brereton, *A History of Modern Trinidad*, p. 110.

13. Brereton, *A History of Modern Trinidad*, pp. 110–11.

14. V. S. Naipaul, *Mr Stone and the Knights Companion* (London: Andre Deutsch, 1963; New York: Vintage Books, 1985), p. 118.

15. See V. S. Naipaul, "Jasmine," *The Overcrowded Barracoon* (London: Andre Deutsch, 1972; New York: Vintage Books, 1984), p. 29.

16. Brereton, *A History of Modern Trinidad*, pp. 112, 110.

17. Brereton, *A History of Modern Trinidad*, pp. 132–33.

18. V. S. Naipaul, *Among the Believers: An Islamic Journey* (New York: Alfred A. Knopf, 1981; New York: Vintage Books, 1982), p. 58.

19. V. S. Naipaul, *The Middle Passage: Impressions of Five Societies—British, French, and Dutch—in the West Indies and South America* (London: Andre Deutsch, 1962; New York: Vintage Books, 1981), pp. 41–42.

20. Naipaul, "Prologue to an Autobiography," *Finding the Center*, pp. 21–25, 66.

21. See also Landeg White, *V. S. Naipaul: A Critical Introduction* (New York: Barnes & Noble, 1975), pp. 28–33.

22. Naipaul, "Prologue to an Autobiography," *Finding the Center*, pp. 71–72.

23. Charles Michener, "The Dark Visions of V. S. Naipaul," *Newsweek*, 16 November 1981, 107–8.

24. Bruce King, "V. S. Naipaul," in *West Indian Literature*, ed. Bruce King (Hamden, Conn.: Archon Books, 1979), p. 165. In *The New English Literatures*,

King writes, interestingly: "If [*A House for Mr Biswas*] is a success story of immigrant life and New World assimilation, it also records the failure of Hindu culture to survive in the West Indies." *The New English Literatures—Cultural Nationalism in a Changing World* (New York: St. Martin's Press, 1980), p. 102.

25. Selwyn R. Cudjoe, *V. S. Naipaul: A Materialist Reading* (Amherst: University of Massachusetts Press, 1988), p. 71.

### 3. Metahistory and Marginality

"Le mythe ne cache rien et il n'affiche rien: il déforme; le mythe n'est ni un mensonge ni un aveu: c'est une inflexion. . . . il transforme l'histoire en nature." Roland Barthes, *Mythologies* (Paris: Editions du Seuil, 1957), p. 215.

1. V. S. Naipaul, *A Turn in the South* (New York: Alfred A. Knopf, 1989; New York: Vintage International, 1990). Henceforth this work will be abbreviated as *TS* in parenthetical citations.

2. V. S. Naipaul, *The Middle Passage: Impressions of Five Societies—British, French and Dutch—in the West Indies and South America* (London, 1962; New York: Vintage Books, 1981), p. 29. All further quotations will be taken from the 1981 edition.

3. Lloyd Best, quoted by Tom Barry, Beth Wood, and Deb Preusch, *The Other Side of Paradise: Foreign Control in the Caribbean* (New York: Grove Press, 1984), p. 4.

4. About 150,000 out of a population of 360,000. Percentages are based on statistics cited in Barry, Wood, and Preusch, *The Other Side of Paradise*.

5. Percentages based on statistics cited in Barry, Wood, and Preusch, *The Other Side of Paradise*, pp. x–xi.

6. Véronique Maurus, "La Martinique retranchée," *Le Monde*, Edition internationale, Sélection hebdomadaire, 12–18 April 1990, 8. Also see Véronique Maurus, "La Guadeloupe entre l'espoir et l'inquiétude," *Le Monde*, 12–18 April 1990, 7.

7. Herbert L. Hiller, "Escapism, Penetration and Response: Industrial Tourism and the Caribbean," *Caribbean Studies* 16.2: 113, quoted in Barry, Wood, and Preusch, *The Other Side of Paradise*, pp. 86, 82. Although Hiller does not use the word *larbin*, a term employed by Aimé Césaire, his critique of tourism seems to share a point with Aimé Césaire's and Frantz Fanon's critiques of colonialism and racism. Fanon, for example, recounts this racist joke that turns on the stereotyped servile attitude of blacks that a certain kind of Western tourism perpetuates:

"One day, Saint Peter sees three men arrive at the gates of heaven: a white man, a mulatto, and a Negro.
"—What do you want? he asks the white man.

## Notes to Metahistory and Marginality

"—Some money.
"—And you? he says to the mulatto.
"—Glory.
"And when it was the turn of the third man, the Negro declared with a big smile:
"—I came to carry the bags of these gentlemen." (39–40)

See Aimé Césaire, *Discours sur le Colonialisme* (Paris: Présence Africaine, 1955) and Frantz Fanon, *Peau noire, masques blancs* (Paris: Editions du Seuil, 1952).

8. Barry, Wood, and Preusch, *The Other Side of Paradise*, p. 81.
9. Eric Williams, *From Columbus to Castro: The History of the Caribbean 1492–1969* (New York: Vintage Books, 1970), p. 142.
10. Albert Memmi, *Portrait du colonisé précedé du portrait du colonisateur* (Utrecht: Jean-Jacques Pauvert, 1966), p. 42.
11. Ian Buruma, "The Bartered Bride," *The New York Review of Books*, 1 June 1989, 8, quoting *The Aquinos of Tarlac: An Essay on History as Three Generations* (Manila: Cacho Hermanos, 1983).
12. See Homi Bhabha, "Of Mimicry and Man: The Ambivalence of Colonial Discourse," *October* 28 (Spring 1984).
13. James Clifford, *The Predicament of Culture: Twentieth-Century Ethnography, Literature, and Art* (Cambridge: Harvard University Press, 1988), p. 15.
14. "La dévaluation du colonisé s'étend ainsi à tout ce qui le touche: A son pays, qui est laid, trop chaud . . . malodorant, au climat vicieux, à la géographie si désespérée qu'elle le condamne au mépris et à la pauvreté, à la dépendance pour l'éternité.

"Cet abaissement du colonisé, qui doit expliquer son dénuement, sert en même temps de repousser à la positivité du colonialiste. Ces accusations, ces jugements irrémédiablement négatifs sont toujours portés *par référence à la métropole*, c'est-à-dire. . . . par référence au colonialiste lui-même." Memmi, *Portrait du colonisé*, p. 105.
15. See Tzvetan Todorov, *La Conquête de l'Amérique: La Question de l'autre* (Paris: Editions du Seuil, 1982), p. 251.
16. V. S. Naipaul, *The Enigma of Arrival* (New York: Alfred A. Knopf, 1987), p. 153.
17. V. S. Naipaul, *The Loss of El Dorado: A History* (London, 1969; New York: Vintage Books, 1984), p. 13. All further quotations are taken from the 1984 edition.
18. V. S. Naipaul, Introduction, *East Indians in the Caribbean: Colonialism and the Struggle for Identity* (Millwood, N.Y.: Kraus International Publications, 1982), p. 4.
19. Barthes, *Mythologies*, p. 230.
20. J. M. G. Le Clézio, *Le Rêve mexicain, ou la pensée interrompue* (Paris: Gallimard, 1988), p. 112.

21. Barthes, *Mythologies*, pp. 208–9, 215.
22. Williams, *From Columbus to Castro*, p. 23.
23. Joseph Conrad, *Heart of Darkness*, ed. Robert Kimbrough (New York: W. W. Norton, 1971), pp. 6–7.
24. In Jamaica as well as other Caribbean islands the claim that Africans, not the Spanish, discovered the New World is popular. See Edwy Plenel, "Le Siècle des éclipses," in "Voyages avec Colomb," *Le Monde*, 31 August 1991, p. 2.
25. Williams, *From Columbus to Castro*, p. 33.
26. See Todorov, *La Conquête*, pp. 138–39.
27. Le Clézio, *Le Rêve mexicain*, p. 213.
28. Todorov, *La Conquête*, pp. 150, 179.
29. Williams, *From Columbus to Castro*, p. 69.
30. Todorov, *La Conquête*, p. 138.
31. Michel Tournier, *Vendredi ou les limbes du Pacifique* (Paris: Gallimard, 1972), p. 246.
32. Julia Kristeva, *Etranges à nous-mêmes* (Paris: Fayard, 1988).

## 4. The Greater Shipwreck

"L'inconvénient, dans la situation de l'exilé . . . réside en ce qu'il renonce . . . aux fortes relations avec ces autres parmi lesquels il vit." Tzvetan Todorov, *Nous et les autres: La Réflexion française sur la diversité humaine* (Paris: Editions de Seuil, 1989), p. 382.

" . . . à mi-distance de ces abîmes et de ces sommets, ils flottaient . . . abandonnés à des jours sans direction et à des souvenirs stériles. . . . Ils éprouvaient ainsi la souffrance profonde de tous les prisonniers et de tous les exilés, qui est de vivre avec une mémoire qui ne sert à rien" Albert Camus, *La Peste* (Paris: Gallimard, 1947), p. 72.

1. V. S. Naipaul, "East Indian," *The Overcrowded Barracoon* (New York: Vintage Books, 1984), p. 32.
2. Quoted by Eric Williams, *From Columbus to Castro: The History of the Caribbean 1492–1969* (New York: Vintage Books, 1970), p. 119.
3. Frantz Fanon, *Peau noire, masques blancs* (Paris: Editions du Seuil, 1952), p. 18. "Le Noir qui entre en France change parce que pour lui la métropole représente le Tabernacle; il change non seulement parce que c'est de là que lui sont venus Montesquieu, Rousseau et Voltaire, mais parce que c'est de là que lui viennent les médecins, les chefs de service, les innombrables petits potentats. . . . Il y a une sorte d'envoûtement à distance, et celui qui part dans une semaine à destination de la Métropole crée autour de lui un cercle magique où les mots Paris, Marseille, la Sorbonne, Pigalle représentent les clés de voûte."
4. Bruce King notes the irony of Singh's middle name: "he has become a cripple incapable of the independence, energy, cunning and will that are required to

make any city or nation fit his longings." See *The New English Literatures— Cultural Nationalism in a Changing World* (New York: St. Martin's Press, 1980), p. 106.

5. V. S. Naipaul, *Mr Stone and the Knights Companion* (London: Andre Deutsch, 1963; New York: Vintage Books, 1985), p. 101. Henceforth abbreviated as *MSK* in parenthetical citations.

6. Bharati Mukherjee and Robert Boyers, "A Conversation with V. S. Naipaul," *The Salmagundi Reader*, ed. Robert Boyers and Peggy Boyers (Bloomington: Indiana University Press, 1983), p. 453.

7. Perhaps an allusion to Isabela, Columbus's failed settlement on the island of Hispaniola. For an explanation of Columbus's method of naming and his "hermeneutic," see Tzvetan Todorov, *La Conquête de l'Amérique: La Question de l'autre* (Paris: Editions du Seuil, 1982), pp. 33–34.

8. V. S. Naipaul, *The Mimic Men* (London: Andre Deutsch, 1967; New York: Vintage Books, 1985), p. 242. All further quotations taken from this edition, which henceforth will be abbreviated as *MM* in parenthetical citations.

9. James Harrington, *Oceana* (1656), quoted by Williams, *From Columbus to Castro*, p. 169.

10. In "A Flag on the Island" the narrator remarks: "All landscapes are in the end only in the imagination; to be faced with reality is to start again." V. S. Naipaul, *A Flag on the Island* (London: Andre Deutsch, 1967), p. 149.

11. C. P. Cavafy, "The City," *The Complete Poems of Cavafy*, expanded ed., trans. Rae Dalven, intro. W. H. Auden (New York: Harcourt Brace Jovanovich, 1976), p. 27.

12. Tom Barry, Beth Wood, and Deb Preusch, *The Other Side of Paradise: Foreign Control in the Caribbean* (New York: Grove Press, 1984), pp. 35–36.

13. Barry, Wood, and Preusch, *The Other Side of Paradise*, pp. 99–109, 13.

14. Barry, Wood, and Preusch, *The Other Side of Paradise*, p. 5.

15. Jeff Drumtra and Thomas George, "The 1980s: A Lost Decade," *World View* 2, no. 3 (1989): 8.

16. *East Indians in the Caribbean: Colonialism and the Struggle for Identity*, intro. V. S. Naipaul (Millwood, N.Y.: Kraus International Publications, 1982), p. 8.

17. For a discussion of "freedom from" and "freedom to," see Erich Fromm, *Escape from Freedom* (New York: Rinehart & Company, 1941).

18. "Stone appears to be a Prufrockian 'little man,'" Robert Hamner has noted. See "Character and Setting," in *Critical Perspectives on V. S. Naipaul*, ed. R. D. Hamner (Washington, D.C.: Three Continents Press, 1977), p. 230.

19. Charles Michener, "The Dark Visions of V. S. Naipaul," *Newsweek*, 16 November 1981, 104.

20. T. F., "Le Goût bourgeois," book review of *Ni Vue Ni Connue* by Béatrix Le Wita, *Le Monde*, 9 December 1988, 24.

21. See Michel Tournier, *Vendredi ou les limbes du Pacifique* (Paris: Gallimard, 1972).
22. This sentence compares closely to a sentence of Conrad's that Naipaul quotes in the essay "Conrad's Darkness": "something inherent in the necessities of successful action . . . carried with it the moral degradation of the idea." See "Conrad's Darkness," *The Return of Eva Perón* (New York: Vintage Books, 1981), p. 233.
23. V. S. Naipaul, *An Area of Darkness* (London: Andre Deutsch, 1964; New York: Vintage Books, 1981), pp. 280–81.
24. Paul Bowles, *Up Above the World* (New York: The Ecco Press, 1966).
25. V. S. Naipaul, *A Bend in the River* (New York: Alfred A. Knopf, 1979; New York: Vintage Books, 1980), p. 241.
26. V. S. Naipaul, *The Enigma of Arrival* (New York: Alfred A. Knopf, 1987), p. 101–2. Henceforth abbreviated as *EA* in parenthetical citations.
27. Tournier, *Vendredi*, p. 181. See, at the end of this edition of Tournier's text, Gilles Deleuze's, "Michel Tournier et le monde sans autrui," pp. 257–83.
28. V. S. Naipaul, "London," *The Overcrowded Barracoon* (London: Andre Deutsch, 1972; New York: Vintage Books, 1984), p. 16.

## 5. An Exile in the Motherland

1. V. S. Naipaul, *An Area of Darkness* (London: Andre Deutsch, 1964; New York: Vintage Books, 1981), p. 29. All further quotations are taken from the 1981 edition, which henceforth will be abbreviated as *AD* in parenthetical citations. *An Area of Darkness* contains three parts plus a prelude and an epilogue. They are entitled: "Traveller's Prelude: A Little Paperwork"; Part I— "A Resting-Place for the Imagination," "Degree," "The Colonial," and "Romancers"; Part II—"A Doll's House on the Dal Lake," "The Medieval City," and "Pilgrimage"; Part III—"Fantasy and Ruins," "The Garland on my Pillow," "Emergency," and "The Village of the Dubes"; Epilogue—"Flight."
2. Naipaul's grandfather "was brought to Trinidad as a baby from eastern Uttar Pradesh"; as a Brahmin boy he received a Hindu education and was trained as a pundit. See the Foreword to *The Adventures of Gurudeva* (London: Andre Deutsch, 1976), pp. 11–12.
3. Bridget Brereton, *A History of Modern Trinidad: 1783–1962* (Kingston: Heinemann, 1981), p. 103, and Eric Williams, *From Columbus to Castro: The History of the Caribbean 1492–1969* (New York: Vintage Books, 1970), p. 348.
4. V. S. Naipaul, *India: A Million Mutinies Now* (New York: Viking, 1990), p. 8. Henceforth abbreviated as *IMMN* in parenthetical citations.
5. "When I was in the fourth form I wrote a vow . . . to leave [Trinidad] within five years. I left after six; and for many years afterwards in England, falling asleep in bedsitters with the electric fire on, I had been awakened by the nightmare that

I was back in the tropical Trinidad." See Charles Michener, "The Dark Visions of V. S. Naipaul," *Newsweek* 16 November 1981, 104–5.

6. See also Frantz Fanon, *Peau noire, masques blancs* (Paris: Editions du Seuil, 1952), p. 18.

7. As Ramchand explains, "By the early 1950s the pattern was established of emigration to the Mother Country for West Indian writers seeking the stamp of approval and wishing to live by their pens; nearly every West Indian novel since then has been first published by London publishing houses for sale to members of the British public." Kenneth Ramchand, *The West Indian Novel and Its Background*, 2d ed. (London: Heinemann, 1983), p. 12.

8. V. S. Naipaul, "East Indian," in *The Overcrowded Barracoon* (London: Andre Deutsch, 1972; New York: Vintage Books, 1984), p. 38.

9. See M. M. Bakhtin, "A Response to a Question from the *Novy Mir* Editorial Staff," *Speech Genres & Other Late Essays*, trans. Vern W. McGee, ed. Caryl Emerson and Michael Holquist (Austin: University of Texas Press, 1986), p. 7.

10. Naipaul, "The Last of the Aryans," in *The Overcrowded Barracoon*, p. 68. Henceforth abbreviated as "LA" in parenthetical citations.

11. For a discussion of castes, see Robert L. Hardgrave, Jr., *India: Government and Politics in a Developing Nation* (New York: Harcourt, Brace & World, 1970), p. 8; Jean Filliozat, *India: The Country and Its Traditions*, trans. Margaret Ledésert (London: George G. Harrap & Co., 1962); and Heinrich Zimmer, *Philosophies of India*, ed. Joseph Campbell (New York: Meridian Books, 1960). Jean Filliozat states that the castes and subcastes are "reputedly over three thousand in number." He writes: "The term 'caste' is a translation of the word 'jati,' used in Sanskrit and most of the modern languages, and denoting 'birth' or 'race'. The castes are closed groups, in theory practising endogamy and not eating with members of another caste. It is in vain that one looks for any precise definition of group. In modern India belonging to a caste implies no more than an acceptance that one is a member of it; intermarriage and fellowship in eating are no longer even fast rules, and belonging to a caste need not even imply recognition by other similar groups" (52).

12. Kathleen Gough, "Criteria of Caste Ranking in South India," *Man in India* 39 (1959): 15–17, quoted by Hardgrave, p. 8.

13. Naipaul, "Jamshed into Jimmy," in *The Overcrowded Barracoon*, p. 52.

14. As noted in chapter 3, for an interpretation that considers the creative and subversive qualities of colonial "mimicry," see Homi Bhabha, "Of Mimicry and Man: The Ambivalence of Colonial Discourse," *October* 28 (Spring 1984).

15. V. S. Naipaul, "A Second Visit," in *The Overcrowded Barracoon*, p. 94. Henceforth abbreviated as "SV" in parenthetical citations.

16. For a discussion of Indian religion and philosophy, see Zimmer, *Philosophies of India*; Filliozat, *India: The Country and Its Traditions*; and Mircea Eliade,

*Yoga: Immortality and Freedom,* trans. Willard R. Trask (New York: Pantheon Books, 1958).

17. In what sense is the West "wise"? Paul Ehrlich, Stanford University professor of population studies, points out that the United States, not the Third World, is the major source of environmental damage. "One American does 20 to 100 times more damage to the planet than one person in the Third World, and one rich American causes 1,000 times more destruction." "We are super consumers . . . and we're extraordinarily . . . sloppy with our technologies," he adds. See "U.S. called major cause of damage to the Earth," Chicago *Tribune,* 8 April 1990, 17.

18. See Edward W. Said, *Orientalism* (New York: Vintage Books, 1979). Critics such as Rana Kabbani have taken Naipaul to task for this: "No contemporary European writer would have dared such a [stereotyped] description . . . but Naipaul feels within his rights to offer whatever description suits his prejudice—for after all, he is 'involved' with this East, having emerged from it and having 'made good.'" See Rana Kabbani, *Europe's Myths of Orient* (Bloomington: Indiana University Press, 1986), p. 130.

19. Muneo Jay Yoshikawa, "The Double-Swing Model of Intercultural Communication between the East and the West," in *Communication Theory: Eastern and Western Perspectives,* ed. D. Lawrence Kincaid (San Diego: Academic Press, 1987), 320–23.

20. See M. M. Bakhtin and P. N. Medvedev, *The Formal Method in Literary Scholarship: A Critical Introduction to Sociological Poetics,* foreword by Wlad Godzich, trans. Albert J. Wehrle (Cambridge: Harvard University Press, 1985), p. 152.

21. V. S. Naipaul, *India: A Wounded Civilization* (New York: Random House, 1976; New York: Vintage Books, 1978), p. 9. All further quotations are taken from the 1978 edition and are abbreviated as *IN* in parenthetical citations.

22. Allan and Anne Findlay, *Population and Development in the Third World* (London: Methuen, 1987), p. 62.

23. Naipaul, "Indian Autobiographies," in *The Overcrowded Barracoon,* pp. 56–57; henceforth abbreviated at "IA" in parenthetical citations.

24. For a discussion of Naipaul's critique of Gandhi, see Sudha Rai, *V. S. Naipaul: A Study in Expatriate Sensibility* (New Delhi: Arnold-Heinemann, 1982), pp. 49–75.

25. Filliozat writes:

Knowledge of India's past varies considerably. Outside truly scholastic circles there are many who believe that the whole scope and chronology of India's past is contained in the Puranas ('old traditions'). . . . According to this tradition the world revolves in an everlasting cyclical and periodic movement around the axis of the North Pole, the home of the gods of nature. At the end of each major period everything is dissolved in chaos, then is reorganized into a new era, at first a kind of Paradise, where Dharma ('Right Order') reigns, only to decline gradually in power until the fourth and worst age, the Kaliyuga, is reached; it is this fourth age in which we are living at present.

Filliozat, *India: The Country and Its Traditions*, p. 120.

26. Dilop Hiro, *Inside India Today*, rev. ed. (New York: Monthly Review Press, 1979), p. 3.

27. "Books of travel will be good in proportion to what a man has previously in his mind; his knowing what to observe; his power of contrasting one mode of life with another. . . . 'He, who would bring home the wealth of the Indies, must carry the wealth of the Indies with him,'" Samuel Johnson writes. Quoted in James Boswell, *The Life of Samuel Johnson* (London, 1791), and in Eric Newby, *A Book of Travellers' Tales* (New York: Viking, 1985), p. 15.

28. On this point Peter Hughes remarks, interestingly: "While the white anthropologist constantly faces the problem of his visible difference and separation from the darker-skinned people he tries to be accepted among, Naipaul's problem is that of his likeness, the danger that he will be confused with the people he lives and travels with. Not only and obviously in India, but also in many parts of Asia, Africa, and even South America, where he can pass for a native or be confused with the Indian traders and merchants long resident there." See *V. S. Naipaul* (London: Routledge, 1988), p. 100.

29. See Bernard Chantebout, *Le Tiers Monde* (Paris: Armand Colin, 1986), pp. 11–28; David Drakakis-Smith, *The Third World City* (London: Methuen, 1987), p. 7; and John Cole, *Development and Underdevelopment: A Profile of the Third World* (London: Methuen, 1987), p. 88.

30. Hiro, *Inside India Today*, p. 18.

31. A. J. Jowett, quoted by Findlay, *Population and Development*, p. 50.

32. Hiro, *Inside India Today*, p. 18.

33. In *India: A Million Mutinies Now* Naipaul makes such a connection:

Independence had come to India like a kind of revolution; now there were many revolutions within that revolution. . . . And it was easy to see how someone . . . who had grown up with another idea of India and its development, could feel alienated and insecure.

Some such feeling of alienation I had know myself when I had gone to India, in 1962. (6)

## 6. The Recursive Voyage

1. Douglas Hofstadter, *Gödel, Escher, Bach: An Eternal Golden Braid: A Metaphorical Fugue on Minds and Machines in the Spirit of Lewis Carroll* (New York: Vintage Books, 1980), p. 127.

2. "You will find no new lands, you will find no other seas. . . . / Always you will arrive in this city." C. P. Cavafy, *The Complete Poems of Cavafy*, expanded ed., trans. Rae Dalven, intro. W. H. Auden (New York: Harcourt Brace Jovanovich, 1976), p. 27.

3. Rana Kabbani, *Europe's Myths of Orient* (Bloomington: Indiana University Press, 1986), p. 136.

4. "Part of the problem of writing is that you use up your experience. The great triumph is to go on," Naipaul has remarked. He goes on to say, "I have to travel. Unless my imagination can be released from all these familiar deadening scenes, I will go stale." Charles Michener, "The Dark Visions of V. S. Naipaul," *Newsweek* 16 November 1981, 105, 109.

5. Naipaul takes his travel writing and social commentary very seriously. He has stated that, for him, the essay can serve as well as fiction as a vehicle for expression of his ideas, and since the early 1960s he has written more "nonfiction" than "fiction." Albert Londres, the peripatetic French journalist, has said that a reporter must know first how to look and listen, for if he knows only how to write he will never amount to anything more than a *littérateur*. Journalism demands as much vision and skill as fiction writing, Londres contends, and Naipaul would no doubt agree. See Nicole Zand, "Albert Londres: 'La Plume dans la plaie,'" *Le Monde*, 6 January 1989, 16. See also, Y. C., "Notre Maître Albert," *L'Express*, 20 January 1989, 63.

6. V. S. Naipaul, "Jacques Soustelle and the Decline of the West," *The Overcrowded Barracoon* (London: Andre Deutsch, 1972; New York: Vintage Books, 1984), p. 193.

7. See Eric Fottorino, "Le Gabon met en cause les contraintes imposées par le FMI," *Le Monde*, Edition internationale, Sélection hebdomadaire, 1–7 March 1990, 9.

8. Naipaul, "Columbus and Crusoe," *The Overcrowded Barracoon*, p. 204. See also Peter Hulme, *Colonial Encounters: Europe and the Native Caribbean, 1492–1797* (London: Methuen, 1986), p. 22; and *The Journal of Christopher Columbus*, trans. Cecil Jane, rev. ed. Louis-André Vigneras (London, 1960), cited by Hulme, p. 23. Tzvetan Todorov interprets Columbus's constant references to gold and gain differently. He argues that Columbus talked about gold for the sake of his crew and the King, but what truly interested Columbus was the discovery of unknown lands and the conversion of their peoples to Christianity. His voyage was thus a crusade in the guise of a business venture. See *La Conquête de l'Amérique: La Question de l'autre* (Paris: Editions du Seuil, 1982), pp. 20–21.

9. Saint Kitts-Nevis became independent from Britain in 1983.

10. This is, as Naipaul puts it, the "deadly comic-strip humour of Negro politics." "St. Kitts: Papa and the Power Set," *The Overcrowded Barracoon*, pp. 229–30.

11. On an island where half the labor force works in the traditional sugar industry and a majority of the other half in new industrial plants paying fifty-two to eighty-eight cents per hour, the causes for unrest and the yearning for a better life are not hard to find; among the impoverished, the need for change, for a new economic power, is real. Tom Barry, Beth Wood, and Deb Preusch, *The Other*

*Side of Paradise: Foreign Control in the Caribbean* (New York: Grove Press, 1984), pp. 352–53.

12. Naipaul, "Anguilla: The Shipwrecked Six Thousand," *The Overcrowded Barracoon*, p. 232.

13. Barry, Wood, and Preusch, *The Other Side of Paradise*, p. 215.

14. In 1971, after the writing of Naipaul's essay, Anguilla again became a British dependency; more recently the island has succeeded in building a tourist industry and supplementing it with "brass-plate development," a system allowing corporations to use the island as a tax haven. Hardly a stage for a "little black comedy," Anguilla has gone in the other direction, turning itself into "the most liberal corporate domicile for offshore companies in the Eastern Caribbean." See Barry, Wood, and Preusch, *The Other Side of Paradise*, p. 131.

15. Errol Hill, *The Trinidad Carnival: Mandate for a National Theatre* (Austin: University of Texas Press, 1972), p. 21.

16. Naipaul, "Power?" *The Overcrowded Barracoon*, p. 247.

17. Eric Williams, former prime minister of Trinidad and Tobago, considers Naipaul's critique "harsh" but "true." Of Caribbean dependency and mimicry he writes: "A too-long history of colonialism seems to have crippled Caribbean self-confidence and Caribbean self-reliance, and a vicious circle has been set up: psychological dependence leads to an ever-growing economic and cultural dependence on the outside world. Fragmentation is intensified in the process. And the greater degree of dependence and fragmentation further reduces local self-confidence." Williams, *From Columbus to Castro: The History of the Caribbean 1492–1969* (New York: Vintage Books, 1970), p. 502.

18. Naipaul, "The Overcrowded Barracoon," *The Overcrowded Barracoon*, p. 255. In the 1973 interview with Ronald Bryden, Naipaul states that an estimated eighty kinds of jobs exist in Mauritius as opposed to ten thousand kinds of jobs in England or France (Bryden, "The Novelist V. S. Naipaul," p. 367). So high is the level of Mauritian unemployment that prostitution has become an acceptable "profession" even for students from the best schools ("OB" 274).

19. In 1986, Mauritius had about 1,100 inhabitants per square mile. Pierre Etienne Dostert, *Africa 1987*, The World Today Series (Washington, D.C.: Skye Corporation, 1986), p. 112. The island's population crisis has resulted, at least in part, from the eradication of malaria in 1949, after which the population zoomed upward carrying with it the problems associated with uncontrolled growth, such as high employment and the degradation of natural resources.

20. Jean-Pierre Langellier, "L'Ile Maurice, nouveau 'petit dragon,'" *Le Monde*, Edition internationale, 9–15 November 1989, 10.

21. Bryden, "The Novelist V. S. Naipaul," p. 368.

22. V. S. Naipaul. *The Return of Eva Perón* (New York: Alfred A. Knopf, 1980; Vintage Books, 1981), p. 24.

23. Naipaul writes: "Writing led both men [Michael X and Yeates] there: for

both of them, uneducated but clever, hustlers with the black cause always to hand . . . writing had for too long been . . . a form of applauded lie" (78).

24. The word *Argentina* means silvery. But, ironically, there are no silver mines in the country, whose name originates from Spanish explorers' belief in a magnificent land of silver that Indians wearing ornaments seemed to promise. This is a variation of the El Dorado theme, which Naipaul reflects on in *The Loss of El Dorado*. John A. Crow and George D. Crow, *Panorama de las Américas*, 7th ed. (Fort Worth, Tex.: Holt, Rinehart and Winston, 1989), p. 116.

25. The author focuses, for example, on machismo and political torture, writing that the "conquest and humiliation of women" is another form of the plunder that characterizes the country's history. It is the "victimization" of the "simple" by the "simpler." Uneducated and with few legal rights, Argentine women are "reared . . . for early marriages or for domestic service"; since few have money or the means of earning it, they "are meant to be victims" and "accept their victim role" (163).

26. Uruguay's reforms included a minimum wage for all workers, pensions, state-provided medical care and social security; it also included nationalization of the railroad and public utilities and a state-controlled chemical industry, banks, hotels, theaters, and casinos. The excesses that this system led to impoverished the country: 90 percent of the work force paid no income tax; of a million workers, 300,000 were on pension and 250,000 were employed by the government. See, for example, Crow, *Panorama de las Américas*, pp. 150–54.

27. Naipaul connects the welfare state with the weakening of the Uruguayan will and the sapping of vitality; words of a Uruguayan businessman sum this up: "'Utopia is the worst thing for a man. He is old at thirty. That happened to us'" (144). Work, struggle, disciplined living: Uruguay abandoned these, it would seem, when it adopted the model of the European welfare state and the good life; even its resources have been its undoing, or so it appears to Naipaul who suggests that the beaches—sun, sand, and surf—have become the country's Land of Cocaigne:

Montevideo is built along a beach; all roads south end in white sand and a bay.

And this is where Uruguayans regularly lose all sense of crisis, and the will to action is weakened: on the too accessible beach, in the resort developments just a few minutes outside Montevideo where many modest people have summer houses amid pines and dunes. (146)

That individuals and societies must struggle in order to create, in order to avoid dependency and parasitism constitutes a recurring theme in Naipaul's works. Interestingly, in the Mukherjee and Boyers interview Naipaul alludes to the decadence of today's North Americans who have been spoiled by their predecessor's successes and have lost the will to struggle that distinguished earlier generations. Mukherjee and Boyers, "A Conversation with V. S. Naipaul," pp. 450–68.

28. Mikhail Bakhtin, *Problems of Dostoevsky's Poetics* (Minneapolis: University of Minnesota Press, 1984), p. 124. For a discussion of the concept of carnival, see primarily pp. 122–37. Emphasis in original.

29. Louis Althusser, "A Letter on Art in Reply to André Daspre," in *Lenin and Philosophy and Other Essays*, trans. Ben Brewster (New York: Monthly Review Press, 1971), p. 222. Emphasis in original.

30. Ideology is a lens, or as Göran Therborn states, it is "the medium through which . . . consciousness and meaningfulness operate." Therborn, *The Ideology of Power and the Power of Ideology* (London: NLB, 1980), pp. 1–2.

31. Bernard Lewis points out that the term *fundamentalism* is a *Western* term originating in the United States in the early twentieth century and referring to certain Protestant groups who asserted their belief in the Bible's literal divine origin and textual inerrancy. The term has found its way into European languages and into Arabic, where it is "used by secularized Muslims to describe their militant compatriots." The term *fundamentalism* is misleading, Lewis notes:

Where the so-called Muslim fundamentalists differ from other Muslims—and incidentally from Christian fundamentalists—is in their scholasticism and their legalism. The gravamen of their case against existing regimes and prevailing ideologies is the abandonment of the *Shari'a*, the systematized law of Islam, and the adoption of what they see as infidel laws and customs. . . . Their critique is not, however, limited to these issues, but covers the whole range of social and cultural modernization. Their declared purpose is to undo all the political, legal, and consequent social changes that have been introduced during the period of Westernization, and to restore the full panoply of the Islamic state and the Islamic holy law.

See Lewis, "Islamic Revolution," *The New York Review of Books*, 21 January 1988, 48–49.

32. For example, Edward Mortimer's *Faith and Power: The Politics of Islam*, written in the wake of the overthrow of the Shah and the occupation of the U.S. embassy in Tehran, includes chapters or case studies of Turkey, Saudi Arabia, Pakistan, Egypt, Syria, Libya, Iran, and the Soviet Union. See *Faith & Power: The Politics of Islam* (New York: Vintage Books, 1982).

33. Jonathan Broder and Ray Moseley, "Islam Fundamentalists—Heralds of a Holy War," *Chicago Tribune*, 8 November 1987, 1, 12.

34. "Muslim countries, where not colonized, were despotisms; and nearly all, before oil, were poor," Naipaul writes. *Among the Believers: An Islamic Journey* (New York: Alfred A. Knopf, 1981; Vintage Books, 1982), p. 12.

35. According to Therborn, ideology operates dialectially by a process of "subjection-qualification" (or, *interpellation*, Althusser's term). Ideologies "subject and qualify subjects by telling them, relating them to, and making them recog-

nize" three things: "what exists," "what is good," and "what is possible." The first element, existence, concerns "who we are, what the world is, what nature, society, men and women are like." Through ideology "we acquire a sense of identity, becoming conscious of what is real and true; the visibility of the world is thereby structured by the distribution of spotlights, shadows, and darkness." The second element, goodness, concerns what is "right, just, beautiful, attractive, enjoyable, and its opposites." Through ideology "our desires become structured and norm-alized." The third element, possibility, concerns the patterning of "our sense of the mutability of our being-in-the-world" and the shaping of "our hopes, ambitions, and fears." Therborn explains that ideological subjection or qualification operates in recognition of a "central Subject" (whether God, Father, Reason, Class, etc.) that "patterns the super-ego" of those subjected and provides them with "ego-ideals." See Therborn, *The Ideology of Power*, p. 18.

36. The concept here is simple: instead of modernizing Islam, fundamentalists seek to Islamize modernity. "Allah contre Satan" in "L'Islam en Fièure," *Le Monde*, 4–13 April 1989, 5.

37. Robin Wright, *Sacred Rage: The Wrath of Militant Islam* (New York: Simon & Schuster, 1985), p. 35.

38. Bruno Etienne, *L'Islamisme radical* (Paris: Hachette, 1987), quoted in "Allah contre Satan," p. 5.

39. Lewis, "Islamic Revolution," p. 49.

40. "Allah contre Satan," p. 1.

41. Objectives Resolution adopted by the Constituent Assembly of Pakistan, Karachi, 12 March 1949; a document cited by Mortimer, *Faith and Power*, pp. 186, 411.

42. The country's name has been attributed to an Indian Moslem, Rahmat Ali, who coined it while a student in England in the 1930s. It signifies "all the territorial constituents" of the ethnic "Fatherland" of the Paks. Khalid bin Sayeed, *Pakistan: The Formative Phase 1857–1948*, 2d ed. (Oxford: Oxford University Press, 1968), p. 48; cited by Mortimer, *Faith and Power*, pp. 199–200. According to Rahmat Ali, Pakistan is an acronym standing for Punjab, Afghania, Kashmir, Iran, Sind, Tukharistan, Afghanistan, and Baluchistan.

43. John Cole, *Development and Underdevelopment: A Profile of the Third World* (London: Methuen, 1987), pp. 88–89.

44. Mortimer, *Faith and Power*, pp. 224–27.

45. The recent past has been a period of decline for Islamic civilization, and Moslems have perceived two possible reasons for and responses to this decline: "Either the claims of Islam were false and the Christian or post-Christian West had finally come up with another system that was superior, or Islam had failed through not being true to itself. In the latter case, once the true Islam had been rediscovered and practised it could not fail to reassert its superiority, in the political domain as in others." Mortimer, *Faith and Power*, p. 87. In *V. S.*

*Naipaul's Later Fiction: The Creative Constraints of Exile* Ling-Mei Lim writes: "Naipaul's objection to the desire for 'cultural purity' stems from its retrogressive tendencies, its inability to face the complexity of the present times. Colonialism, though reprehensible in its morality, has opened up for Third World societies a pandora's box of mixed possibilities which cannot be dealt with simply by reasserting ancestral ways. By intruding into 'closed' indigenous cultures, colonialism has brought irreversibly the awareness of a movement of history and human activities beyond the confines of these societies. The awareness of other races and other values brings dislocations to the native worlds, setting up other standards by which their own activities must be evaluated." Lim, *V. S. Naipaul's Later Fiction: The Creative Constraints of Exile* (Ph.D. diss., Indiana University, 1986), p. 278.

46. About 38 percent of Malaysians are Muslim. Broder and Moseley, "Islam Fundamentalists," pp. 1, 8.

47. Malaysia has 15.7 million inhabitants. Cole, *Development and Underdevelopment*, pp. 88–90.

48. David Drakakis-Smith, *The Third World City* (London: Metheun, 1987), pp. 82–85. Drakakis-Smith writes: "inequality actually increased in Malaysia in the decade following independence . . . and inter-ethnic tensions built up considerably. The Malay peasants resented their worsening plight and blamed those in the cities (who were mainly Chinese); the poor urban Malays resented Chinese domination of industrial and commercial employment; the Chinese proletariat resented their low wages and blamed the Malaysian government's repression of trade unions; the Chinese bourgeoisie resented their exclusion from government and new industrial development. All of this resentment was ignited by the 1969 elections which resulted in major urban ethnic rioting and several hundred deaths" (85).

49. Ninety percent of Indonesia's population is Muslim. Broder and Moseley, "Islam Fundamentalists," pp. 1, 8.

50. The Indonesian government is distrustful of the fundamentalist movement, and since 1985 all religions in Indonesia have been forbidden to engage in political activities. See "Asie de Sud-Est: Tolérance sous les tropiques," *Le Monde*, 12 April 1989: 7.

51. This analysis also differs from that of Marvin Zonis, director of the Middle East Institute of the University of Chicago, who calls Iran's revolutionary Islam "the single most impressive political ideology which has been proposed in the 20th century since the Bolshevik Revolution." See Zonis, "Psychological Roots of Shi'ite Muslim Terrorism," quoted by Robin Wright, *Sacred Rage*, p. 31.

52. An ideology does not exist in isolation but in dialogic relationship with other ideologies; as such, "ideologies overlap, compete and clash, drown or reinforce each other." Therborn comments that the operation of ideology in society is "better illustrated by the cacophony of sounds and signs of a big city street than

by the text serenely communicating with the solitary reader, or the teacher or TV-personality addressing a quiet, domesticated audience." Therborn, *Ideology of Power*, p. vii.

53. In 1988 Benazir Bhutto became the prime minister and first female head of state of an Islamic country. See J.-P. Péroncel-Hugoz, "Islam et deuxième sexe," *Le Monde*, 2 December 1988, 6.

54. Kabbani, *Europe's Myths of Orient*, p. 134.

55. Within the Islamic diaspora, there are differences, as any traveler who has visited a Muslim country like Saudi Arabia, on the one hand, and Tunisia, on the other hand, will observe. Social attitudes toward women's identities and roles can vary significantly from one Muslim country to another. In Saudi Arabia, women wear veils in public, do not drive cars, and attend sexually segregated schools. In Tunisia, where polygamy has been abolished, judiciary divorce in lieu of "repudiation" has been instituted, and political rights, including suffrage, have been extended to women, women are superficially and perhaps profoundly different from their Saudi counterparts. What is true of social attitudes toward women is also true of myriad other attitudes and responses. When the Ayatollah Khomeini condemned British author Salman Rushdie for blasphemy against Islam, many Muslims around the world looked up to Khomeini as their spiritual leader and expressed their anger against Rushdie and the publishers of his book—but many Muslims did not. At that time the Tunisian daily newspaper *La Presse* carried a front-page editorial entitled "Peut-on convaincre par la violence?" (Can one convince through violence?) in which the representative of the Arab League in Paris sought to recast the image of crazed, sword-bearing Islam that Khomeini had once again encouraged. See J. de L. G., "Un 'acquis' irréversible," *Le Monde*, 6–7 November 1988, 9; Ray Moseley, "Women search for new roles in Islamic settings," *Chicago Tribune*, 11 November 1987, 1, 8; and Hamadi Essid, "Peut-on convaincre par la violence?" *La Presse de Tunisie*, 23 February 1989, 1. Also see Sylvaine Pasquier, with Elie Marcuse, "Le Livre qui enflamme l'Islam," *L'Express*, 24 February 1989, 22–24; "L'Imam Khomeiny confirme sa condamnation de Salman Rushdie et attaque les 'libéraux' en Iran," *Le Monde*, 24 February 1989, 3; André Fontaine, "Entre la flèche et la cible," *Le Monde*, 24 February 1989, 1, 3.

56. J.-P. Péroncel-Hugoz, "Un Génial attentat contre le Coran," review of *Le Coran*, by Jacques Berque, *Le Monde*, Sélection hebdomadaire, 14–20 February 1991, 12.

57. V. S. Naipaul, *Finding the Center: Two Narratives* (New York: Alfred A. Knopf, 1984; Vintage Books, 1986), p. vii.

58. Janet Varner Gunn, *Autobiography: Toward a Poetics of Experience* (Philadelphia: University of Pennsylvania Press, 1982), pp. 33–35.

59. See Mircea Eliade, *Yoga: Immortality and Freedom*, trans. Willard R. Trask, Bollingen Series 56 (New York: Pantheon Books, 1958), p. 13.

60. During 1989 and 1990 the Ivory Coast (and other West African countries) experienced the most severe crisis since its independence; strikes and riots fractured the country's reputation for stability. See, for example, Jose-Alain Fralon, "Vent de fronde sur la Côte-d'Ivoire," *Le Monde*, Sélection hebdomadaire, 1–7 March 1990, 1, 7; and "Côte-d'Ivoire: Les Libanais, boucs émissaires de la crise," Sélection hebdomadaire, 22–28 March 1990, 5. See also Eric Fottorino, "Le Gabon met en cause les contraintes imposées par le FMI," *Le Monde*, Sélection hebdomadaire, 1–7 March 1990, 7.

61. See the chapter on Jules Verne in Pierre Macherey, *Pour une théorie de la production littéraire* (Paris: François Maspero, 1978), pp. 183–254.

## 7. The Fourth World

1. V. S. Naipaul, "The Novelist V. S. Naipaul Talks About His Work to Ronald Bryden," *The Listener* 89 (22 March 1973): 368.

2. *Libanisation* refers to the splintering of a country, Lebanon, into small warring factions.

3. Many of these statistics are cited by David Lamb, *The Africans* (New York: Vintage Books, 1985), p. 109; also see Pierre Etienne Dostert, *Africa 1987*, The World Today Series (Washington, D.C.: Skye Corporation, 1986).

4. The countries or regions in which fighting of one sort or another was taking place are Angola, Ethiopia, Liberia, Mali, Mauritania, Mozambique, Uganda, Rwanda, the West Sahara, Senegal, Somalia, Sudan, and Chad. See Jacques de Barrin, "Les treize guerres du continent noir," *Le Monde*, Edition internationale, Sélection hebdomadaire, 18–24 October 1990, 5.

5. Lamb, *The Africans*, pp. 113–20.

6. See Jean de la Guérivière, "Le Président Adhmed Abdallah a été assassiné," *Le Monde*, Edition internationale, Sélection hebdomadaire, 23 November 1989, 6.

7. "Conrad's Darkness," *The Return of Eva Péron* (New York: Vintage Books, 1981), p. 233.

8. V. S. Naipaul, *The Enigma of Arrival* (New York: Alfred A. Knopf, 1987), p. 166.

9. V. S. Naipaul, *In a Free State* (London: Andre Deutsch, 1971; New York: Vintage Books, 1984), p. 9. All further quotations taken from the 1984 edition.

10. See Erich Fromm, *Escape from Freedom* (New York: Rinehart & Company, 1941), p. 256.

11. Although the terms *Third World* and *First World* have become outdated, no alternate terms have yet taken their place. Of a new actuality in the world, Alvin Toffler writes, in *Powershift*, "from now on the world will be split between the fast and the slow." See *Powershift: Knowledge, Wealth, and Violence at the Edge of the 21st Century* (New York: Bantam Books, 1990), p. 397.

12. From Naipaul's interviews and works, especially the semiautobiographical *Enigma of Arrival*, the reader can gain an insight into the construction of images of Africa in the novel. "In a Free State" refers to events in Rwanda, Kenya, and Uganda, and it anticipates the breakdown and horror that overtook the latter country in the 1970s. "I got very frightened being [in Uganda] in 1966," Naipaul has commented. "I used to think, 'I'm alone here . . . terrible things are coming here.'" And terrible things did come. Once considered Britain's most promising African colony, "the pearl of Africa" in the words of Winston Churchill, Uganda's natural and man-made assets included fertile farmland, rich forests, abundant wildlife, a solid economy, the continent's top university, excellent hospitals, a thousand miles of paved roads, and a rail network, yet Uganda's postcolonial history rivals any in tragedy, chaos, and horror. By 1977, fifteen years after its independence, the country had fallen apart, descending into what seemed an unending nightmare in which many thousands of people were tortured and killed. At the height of the horror, dump trucks plied the streets of Kampala collecting bodies of victims. A reported 200,000 people were killed during the Amin years, though the actual figure probably approached one million. Another 300,000 people were killed during the reprisal after Amin's ouster. Also see Lamb, *The Africans*, pp. 83–93, and Dostert, *Africa 1987*, pp. 126–27. Also see Bharati Mukherjee and Robert Boyers, "A Conversation with V. S. Naipaul," *The Salmagundi Reader*, ed. Robert Boyers and Peggy Boyers (Bloomington: Indiana University Press, 1983), 459, 464.
13. V. S. Naipaul, "Jacques Soustelle and the Decline of the West," *The Overcrowded Barracoon* (London: Andre Deutsch, 1972; New York: Vintage Books, 1984), p. 200.
14. V. S. Naipaul, *Guerrillas* (London: Andre Deutsch, 1975; New York: Vintage Books, 1980), p. 215. All further quotations are taken from the 1980 edition.
15. Tom Barry, Beth Wood, and Deb Preusch, *The Other Side of Paradise: Foreign Control in the Caribbean* (New York: Grove Press, 1984), p. 364.
16. See Jean-Michel Caroit, "Les Rebelles musulmans se sont rendus sans conditions," *Le Monde*, Edition internationale, Sélection hebdomadaire, 2–9 August 1990, 6.
17. Mukherjee and Boyers, "A Conversation with the V. S. Naipaul," p. 459.
18. Bakhtin explains the process of appropriation in this way: "The word in language is half someone else's. It becomes 'one's own' only when the speaker populates it with his own intentions, his own accent, when he appropriates the word, adapting it to his own semantic and expressive intention. Prior to this moment of appropriation, the word does not exist in a neutral and impersonal language . . . but rather it exists in other people's intentions: it is from there that one must take the word, and make it one's own." See M. M. Bakhtin, "Discourse in the Novel," *The Dialogic Imagination: Four Essays of M. M. Bakhtin* (Austin: University of Texas Press, 1981), pp. 293–94.

19. In a world of mixing races and cultures, who is "black," who is "brown," and who is "white"? *Guerrillas* has a racist element, but it also offers an insight: "pure things fall apart." For a discussion of this idea, see James Clifford, *The Predicament of Culture: Twentieth-Century Ethnography, Literature, and Art* (Cambridge: Harvard University Press, 1988).

20. Mukherjee and Boyers, "A Conversation with V. S. Naipaul," p. 462.

21. V. S. Naipaul, *A Bend in the River* (New York: Alfred A. Knopf, 1979; New York: Vintage Books, 1980), p. 11. All further quotations taken from the 1980 edition.

22. The "Big Man" is of course modeled on Zaire's president Mobutu, whose ideological program, originally called *authenticité* and later "Mobutuism," was promulgated through his self-created political party, *le Mouvement Populaire de la Révolution*. The program and party's objective, the fostering of an "authentic" African spirit in those who had lost it through the processes of colonialism, was worthy, but the party thrived on exclusion and corruption and became a vehicle for the personality cult of the president. Mobutu ruled absolutely, controlling appointments and promotions, and by appropriating revenues he accumulated more and more power. He assumed grandiose titles such as "Guide" and "Messiah" and had himself praised in Zairian song and dance. Officials wore badges with his portrait on them; each day's television programming began with his image descending as if from heaven. See Martin Meredith, *The First Dance of Freedom: Black Africa in the Postwar Era* (New York: Harper & Row, 1984), p. 344.

23. The recent Liberian conflict is a good example. Gios, Krahns, and Manos have long distrusted one another, but it was a mix of socioeconomic elements that brought about the Liberian civil war. See C. S., "Le Libériens tentent de se doter d'un régime de transition," *Le Monde*, Edition internationale, Sélection hebdomadaire, 14–20 March 1990, 7.

24. Meredith, *First Dance of Freedom*, p. 139.

25. Lamb, *The Africans*, p. 172; also, Paul Cammack, David Pool, and William Tordoff, *Third World Politics: A Comparative Introduction* (Baltimore: The Johns Hopkins University Press, 1988), p. 52.

26. See, for example, Henri Rouillé d'Orfeuil, *Le Tiers Monde: Repères* (Paris: Editions La Découverte, 1987), and Walter Rodney, *How Europe Underdeveloped Africa* (Washington, D.C.: Howard University Press, 1982).

27. See, for example, Christopher L. Miller, *Blank Darkness: Africanist Discourse in French* (Chicago: University of Chicago Press, 1985).

28. Jeff Drumta and Thomas George, "The 1980s: A Lost Decade," *WorldView* 2, no. 3 (1989), 11.

29. Drumta and George, "The 1980s," p. 11.

30. According to the United Nations "misery index," the following African countries are among the twenty-five poorest: Niger, Mali, Burkina Faso, Sierra

Leone, Chad, Guinea, Somalia, Mauretania, Benin, Mozambique, Malawi, Sudan, Central African Republic, Senegal, Ethiopia, Zaire, Rwanda, Angola, and Nigeria. See "Poverty's Human Face," *WorldView* 4 (Spring 1991): 14–16.

31. Lamb, *The Africans*, p. 173.

32. See Laurent Zecchini, "Peut-on filmer la pauveté?" *Le Monde*, Edition internationale, Sélection hebdomadaire, 7–13 March 1991, 15.

33. Andrew Young made these comments during an interview with the African service of La Voix de l'Amérique, broadcast September 1991.

34. Jeff Drumtra, "Power to the People," *WorldView* 4, no. 4 (1991–92):8–13.

## 8. Exile and Enigma of Arrival

1. V. S. Naipaul, "The Mourners," *A Flag on the Island* (London: Andre Deutsch, 1967), p. 61. There is apparently another version of this story, which Selwyn Cudjoe discusses in his book on Naipaul. The narrator of the version from which Cudjoe quotes is named Ann, not Romesh. See *V. S. Naipaul: A Materialist Reading* (Amherst: University of Massachusetts Press, 1988), pp. 22, 236.

2. V. S. Naipaul, *The Enigma of Arrival* (New York: Alfred A. Knopf, 1987), p. 346. All further quotations are taken from this edition. Mourning is also the theme of Naipaul's 1950 poem, "Two Thirty A.M.," whose speaker is overpowered by a sense of "death / and nothing / and mourning." See Cudjoe, *V. S. Naipaul*, pp. 20–21.

3. Frank Kermode, *The Sense of Ending: Studies in the Theory of Fiction* (New York: Oxford University Press, 1967), p. 7. Quoted by Janet Varner Gunn, *Autobiography: Toward a Poetics of Experience* (Philadelphia: University of Pennsylvania Press, 1982), p. 36.

4. Naipaul's sister Sati died in 1984.

5. Peter Hughes has written: "Naipaul to my mind stands and rises to greatness as a writer because his prose has such precision and strength. His feelings for language, his mastery of style, show that Gibbon was right. However belated and Byzantine the cultural conditions may be, however sunk in servitude and depression, the discourse of literature can still restore to the human spirit what might otherwise seem lost beyond recall." See *V. S. Naipaul* (London: Routledge, 1988), p. 93. Selwyn Cudjoe judges that although Naipaul's technical proficiency has improved through the years, his works have declined since *The Mimic Men*. Cudjoe writes: "Naipaul was unable to go beyond an examination of what it means to be a subject in a postcolonial world and thus he repeats the same tirades against these societies. . . . his range of examination ha[s] narrowed and his insights ha[ve] become repetitious." See *V. S. Naipaul: A Materialist Reading*, p. 14. I believe that *The Enigma of Arrival* goes beyond Naipaul's earlier works in that it critiques them: whereas *The Mimic Men*, for example, allows Singh his fantasies of "Old England," this novel exposes that fantasy and finally rejects it.

6. Interestingly, Naipaul used the phrase "second childhood" many years

before in an interview with Ian Hamilton, in which he commented: "I was eighteen, when I came [to England], and in a way, I have grown up here. I've had a second childhood, a second becoming aware of the world. I've grown out of one attitude and begun to understand the world from another point of view in my maturity." See "Without a Place: Interview, Ian Hamilton," 1971, reprinted in *Savacou* 9–10 (1974) and *Critical Perspectives on V. S. Naipaul*, ed. R. D. Hamner (Washington, D.C.: Three Continents Press, 1977), pp. 39–40.

7. See the essay "Jasmine," discussed in the introduction of this book.

8. Dubrovsky made this remark in an interview with La Voix de l'Amérique broadcast in May 1990.

9. A quaint Waldenshaw neologism, the narrator points out.

10. Albert Camus, *Le Mythe de Sisyphe: Essai sur l'absurde* (Paris: Gallimard, 1942), p. 168.

11. In other words, Naipaul has said, "All my work is really one." "The Novelist V. S. Naipaul Talks About His Work to Ronald Bryden," *The Listener* 89 (22 March 1973): 367.

12. M. M. Bakhtin and P. N. Medvedev, *The Formal Method of Literary Scholarship: A Critical Introduction to Sociological Poetics*, trans. Albert J. Wehrle (Cambridge: Harvard University Press, 1985), p. 131.

13. The short story "Tell Me Who to Kill" from *In a Free State* is, of course, set in London.

14. See Erich Fromm, *Escape from Freedom* (New York: Rinehart & Company, 1941).

15. For an alternate reading, see Cudjoe, *V. S. Naipaul*, p. 15.

16. M. M. Bakhtin and P. N. Medvedev, *Formal Method*, p. 154.

17. Douglas Hofstadter, *Gödel, Escher, Bach: An Eternal Golden Braid: A Metaphorical Fugue on Minds and Machines in the Spirit of Lewis Carroll* (New York: Vintage Books, 1980), pp. 13, 690.

18. See H. H. Arnason, *History of Modern Art* (Englewood Cliffs, N.J.: Prentice-Hall, [1968]), p. 708.

19. Bakhtin and Medvedev, *Formal Method*, p. 29.

20. Jorge Luis Borges, "The Circular Ruins," in *Labyrinths: Selected Stories and Other Writings*, ed. Donald A. Yates and James E. Irby, preface André Maurois (Harmondsworth, Middlesex: Penguin Books, 1976), pp. 72–74.

21. Gunn, *Autobiography*, p. 17.

## 9. Toward a New Pluralism

1. Bruce King has written: "Autobiography is particularly relevant to those in an emerging nation or rapidly changing society and has resulted in some of the best West Indian and African literature." *The New English Literatures—Cultural Nationalism in a Changing World* (New York: St. Martin's Press, 1980), p. 129.

2. In this and the previous sentence, I have adapted the concept of "*entre-*

*deux.*" See Daniel Sibony, *L'Entre-deux ou l'origine en partage* (Paris: Editions du Seuil, 1991).

3. Julia Kristeva, *Etrangers à nous-mêmes* (Paris: Fayard, 1988), p. 13.

4. C. L. R. James, *Beyond a Boundary* (London, 1963; New York: Pantheon Books, 1983), p. 9.

5. Albert Camus, *Le Mythe de Sisyphe: Essai sur l'absurde* (Paris: Gallimard, 1942), p. 104.

6. The concept of decline or decay constitutes what Bakhtin calls a "transpositioning" of time in which the present and past are "enriched at the expense of the future." In this "historical inversion" or transposition, Bakhtin explains, the "future is not homogeneous with the present and the past, and no matter how much time it occupies it is denied a basic concreteness." See M. M. Bakhtin, "Forms of Time and of the Chronotope in the Novel," *The Dialogic Imagination: Four Essays*, ed. Michael Holquist, trans. Caryl Emerson and Michael Holquist (Austin: University of Texas Press, 1981), p. 147.

7. V. S. Naipaul, "V. S. Naipaul Tells How Writing Changes a Writer," *Tapia*, 2 December 1973, 11. Selwyn R. Cudjoe quotes this in *V. S. Naipaul: A Materialist Reading* (Amherst: University of Massachusetts Press, 1988), pp. 162–63.

8. Charles Michener, "The Dark Visions of V. S. Naipaul," *Newsweek*, 16 November 1981, 104–12.

9. Harris writes: "Culture is deed, instantaneous bright deed, as well as active reflection in the depths of otherness. The nature of that reflection is sometimes akin to darkness, sometimes akin to the nightsky, the dark night which alone mirrors constellations and stars invisible in day." Wilson Harris, *The Womb of Space: The Cross-Cultural Imagination* (Westport, Conn.: Greenwood Press, 1983), p. 9.

10. For a discussion of various modes of intercultural encounter, see Muneo Jay Yoshikawa, "The Double-Swing Model of Intercultural Communication between the East and the West," in *Communication Theory: Eastern and Western Perspectives*, ed. D. Lawrence Kincaid (San Diego: Academic Press, 1987), pp. 320–23.

11. Bakhtin and Medvedev describe this writer-reader interrelationship and the social nature of the literary work in these words: "Every element of the work can be compared to a thread stretching between people. The work is a network of such threads, which creates a complex and differentiated social interrelationship between the people who have access to it." Bakhtin and Medvedev state that the interrelationships of similarity and difference between the writer and readers not only structure the literary work but also have an impact on even "the most changeable and individual aspects" of it such as intonation, word and phrase selection. To understand a literary work, they emphasize, one must consider "the organized interrelationships of the people between whom the work is situated as the ideological body of their intercourse." See M. M. Bakhtin and P. N. Medvedev, *The Formal Method in Literary Scholarship: A Critical Introduction to*

*Sociological Poetics*, trans. Albert J. Wehrle (Cambridge: Harvard University Press, 1985), p. 153.

12. See V. S. Naipaul, "The Writer," review of *Exhumations* by Christopher Isherwood, reprinted in *Critical Perspectives on V. S. Naipaul*, ed. R. D. Hamner (Washington, D.C.: Three Continents Press, 1977), p. 30; and "V. S. Naipaul," interview with Israel Shenker, in Hamner, *Critical Perspectives on V. S. Naipaul*, p. 53.

13. Like the narrator of *The Enigma of Arrival*, Naipaul may have decided during this period to leave England permanently: "I thought I would put an end to my time [there]; shed weariness, not only the weariness of the writing, but also the weariness of being in England, the rawness of my nerves as a foreigner . . . put an end to the distortion of my personality that had begun on the very day I had left home" (*EA* 157). The plans of the narrator go awry; after leaving for the Americas, he must return to England to take care of an unexpected complication regarding a manuscript.

# Bibliography

**Works by Naipaul**
**Listed chronologically**

*Interviews, Reviews, and Short Articles*

"The Little More." *The Times* [London], 13 July 1961. Reprinted in *Critical Perspectives on V. S. Naipaul*, ed. R. D. Hamner, 13–15. Washington, D.C.: Three Continents Press, 1977.

"Critics and Criticism." *Bim* 10 (January–June 1964): 74–77.

"The Documentary Heresy." *Twentieth Century* (Winter 1964). Reprinted in *Critical Perspectives on V. S. Naipaul*, ed. R. D. Hamner, 23–25. Washington, D.C.: Three Continents Press, 1977.

"Images." *New Statesman* (24 September 1965). Reprinted in *Critical Perspectives on V. S. Naipaul*, ed. R. D. Hamner, 26–29. Washington, D.C.: Three Continents Press, 1977.

"What's Wrong with Being a Snob?" *Saturday Evening Post* (3 June 1967). Reprinted in *Critical Perspectives on V. S. Naipaul*, ed. R. D. Hamner, 34–38. Washington, D.C.: Three Continents Press, 1977.

"The Novelist V. S. Naipaul Talks to Nigel Bingham About His Childhood in Trinidad." Interview. *The Listener* 88 (7 September 1972): 306–7.

"The Novelist V. S. Naipaul Talks About His Work to Ronald Bryden." Interview. *The Listener* 89 (22 March 1973): 367–70.

"Without a Place." *Savacou* 9–10 (1974). Reprinted as "Without a Place: Interview, Ian Hamilton." In *Critical Perspectives on V. S. Naipaul*, ed. R. D. Hamner, 39–47. Washington, D.C.: Three Continents Press, 1977.

Foreword to *The Adventures of Gurudeva*, by Seepersad Naipaul. London: Andre Deutsch, 1976.

"V. S. Naipaul." Interview with Israel Shenker. In *Critical Perspectives on V. S.

*Naipaul*, ed. R. D. Hamner, 48–53. Washington, D.C.: Three Continents Press, 1977.
"The Writer." Review of *Exhumations* by Christopher Isherwood. Reprinted in *Critical Perspectives of V. S. Naipaul*, ed. R. D. Hamner, 30–33. Washington, D.C.: Three Continents Press, 1977.
Introduction to *East Indians in the Caribbean: Colonialism and the Struggle for Identity*. Millwood, N.Y.: Kraus International Publications, 1982.
"A Conversation with V. S. Naipaul." Interview with Bharati Mukherjee and Robert Boyers. In *The Salmagundi Reader*, ed. Robert Boyers and Peggy Boyers, 450–68. Bloomington: Indiana University Press, 1983.

## Books

*The Mystic Masseur*. London: Andre Deutsch, 1957; New York: Vintage Books, 1984.
*The Suffrage of Elvira*. London: Andre Deutsch, 1958; New York: Penguin, 1969.
*Miguel Street*. London: Andre Deutsch, 1959; New York: Penguin, 1971.
*A House for Mr Biswas*. London: Andre Deutsch, 1961; New York: Penguin, 1981.
*The Middle Passage: Impressions of Five Societies—British, French and Dutch—in the West Indies and South America*. London: Andre Deutsch, 1962; New York: Penguin, 1981.
*Mr Stone and the Knights Companion*. London: Andre Deutsch, 1963; New York: Vintage Books, 1985.
*An Area of Darkness*. London: Andre Deutsch, 1964; New York: Vintage Books, 1981.
*The Mimic Men*. London: Andre Deutsch, 1967; New York: Vintage Books, 1985.
*A Flag on the Island*. London: Andre Deutsch, 1967.
*The Loss of El Dorado: A History*. London: Andre Deutsch, 1969; New York: Vintage Books, 1984.
*In a Free State*. London: Andre Deutsch, 1971; New York: Vintage Books, 1984.
*The Overcrowded Barracoon*. London: Andre Deutsch, 1972; New York: Vintage Books, 1984.
*Guerrillas*. London: Andre Deutsch, 1975; New York: Vintage Books, 1980.
*India: A Wounded Civilization*. New York: Alfred A. Knopf, 1977; Vintage Books, 1978.
*A Bend in the River*. New York: Alfred A. Knopf, 1979; Vintage Books, 1980.
*A Congo Diary*. Los Angeles: Sylvester and Orphanos, 1980.
*The Return of Eva Perón*. New York: Alfred A. Knopf, 1980; Vintage Books, 1981.
*Among the Believers: An Islamic Journey*. New York: Alfred A. Knopf, 1981; Vintage Books, 1982.

*Finding the Center: Two Narratives.* New York: Alfred A. Knopf, 1984; Vintage Books, 1986.
*The Enigma of Arrival.* New York: Alfred A. Knopf, 1987.
*A Turn in the South.* New York: Alfred A. Knopf, 1989; Vintage International, 1990.
*India: A Million Mutinies Now.* New York: Viking, 1990.

## Works about Naipaul
## Listed alphabetically

Boxill, Anthony. *V. S. Naipaul's Fiction: In Quest of the Enemy.* Fredericton, Canada: York Press, 1983.

———. "V. S. Naipaul's Starting Point." *The Journal of Commonwealth Literature* 10 (1975): 1–9.

Boyers, Robert. "Confronting the Present." *Salmagundi* 54 (1981): 77–97.

———. "Politics, Fiction, Autobiography." The Edwin M. Moseley Faculty Research Lecture 1979. Saratoga Springs, N.Y.: Skidmore College, 1980.

Cudjoe, Selwyn R. *V. S. Naipaul: A Materialist Reading.* Amherst: University of Massachusetts Press, 1988.

Derrick, A. C. "Naipaul's Technique as a Novelist." In *Critical Perspectives on V. S. Naipaul,* ed. R. D. Hamner, 194–207. Washington, D.C.: Three Continents Press, 1977.

Garebian, Keith. "V. S. Naipaul's Negative Sense of Place." *The Journal of Commonwealth Literature* 10 (1975): 23–35.

Goodheart, Eugene. "Naipaul and the Voices of Negation." *Salmagundi* 54 (1981): 44–58.

Gurr, Andrew. *Writers in Exile: The Identity of Home in Modern Literature.* Sussex: The Harvester Press, 1981.

Hamner, Robert. "Character and Setting." In *Critical Perspectives on V. S. Naipaul,* ed. R. D. Hamner, 208–41. Washington, D.C.: Three Continents Press, 1977.

———. *V. S. Naipaul.* New York: Twayne Publishers, 1973.

———. "V. S. Naipaul: A Selected Bibliography." *The Journal of Commonwealth Literature* 10 (1975): 36–45.

———, ed. *Critical Perspectives on V. S. Naipaul.* Washington, D.C.: Three Continents Press, 1977.

Hughes, Peter. *V. S. Naipaul.* London: Routledge, 1988.

King, Bruce. "V. S. Naipaul." In *West Indian Literature,* ed. Bruce King, 161–78. Hamden, Conn.: Archon Books, 1979.

Lim, Ling-Mei. *V. S. Naipaul's Later Fiction: The Creative Constraints of Exile.* Ph.D. diss., Indiana University, 1984.

Mason, Nondita. *The Fiction of V. S. Naipaul.* Calcutta: The World Press Private Limited, 1986.

McSweeney, Kerry. *Four Contemporary Novelists*. Montreal: McGill-Queen's University Press, 1983.

McWatt, Mark, ed. *West Indian Literature and Its Social Context: Proceedings of the Fourth Annual Conference on West Indian Literature*. St. Michael, Barbados: Department of English U.W.I., 1985.

Michener, Charles. "The Dark Visions of V. S. Naipaul." *Newsweek*, 16 November 1981, 104–12.

Morris, Robert K. *Paradoxes of Order: Some Perspectives on the Fiction of V. S. Naipaul*. Colombia: University of Missouri Press, 1975.

Nightingale, Peggy. *Journey Through Darkness: The Writings of V. S. Naipaul*. Saint Lucia: University of Queensland Press, 1987.

Parrinder, Patrick. "A Novel for Our Time: V. S. Naipaul's *Guerrillas*." In *The Failure of Theory: Essays on Criticism and Contemporary Fiction*, 185–206. Totowa, N.J.: Barnes & Noble Books, 1987.

Rai, Sudha. *V. S. Naipaul: A Study in Expatriate Sensibility*. New Delhi: Arnold-Heinemann, 1982.

Ramchand, Kenneth. *The West Indian Novel and Its Background*. New York: Barnes & Noble, 1970.

Rao, K. I. Madhusudana. *Contrary Awareness: A Critical Study of the Novels of V. S. Naipaul*. Madras, India: Centre for Research on New International Economic Order, 1982.

Rohlehr, Gordon. "The Ironic Approach: The Novels of V. S. Naipaul." In *Critical Perspectives on V. S. Naipaul*, ed. R. D. Hamner, 178–93. Washington, D.C.: Three Continents Press, 1977.

St. Omer, Garth. *The Colonial Novel: Studies in the Novels of Albert Camus, V. S. Naipaul and Alejo Carpentier*. Ph.D. diss., Princeton University, 1975.

Theroux, Paul. *V. S. Naipaul: An Introduction to His Work*. New York: Africana Publishing Corporation, 1972.

Thieme, John. "V. S. Naipaul's Third World: A Not So Free State." *The Journal of Commonwealth Literature* 10 (1975): 11–22.

Walsh, William. *V. S. Naipaul*. Edinburgh: Oliver & Boyd, 1973.

White, Landeg. *V. S. Naipaul: A Critical Introduction*. New York: Barnes & Noble, 1975.

## General Works
### Listed alphabetically

Achebe, Chinua. *Morning Yet on Creation Day*. Garden City, N.Y.: Anchor Press/Doubleday, 1976.

Althusser, Louis. *Lenin and Philosophy and Other Essays*. Trans. Ben Brewster. New York: Monthly Review Press, 1971.

———. *Positions*. Paris: Editions sociales, 1976.

# Bibliography

Amalric, Jacques. "La France embourbée." No. 5 in "Plaies d'Afrique." *Le Monde*, Edition internationale, Sélection hebdomadaire, 14–20 June 1990, 2.

"Amnesty International dénonce une 'vague d'exécutions politiques.'" *Le Monde*, 14 December 1988, 6.

Arnason, H. H. *History of Modern Art: Painting, Sculpture, Architecture.* Englewood Cliffs, N.J.: Prentice-Hall, 1968.

Ashcroft, Bill, Gareth Griffiths, and Helen Tiffin. *The Empire Writes Back: Theory and Practice in Post-Colonial Literatures.* London and New York: Routledge, 1989.

"Asie de Sud-Est: Tolérance sous les tropiques." *Le Monde*, 12 April 1989, 7.

Bakhtin, M. M. "The *Bildungsroman*." *Speech Genres & Other Late Essays.* Trans. Vern W. McGee, ed. Caryl Emerson and Michael Holquist. Austin: University of Texas Press, 1986.

———. *The Dialogic Imagination: Four Essays.* Ed. Michael Holquist, trans. Caryl Emerson and Michael Holquist. Austin: University of Texas Press, 1981.

———. *Problems of Dostoevsky's Poetics.* Ed. and trans. Caryl Emerson, introd. by Wayne C. Booth. Minneapolis: University of Minnesota Press, 1984.

———. "A Response to a Question from the *Novy Mir* Editorial Staff." *Speech Genres & Other Late Essays.* Trans. Vern W. McGee, ed. Caryl Emerson and Michael Holquist. Austin: University of Texas Press, 1986.

———. *Speech Genres & Other Late Essays.* Trans. Vern W. McGee, ed. Caryl Emerson and Michael Holquist. Austin: University of Texas Press, 1986.

Bakhtin, M. M., and P. N. Medvedev. *The Formal Method in Literary Scholarship: A Critical Introduction to Sociological Poetics.* Foreword by Wlad Godzich. Trans. Albert J. Wehrle. Cambridge: Harvard University Press, 1985.

Barry, Tom, Beth Wood, and Deb Preusch. *The Other Side of Paradise: Foreign Control in the Caribbean.* New York: Grove Press, 1984.

Barthes, Roland. *Mythologies.* Paris: Editions du Seuil, 1957.

Bastide, Roger. *Les Amériques noires: Les Civilisations africaines dans le nouveau monde.* Paris: Payot, 1967.

Berque, Jacques. *Arab Rebirth: Pain and Ecstasy.* London: Al Saqi, 1983.

———. *L'Islam au temps du monde.* Paris: Sinbad, 1984.

———. *Mémoires des deux rives.* Paris: Editions du Seuil, 1989.

Bhabha, Homi. "Of Mimicry and Man: The Ambivalence of Colonial Discourse." *October* 28 (Spring 1984).

———, ed. *Nation and Narration.* London: Routledge, 1990.

Borges, Jorge Luis. "The Circular Ruins." *Labyrinths: Selected Stories and Other Writings.* Ed. Donald A. Yates and James E. Irby, preface André Maurois. Harmondsworth, Middlesex: Penguin Books, 1976.

Bowles, Paul. *Their Heads Are Green and Their Hands Are Blue.* New York: Random House, 1957.

———. *Up Above the World.* New York: The Ecco Press, 1966.

Braillard, Philippe, and Mohammad-Reza Djalili. *Tiers monde et relations internationales.* Paris: Masson, 1984.

Brandt Commission. *Common Crisis: North-South Co-Operation for World Recovery.* Cambridge: MIT Press, 1983.

Brereton, Bridget. *A History of Modern Trinidad: 1783–1962.* Kingston: Heinemann, 1981.

Broder, Jonathan, and Ray Moseley. "Islam Fundamentalists—Heralds of a Holy War." *Chicago Tribune,* 8 November 1987, 1, 12.

Brown, Judith. *Modern India: The Origins of an Asian Democracy.* Delhi: Oxford University Press, 1985.

Bryden, Ronald. "Between the Epics." *New Statesman,* 7 November 1969, 661–62.

Buruma, Ian. "The Bartered Bride." *The New York Review of Books,* 1 June 1989, 7–11.

Callinicos, Alex. *Marxism and Philosophy.* Oxford: Oxford University Press, 1985.

Camilleri, Carmel, and Margalit Cohen-Emerique, eds. *Chocs de cultures: Concepts et enjeux pratiques de l'interculturel.* Paris: Editions L'Harmattan, 1989.

Cammack, Paul, David Pool, and William Tordoff. *Third World Politics: A Comparative Introduction.* Baltimore: The Johns Hopkins University Press, 1988.

Camus, Albert. *L'Homme révolté.* Paris: Gallimard, 1951.

———. *Le Mythe de Sisyphe: Essai sur l'absurde.* Paris: Gallimard, 1942.

———. *La Peste.* Paris: Gallimard, 1947.

Caroit, Jean-Michel. "Les Rebelles musulmans se sont rendus sans conditions." *Le Monde,* Edition internationale, Sélection hebdomadaire, 2–9 August 1990, 6.

Cavafy, C. P. *The Complete Poems of Cavafy.* Expanded ed., trans. Rae Dalven, intro. W. H. Auden. New York: Harcourt Brace Jovanovich, 1976.

Césaire, Aimé. *Discours sur le colonialisme.* Paris: Présence Africaine, 1955.

———. *Une Saison au Congo.* Paris: Editions du Seuil, 1967.

———. *La Tragédie du roi Christophe.* Paris: Présence Africaine, 1963.

Chantebout, Bernard. *Le Tiers Monde.* Paris: Armand Colin, 1986.

Cleveland, Ray L. *The Middle East and South Asia 1987.* The World Today Series. Washington, D.C.: Skye Corporation, 1986.

Clifford, James. *The Predicament of Culture: Twentieth-Century Ethnography, Literature, and Art.* Cambridge: Harvard University Press, 1988.

Cole, John. *Development and Underdevelopment: A Profile of the Third World.* London: Methuen, 1987.

Conrad, Joseph. *Great Short Works of Joseph Conrad.* New York: Harper & Row, 1967.
———. *Heart of Darkness.* Ed. Robert Kimbrough. New York: W. W. Norton, 1971.
———. *Lord Jim.* Ed. Thomas C. Moser. New York: W. W. Norton, 1968.
———. Preface to *The Nigger of the 'Narcissus.'* In *Heart of Darkness*, by Joseph Conrad. Ed. Robert Kimbrough. New York: W. W. Norton, 1971.
Coron, Edith. "Le Président face aux décus du 'menemisme.'" *Le Monde*, Edition internationale, Sélection hebdomadaire, 25 January 1990, 5.
Cros, Edmund. *Theory and Practice of Sociocriticism.* Trans. Jerome Schwartz, foreword Jürgen Link and Ursula Link-Herr. Theory and History of Literature, vol. 53. Minneapolis: University of Minnesota Press, 1988.
Crow, John A., and George D. Crow. *Panorama de las Américas.* 7th ed. Fort Worth, Tex.: Holt, Rinehart and Winston, 1989.
Dance, Daryl Cumber, ed. *Fifty Caribbean Writers: A Bio-Biographical Critical Sourcebook.* New York: Greenwood Press, 1986.
de Barrin, Jacques. "Des centaines de Touregs tués au Niger." *Le Monde*, Edition internationale, Sélection hebdomadaire, 14–20 June 1990, 3.
———. "Les treize guerres du continent noir." *Le Monde*, Edition internationale, Sélection hebdomadaire, 18–24 October 1990, 5.
de la Croix, Horst, and Richard G. Tansey. *Gardner's Art Through the Ages.* 5th ed. New York: Harcourt, Brace & World, 1970.
de la Guérivière, Jean. "Le Président Adhmed Abdallah a été assassiné," *Le Monde*, Edition internationale, Sélection hebdomadaire, 23 November 1989, 6.
Deleuze, Gilles. "Michel Tournier et le monde sans autrui." *Vendredi ou les limbes du Pacifique*, by Michel Tournier, 257–83. Paris: Gallimard, 1972.
———. *Le Pli.* Paris: Les Editions de Minuit, 1988.
Dostert, Pierre Etienne. *Africa 1987.* The World Today Series. Washington, D.C.: Skye Corporation, 1986.
Drakakis-Smith, David. *The Third World City.* London: Methuen, 1987.
Droit, Roger-Pol. *L'Oubli de l'Inde: Une Amnésie philosophique.* Paris: Presses Universitaires de France, 1989.
Drouin, Pierre. "La 'force terrifiante' de l'Occident." Review of *L'Occidentalisation du monde*, by Serge Latouche. *Le Monde*, 24 February 1989, 17.
Drumtra, Jeff. "Power to the People." *WorldView* 4, no. 4 (1991–92): 8–13.
Drumtra, Jeff, and Thomas George. "The 1980s: A Lost Decade." *WorldView* 2, no. 3 (1989): 8–12.
Dumont, René. *Un Monde intolérable: Le Libéralisme en question.* Paris: Editions du Seuil, 1988.
Eagleton, Terry. *Marxism and Literary Criticism.* Berkeley: University of California Press, 1976.
Eliade, Mircea. *Yoga: Immortality and Freedom.* Trans. Willard R. Trask. Bollingen Series 56. New York: Pantheon Books, 1958.

Essid, Hamadi. "Peut-on convaincre par la violence?" *La Presse de Tunisie*, 23 February 1989, 1.
Fanon, Frantz. *Les Damnés de la terre*. Paris: François Maspero, 1981.
———. *Peau noire, masques blancs*. Paris: Editions du Seuil, 1952.
Filliozat, Jean. *India: The Country and Its Traditions*. Trans. Margaret Ledésert. London: George G. Harrap & Co., 1962.
Findlay, Allan, and Anne Findlay. *Population and Development in the Third World*. London: Methuen, 1987.
Fontaine, André. "Entre la flèche et la cible." *Le Monde*, 24 February 1989, 1, 3.
Fottorino, Eric. "Dette: paiera, paiera pas . . . ," in "Plaies d'Afrique." *Le Monde*, Edition internationale, Sélection hebdomadaire, 7–13 June 1990, 6–7.
———. "Le Gabon met en cause les contraintes imposées par le FMI." *Le Monde*, Edition internationale, Sélection hebdomadaire, 1–7 March 1990, 7.
———. "Matiéres premiéres: Du miracle au mirage," in "Plaies d'Afrique." *Le Monde*, Edition internationale, Sélection hebdomadaire, 7–13 June 1990, 6–7.
Fralon, José-Alain. "Côte-d'Ivoire: Les Libanais, boucs émissaires de la crise." *Le Monde*, Edition internationale, Sélection hebdomadaire, 22–28 March 1990, 5.
———. "Vent de fronde sur la Côte-d'Ivoire." *Le Monde*, Edition internationale, Sélection hebdomadaire, 1–7 March 1990, 1, 7.
Fromm, Erich. *Escape from Freedom*. New York: Rinehart & Company, 1941.
Gérard, Albert. *Etudes de littérature africane francophone*. Dakar: Les Nouvelles Éditions Africaines, 1977.
Gikandi, Simon. *Reading the African Novel*. London: Heinemann, 1987.
Glissant, Edouard. *Le Discours antillais*. Paris: Editions du Seuil, 1981.
Gombrich, E. H. *Art and Illusion: A Study in the Psychology of Pictorial Representation*. Bollingen Series 35, 5. Princeton: Princeton University Press, 1972.
Gouldner, Alvin W. *The Dialectic of Ideology and Technology*. New York: Oxford University Press, 1976.
Griffiths, Gareth. *A Double Exile: African and West Indian Writing Between Two Cultures*. London: Marion Boyars, 1978.
Gugelberger, Georg, ed. *Marxism and African Literature*. Trenton, N.J.: Africa World Press, 1985.
Gunn, Janet Varner. *Autobiography: Toward a Poetics of Experience*. Philadelphia: University of Pennsylvania Press, 1982.
Hall, Edward T. *Beyond Culture*. Garden City, N.Y.: Anchor Books, 1977.
Hardgrave, Robert L., Jr. *India: Government and Politics in a Developing Nation*. New York: Harcourt, Brace & World, 1970.

Harris, Wilson. *The Womb of Space: The Cross-Cultural Imagination*. Westport, Conn.: Greenwood Press, 1983.
Hayakawa, S. I., and Alan R. Hayakawa. *Language and Thought*. 5th ed. San Diego: Harcourt Brace Jovanovich, 1990.
Hélène, Jean. "Somalie: Modagiscio exsangue." *Le Monde*, Edition internationale, Sélection hebdomadaire, 20–27 February, 1991, 9.
Hill, Errol. *The Trinidad Carnival: Mandate for a National Theatre*. Austin: University of Texas Press, 1972.
Hiro, Dilop. *Inside India Today*. Rev. ed. New York: Monthly Review Press, 1979.
Hodges, Donald C. *Argentina 1943–1976: The National Revolution and Resistance*. Albuquerque: University of New Mexico Press, 1976.
Hofstadter, Douglas. *Gödel, Escher, Bach: An Eternal Golden Braid: A Metaphorical Fugue on Minds and Machines in the Spirit of Lewis Carroll*. New York: Vintage Books, 1980.
Hulme, Peter. *Colonial Encounters: Europe and the Native Caribbean, 1492–1797*. London: Methuen, 1986.
Huxley, Aldous. *The Olive Tree*. London: Chatto & Windus, 1947.
J. de L. G. "Un 'Acquis' irréversible." *Le Monde*, 6–7 November 1988, 9.
"L'Imam Khomeiny confirme sa condamnation de Salman Rushdie et attaque les 'libéraux' en Iran." *Le Monde*, 24 February 1989, 3.
"L'Islam en fièvre": "Allah contre Satan" (4 April); "Egypte, Soudan, Arabie saoudite, Bahreïn" (5 April); "Irak, Syrie, Oman" (6 April); "Israël et les territoires occupés" (7 April); "Maghreb: De clandestinité au légalisme" (8 April); "Sahel: Tentations intégristes" (9 April); "Soucontinent indien: Toujours l'éclatement de l'Empire" (11 April); "Asie du Sud-Est: Tolérance sous les tropiques" (12 April); "Turquie: Reconquérir l'individu avant l'Etat" (13 April). *Le Monde*, 4–13 April, 1989.
James, C. L. R. *Beyond a Boundary*. London, 1963; New York: Pantheon Books, 1983.
Jameson, Fredric. *Marxism and Form: Twentieth-Century Dialectical Theories of Literature*. Princeton: Princeton University Press, 1971.
———. *The Political Unconscious: Narrative as a Socially Symbolic Act*. Ithaca, N.Y.: Cornell University Press, 1981.
———. *The Prison-House of Language: A Critical Account of Structuralism and Russian Formalism*. Princeton: Princeton University Press, 1972.
JanMohamed, Abdul R. *Manichean Aesthetics: The Politics of Literature in Colonial Africa*. Amherst: University of Massachusetts Press, 1983.
Joyce, James. *Portrait of the Artist as a Young Man*. New York: Viking Press, 1966.
Kabbani, Rana. *Europe's Myths of Orient*. Bloomington: Indiana University Press, 1986.

Kane, Cheikh Hamidou. *L'Aventure ambiguë.* Paris: Union Generale d'Editions, 1961.
Kepel, Gilles. "Impasses arabes." *Le Monde*, Edition internationale, Sélection hebdomadaire, 7–13 March 1991, 1.
King, Bruce. *Literatures of the World in English.* London: Routledge & Kegan Paul, 1974.
———. *The New English Literatures—Cultural Nationalism in a Changing World.* New York: St. Martin's Press, 1980.
———. *West Indian Literature.* Hamden, Conn.: Archon Books, 1979.
Knowles, Roberta, and Erika Smilowitz, eds. *Conference on Critical Approaches to West Indian Literature.* St. Thomas, Virgin Islands: College of the Virgin Islands, 1981.
Korzybski, Alfred. *Science and Sanity: An Introduction to Non-Aristotelian Systems and General Semantics.* Lancaster, Penn.: Science Press Printing Company, 1933.
Kristeva, Julia. *Etrangers à nous-mêmes.* Paris: Fayard, 1988.
Kupperman, Fred. "Babel: Bleu-blanc-rouge." In *L'Express: Ainsi Va La France*, ed. Ross Steele and Jacqueline Gaillard, 20–21. Lincolnwood, Ill.: NTC, 1985.
Kuppuswamy, B. *Population and Society in India.* Bombay: Popular Prakashan, 1975.
Kurlansky, Mark. "Reluctant destination: Trinidad not ready for tourism." *Chicago Tribune*, 10 December 1989, 10.
Lamb, David. *The Africans.* New York: Vintage Books, 1985.
Lamming, George. *The Emigrants.* London: Michael Joseph, 1954.
———. *The Pleasures of Exile.* London: Allison & Busby, 1984.
Langellier, Jean-Pierre. "L'Ile Maurice, nouveau 'petit dragon.'" *Le Monde*, Edition internationale, Sélection hebdomadaire, 9–15 November 1989, 10.
———. "La Peur de l'oubli," in "Plaies d'Afrique." *Le Monde*, Edition internationale, Sélection hebdomadaire, 31 May–6 June 1990, 1, 6.
Laye, Camara. *L'Enfant noir.* Paris: Plon, 1953.
Le Clézio, J. M. G. *Le Rêve Mexicain, ou la pensée interrompue.* Paris: Gallimard, 1988.
Lewis, Bernard. "Islamic Revolution." *The New York Review of Books*, 21 January 1988, 48–49.
Macdonnell, Diane. *Theories of Discourse: An Introduction.* Oxford: Basil Blackwell, 1986.
Macherey, Pierre. *Pour une théorie de la production littéraire.* Paris: François Maspero, 1978.
Marion, Georges. "'Ordre moral' islamique en Algérie." *Le Monde*, Edition internationale, Sélection hebdomadaire, 12–18 July 1990, 5.

Marx, Karl, and Frederic Engels. *Basic Writings on Politics and Philosophy.* Ed. Lewis S. Feuer. Garden City, N.Y.: Anchor Books, 1959.
———. *The Marx-Engels Reader.* 2d ed. Ed. Robert C. Tucker. New York: W. W. Norton, 1978.
Maurus, Véronique. "La Guadeloupe entre l'espoir et l'inquiétude." *Le Monde,* Edition internationale, Sélection hebdomadaire, 12–18 April 1990, 7.
———. "La Martinique retranchée." *Le Monde,* Edition internationale, Sélection hebdomadaire, 12–18 April 1990, 8.
Meaudre, Yves. *France, terre d'exil.* Paris: Fayard, 1989.
Memmi, Albert. *La Statue de sel.* Paris: Gallimard, 1966.
———. *Portrait du colonisé précédé du portrait du colonisateur.* Utrecht: Jean-Jacques Pauvert, 1966.
Meredith, Martin. *The First Dance of Freedom: Black Africa in the Postwar Era.* New York: Harper & Row, 1984.
Merleau-Ponty, Maurice. *Phénoménologie de la perception.* Paris: Gallimard, 1945.
Mesarovic, Mihajlo, and Eduard Pestel. *Mankind at the Turning Point: The Second Report to the Club of Rome.* New York: E. P. Dutton & Co., 1974.
Miller, Christopher L. *Blank Darkness: Africanist Discourse in French.* Chicago: University of Chicago Press, 1985.
Mirville, Ernest. *Considérations ethno-psychanlytiques sur le carnaval Haïtien.* Série Anthropologie. Port-au-Prince, Haiti: Collection Coucouille, 1978.
Mortimer, Edward. *Faith & Power: The Politics of Islam.* New York: Vintage Books, 1982.
Moseley, Ray. "Women search for new roles in Islamic settings." *Chicago Tribune,* 11 November 1987, 1, 8.
Nazareth, Peter. *The Third World Writer: His Social Responsibility.* Nairobi: Kenya Literature Bureau, 1978.
Newby, Eric. *A Book of Travellers' Tales.* New York: Viking, 1985.
Ngara, Emmanuel. *Art and Ideology in the African Novel: A Study of the Influence of Marxism on African Writing.* London: Heinemann, 1985.
Ortega y Gasset, José. "History as a System." *History as a System and Other Essays Toward a Philosophy of History.* New York: W. W. Norton, 1961.
———. *Meditations on Quixote.* Trans. Evelyn Rugg and Diego Marin. New York: W. W. Norton, 1975.
Oyono, Ferdinand. *Une Vie de boy.* Paris: Julliard, 1957.
Parry, J. H., Philip Sherlock, and Anthony Maingot. *A Short History of the West Indies.* 4th ed. New York: Saint Martin's Press, 1987.
Pasquier, Sylvaine, with Elie Marcuse. "Le Livre qui enflamme l'Islam." *L'Express,* 24 February 1989, 22–24.
Péroncel-Hugoz, J.-P. "Islam et deuxième sexe." *Le Monde,* 2 December 1988, 6.

———. "Un génial attentat contre le Coran." Review of *Le Coran*, by Jacques Berque. *Le Monde*, Sélection hebdomadaire, 14–20 February 1991, 12.
Plenel, Edwy. "La siècle des éclipses," in "Voyages avec Colomb." *Le Monde*, 31 August 1991, 2.
Porte, Guy. "Un Mort et une dizaine de blessés dans un attentat contre au foyer SONACOTRA." *Le Monde*, 20 December 1988, 40.
R. -P. P. "Le Rapport annuel d'Amnesty International: Forte augmentation des 'exécutions extra-judiciares.'" *Le Monde*, Edition internationale, Sélection hebdomadaire, 26 October–2 November 1989, 5.
Ramchand, Kenneth. *The West Indian Novel and Its Background*. 2d ed. London: Heinemann, 1983.
Rodney, Walter. *How Europe Underdeveloped Africa*. Washington, D.C.: Howard University Press, 1982.
Rouillé d'Orfeuil, Henri. *Le Tiers Monde: Repères*. Paris: Editions La Decouverte, 1987.
Rubin, Barry. *Paved with Good Intentions: The American Experience and Iran*. New York: Penguin Books, 1982.
Ryan, Michael. *Marxism and Deconstruction: A Critical Articulation*. Baltimore: The Johns Hopkins University Press, 1982.
Said, Edward W. "The Mind of Winter: Reflections on Life in Exile." *Harper's Magazine*, 269 (September 1984).
———. *Orientalism*. New York: Vintage Books, 1979.
Sammut, Carmel. *L'Impérialisme capitaliste français et le nationalisme tunisien (1881–1914)*. Paris: Publisud, 1983.
Seurat, Michel. *L'État de barbarie*. Paris: Editions du Seuil, 1989.
Seymour, J. -J., and H. Elisabeth. *Les Caraïbes: Des brûlots sur la mer*. Paris: Editions Caribéennes, 1981.
Sibony, Daniel. *L'Entre-deux ou l'origine en partage*. Paris: Editions du Seuil, 1991.
Simon, Catherine. "La Boîte de Pandore du président Mobutu." *Le Monde*, Edition internationale, Sélection hebdomadaire, 20–26 December 1990, 1.
———. "Démocratie: Adieu au parti unique?" in "Plaies d'Afrique." *Le Monde*, Edition internationale, Sélection hebdomadaire, 7–13 June 1990, 6–7.
Simpson, George Eaton. "Religion and Justice: Some Reflections on the Ras Tafari Movement." *Journal of Caribbean Studies* 5 (1986): 145–53.
Singham, A. W. *The Hero and the Crowd in a Colonial Polity*. New Haven, Conn.: Yale University Press, 1968.
Smilowitz, Erika Sollish, and Roberta Quarles Knowles, eds. *Critical Issues in West Indian Literature*. Parkersburg, Iowa: Caribbean Books, 1984.
Soustelle, Jacques. *Les Quatre Soleils: Souvenirs et réflexions d'un ethnologue au Mexique*. Paris: Plon, 1967.

Stanzel, F. K. *A Theory of Narrative*. Trans. Charlotte Goedsche, preface Paul Hernadi. Cambridge: Cambridge University Press, 1984.
T. F. "Le Gout bourgeois." Review of *Ni Vue Ni Connue*, by Béatrix La Wita, *Le Monde*, 9 December 1988, 24.
Therborn, Göran. *The Ideology of Power and the Power of Ideology*. London: NLB, 1980.
Todorov, Tzvetan. *La Conquête de l'Amérique: La Question de l'autre*. Paris: Editions du Seuil, 1982.
———. *Mikhail Bakhtin: The Dialogic Principle*. Trans. Wlad Godzich. Minneapolis: University of Minnesota Press, 1984.
———. *Nous et les autres: La Réflexion française sur la diversité humaine*. Paris: Editions du Seuil, 1989.
———. *Théories du symbole*. Paris: Editions du Seuil, 1977.
Toffler, Alvin. *Powershift: Knowledge, Wealth, and Violence at the Edge of the 21st Century*. New York: Bantam Books, 1990.
Tournier, Michel. *Vendredi ou les limbes du Pacifique*. Paris: Gallimard, 1972.
Vanhecke, Charles. "Carlos Menem, péroniste en diable." *Le Monde*, 20 January 1989, 6.
Volosinov, V. N. *Marxism and the Philosophy of Language*. Trans. Ladislav Matejka and I. R. Titunik. Cambridge: Harvard University Press, 1986.
Watson, Francis. *A Concise History of India*. London: Thames and Hudson, 1974.
Williams, Eric. *From Columbus to Castro: The History of the Caribbean 1492–1969*. New York: Vintage Books, 1984.
Wright, Elizabeth. *Psychoanalytic Criticism: Theory in Practice*. London: Methuen, 1984.
Wright, Robin. *Sacred Rage: The Wrath of Militant Islam*. New York: Simon & Schuster, 1985.
Y.C. "Notre Maître Albert." *L'Express*, 20 January 1989, 63.
Yoshikawa, Muneo Jay. "The Double-Swing Model of Intercultural Communication between the East and the West." In *Communication Theory: Eastern and Western Perspectives*, ed. D. Lawrence Kincaid, 319–29. San Diego: Academic Press, 1987.
Zand, Nicole. "Albert Londres: 'La Plume dans la plaie.'" *Le Monde*, 6 January 1989, 16.
———. "Le Serpent de mer de l'Europe." *Le Monde*, 2 December 1988, 24.
Zecchini, Laurent. "Peut-on filmer la pavreté?" *Le Monde*, Edition internationale, Sélection hebdomadaire, 7–13 March 1991, 15.
Zimmer, Heinrich. *Philosophies of India*. Ed. Joseph Campbell. New York: Meridian Books, 1960.

# Index

*The Adventures of Gurudeva*, 11, 42, 230, 232, 234–35, 240
alienation, 3, 6, 18, 21, 48, 62–64, 76, 85, 88–89, 97, 104, 108–11, 114, 130, 132, 163, 169, 171, 204–5, 215–16, 220, 222
Althusser, Louis, 146, 247
*Among the Believers: An Islamic Journey*, 147–59
"Anguilla: The Shipwrecked Six Thousand," 137–38
*An Area of Darkness*, 11, 104, 108, 113–20, 122, 127, 131, 133, 147, 159, 189, 203, 209, 217
Argentina, 142–43, 183
Ashcroft, Bill, 13

Bakhtin, Mikhail, 12, 22, 31, 165, 194, 202, 210, 212, 252, 256
Barthes, Roland, 65, 79
*A Bend in the River*, 11, 19, 109, 135, 144, 163, 165, 167, 184–93, 209, 220
Berque, Jacques, 158
Bowles, Paul, 6, 13, 229
Boyers, Robert, 182, 246–47
Brereton, Bridget, 32, 58–59
Buruma, Ian, 74

Camilleri, Carmel, 15
Camus, Albert, 87, 94, 202, 217
Carew, Jan, 3
carnival, 17, 21–22, 30–31, 36, 42, 44–45, 72, 138–39, 141, 145, 162, 165, 183
Cavafy, C.P., 10, 95, 134
Césaire, Aimé, 74
Chaudhuri, Nirad, 116, 128
Chauveton, Urbain, 6
"The Circus at Luxor," 176, 209
Columbus, Christopher, 6, 8, 48, 66–68, 78, 80, 90, 136
"Columbus and Crusoe," 136–37
Congo (Zaire), 144–46, 167, 184, 189, 191
Conrad, Joseph, 46, 80, 142, 146, 153, 163, 167
"Conrad's Darkness," 146, 163
"The Crocodiles of Yamoussoukro," 136, 161–63
Crusoé, Robinson, 85, 111–12
Crusoe, Robinson, 18, 79, 89, 91–92, 105–6, 110, 136
Cudjoe, Selwyn, 63, 230, 233, 254

decay, sense of, 95, 102, 106, 108, 113, 118–19, 121–22, 129, 136, 139, 161,

decay, sense of (*cont.*)
  163, 173, 182, 190, 197, 199, 201, 204, 206–7, 218, 220, 222
decolonization, 99–103
Descartes, René, 7–9
dialogism, 6, 8, 13–15, 131, 156, 168, 186, 192, 220–22
double-voicedness, 22–23, 31, 36–37, 44, 217
Drakakis-Smith, David, 154, 249
*Dubliners*, 23–24
Dubrovsky, Serge, 197

"East Indian," 10–11, 87, 90
East Indians, 40, 42–43, 48, 52, 54–55, 58–59, 90, 130, 179, 203, 207, 216
*East Indians in the Caribbean: Colonialism and the Struggle for Identity* (introduction), 78, 102
Ehrlich, Paul, 242
Eliade, Mircea, 8
*The Empire Writes Back*, 4, 13
*The Enigma of Arrival*, 11–12, 19, 48, 64, 76, 92, 103, 110–12, 136, 141, 164, 168, 176, 179, 194–214, 217, 219–22
Escher, M. C., 211
Etienne, Bruno, 148
exile, 4–19, 21–22, 24–25, 46–48, 53, 55, 61–64, 66, 74, 76–77, 84–99, 102–4, 106, 108–15, 117, 119, 122–23, 130–35, 140–41, 146, 149, 158–65, 168–69, 171–72, 177, 180–83, 185, 187, 193, 195, 198–99, 201–11, 215–25; as an in-between, 5, 19, 159, 215, 221; as a lens, 4–6, 15; as a search for origins, 10, 18, 159, 195, 215, 217, 221, 224; as a split, 5, 9–11, 18–19, 23, 66, 76, 94, 111, 114, 135, 162–63, 199, 204, 206, 209–10, 213; as a wound, 6, 8, 49, 102, 114–15, 117, 159, 195, 199, 216

exotopy, 12, 14, 62, 99, 115, 123, 229

Fanon, Frantz, 88, 181, 236–38
Fillozat, Jean, 241–43
*Finding the Center: Two Narratives*, 11–12, 159–64, 197, 221
"A Flag on the Island," 239
Fromm, Erich, 168, 208, 233
Froude, James, 73

Gandhi, Mohandas Karamchand, 6, 122, 124, 127–29, 203
Ganesh, 37–44, 47, 61, 92, 204
Gombrich, E. H., 16
Greene, Graham, 15–16, 72
Griffiths, Gareth, 13
*Guerrillas*, 11, 19, 135, 144, 163, 165, 167–68, 173, 177–85, 209, 220
Gunn, Janet Varner, 160, 213
Guyana, 67, 69, 70, 79, 216

Hamilton, Ian, 6, 255
Hammer, R. D., 239
Harris, Wilson, 7, 256
*Heart of Darkness*, 144, 172–73
Hill, Errol, 21, 231
Hiller, Herbert, 71–72
*A House for Mr Biswas*, 10, 17, 37, 46–64, 88, 90, 195, 203, 206, 208
Hughes, Peter, 254
humor, 21, 23, 26, 30–31, 35–38, 44, 62, 76
hybridity, 23, 33, 90, 156, 158, 185, 231

*In a Free State*, 11, 19, 138, 163, 165, 167–77, 185, 189, 209, 220
"India," 120–23
*India: A Million Mutinies Now*, 19, 116, 123, 129, 131, 141, 193, 215–16, 219–25, 243
*India: A Wounded Civilization*, 116, 123–29, 147, 170, 203

## Index

Indonesia, 154–56
Iran, 147–51, 153, 156–57
irony, 18, 23, 25, 27–29, 33, 36, 48, 50, 54, 62, 64, 68, 70, 89, 93, 103–4, 106, 114, 128, 136–37, 139, 141, 143, 145, 150, 156, 167–69, 175, 177, 190, 192, 199, 209, 217, 220

"Jacques Soustelle and the Decline of the West," 135–36
Jamaica, 67, 71, 145, 147
James, C. L. R., 3, 216, 232
Jameson, Fredric, 46
"Jamshed into Jimmy," 120–21
"Jasmine," 3–4, 216
Johnson, Samuel, 243

Kabbani, Rana, 134, 158, 242
"Kamikaze in Montevideo," 143
Kane, Cheikh Hamidou, 9, 227
King, Bruce, 62, 236, 255
Kristeva, Julia, 8–9, 85, 216

Lamb, David, 167, 252
Laye, Camara, 9
Le Clézio, J. M. G., 81
Lewis, Bernard, 148, 247
Lim, Ling-Mei, 13, 249
London, 90, 92, 107, 112
Londres, Albert, 244
*The Loss of El Dorado*, 17–18, 65–66, 75, 77–86, 137, 147, 209

Macherey, Pierre, 164
Malaysia, 153–54
marginality, 3–5, 13, 16–17, 60, 63, 65–67, 69, 73–74, 88–89, 92, 94, 96, 98, 139–41, 146, 163, 171, 217
Martinique, 67, 70–71, 75, 147
Mauritius, 139–41
Medvedev, P. N., 194, 210, 212, 256
Memmi, Albert, 73, 75, 237

Meredith, Martin, 253
Michael X, 141, 144, 162, 168, 173, 182, 241
Michener, Charles, 218, 244
*The Middle Passage*, 17–18, 31, 34, 44, 60, 65–78, 83–85, 92–93, 114, 137, 147, 159, 163, 203, 209, 217
*Miguel Street*, 17, 23–31, 35–37, 39, 41–42, 47, 53, 61, 74–75, 88, 203, 207–8, 219, 221
*The Mimic Men*, 6, 11, 18, 69, 77, 88–89, 92–104, 106, 109–11, 114, 116, 135, 159, 177, 183, 195, 204–5, 209, 213, 220
mimicry, 28, 43, 69, 74–76, 101, 103–5, 108, 120–21, 124, 128, 141, 148, 162, 181, 220
Mirville, Ernest, 22
modes of intercultural encounter and communication, 14–16
Mortimer, Edward, 248–49
"The Mourners," 194–95, 206
*Mr Stone and the Knights Companion*, 11, 18, 88–89, 92, 104–10, 114, 204, 220
Mukherjee, Bharati, 182, 246–47
*The Mystic Masseur*, 17, 23, 37–45, 47, 61, 75, 92, 204
myth, 4, 18–19, 65, 69, 75, 78–80, 82–86, 88–89, 101–2, 116, 118, 121, 124, 127–29, 142–43, 146–47, 152–53, 159, 167–68, 175–76, 179, 184, 189–92, 196, 203–5, 217–18

Naipaul, Seepersad, 11, 17, 42, 47, 61–62, 232
Naipaul, Shiva, 195
Naipual, V. S.: grandparents of, 49, 113, 116, 131, 216, 234; works of, *see* individual titles
Narayan, R. K., 124–25
"A New King for the Congo: Mobutu and the Nihilism of Africa," 142, 144–45, 163

"One Out of Many," 10–12, 169–71
Ortega y Gasset, José, 194
*The Other Side of Paradise: Foreign Control in the Caribbean*, 72, 101, 244–45
*The Overcrowded Barracoon*, 135–41, 163

Pakistan, 113, 147, 150–53, 157, 163, 216
picaroon society, 31, 43–44, 59–60, 232
Picton, Thomas, 82–83
pluralism, 215–25
Port of Spain, 23, 25, 27, 30, 37, 46, 48, 50–51, 56, 59, 63, 72, 77, 111, 207–8
postcolonial world, 5, 15, 19–20, 65, 92, 128–29, 134–36, 141–42, 144–46, 160, 162, 165, 167, 172, 174–77, 179, 182, 184–87, 189, 191–93, 215, 217, 220, 222
"Power?" 137–39, 141
"Prologue to an Autobiography," 47, 61, 159–61, 197

Rachlin, Nahid, 148
Rai, Sudha, 128
Raleigh, Walter, 78–80, 84
Ramchand, Kenneth, 7, 46, 231, 241
recursion, 12, 17, 133–35, 146, 159–60, 163–64, 202, 210, 212, 220
*The Return of Eva Perón*, 141–46

Said, Edward, 6
satire, 23, 31, 33, 35–36, 38, 40, 42, 44, 52, 61, 76, 120, 146, 204, 217, 220
"A Second Visit," 121–23
Sibony, Daniel, 228, 255–56
Stanzel, F. K., 232
"St Kitts: Papa and the Power Set," 137
*The Suffrage of Elvira*, 17, 23, 31–37, 40, 47, 177, 182, 204

Suriname, 67, 70, 101
syncretism, 5, 9, 11–13, 17, 74, 90–91, 112, 138, 161, 187, 210–11, 215, 220, 222, 231

"Tell Me Who To Kill," 169, 171–72, 209
Therborn, Göran, 156, 247–50
Tiffin, Helen, 13
Todorov, Tzvetan, 5, 7–8, 12, 81, 87, 229, 244
Toffler, Alvin, 251
tourism, 71–72
Tournier, Michel, 85, 107, 111
travel books, 9, 37, 134–35, 160, 209, 219–20
Trinidad, 3, 4, 11, 16–18, 21–23, 30–32, 38–41, 43–45, 47–50, 53–54, 58, 61–62, 65–69, 73–75, 77–78, 80–82, 85, 88–91, 113–15, 117, 130–31, 134, 138–40, 142, 162, 179, 182, 195, 196–99, 203, 209–10, 216, 218–22
*A Turn in the South*, 19, 66, 215, 219, 221–22

Uruguay, 143

*Vendredi ou les limbes du Pacifique*, 85, 111

West Indies and Caribbean, 17, 65–66, 73, 76, 85–86, 205, 220
White, Landeg, 232
Williams, Eric, 48, 73, 80, 234, 245

Yoshikawa, Muneo Jay, 14–15

Zaire. *See* Congo